SILVER·BURDETT

Making Music

Coordinating Authors

Hunter C. March   Will Schmid   Sandra L. Stauffer

Program Authors

Jane Beethoven   Judith A. Jellison   Konnie Saliba
Susan Brumfield   Rita Klinger   Carol Scott-Kassner
Patricia Shehan Campbell   Rochelle Mann   Mary E. Shamrock
David N. Connors   Nan L. McDonald   Judith Thomas
Robert A. Duke   Marvelene C. Moore   Jill Trinka
                     Mary Palmer

PEARSON
Scott Foresman

Editorial Offices: Glenview, Illinois • Parsippany, New Jersey • New York, New York
Sales Offices: Needham, Massachusetts • Duluth, Georgia • Glenview, Illinois
Coppell, Texas • Sacramento, California • Mesa, Arizona

ISBN: 0-382-36576-3

Contributing Authors

Audrey A. Berger
Roslyn Burrough
J. Bryan Burton
Jeffrey E. Bush
John M. Cooksey
Shelly C. Cooper
Alice-Ann Darrow
Scott Emmons
Debra Erck
Anne M. Fennell
Doug Fisher
Carroll Gonzo
Larry Harms
Martha F. Hilley
Debbie Burgoon Hines

Mary Ellen Junda
Donald Kalbach
Shirley Lacroix
Henry Leck
Sanna Longden
Glenn A. Richter
Carlos Xavier Rodriguez
Kathleen Donahue Sanz
Julie K. Scott
Gwen Spell
Barb Stevanson
Kimberly C. Walls
Jackie Wiggins
Maribeth Yoder-White

Listening Map Contributing Authors

Patricia Shehan Campbell
Jackie Chooi-Theng Lew
Ann Clements
Kay Edwards
Scott Emmons
Sheila Feay-Shaw

Kay Greenhaw
David Hebert
Hunter C. March
Carol Scott-Kassner
Mary E. Shamrock
Sandra L. Stauffer

Movement Contributing Authors

Judy Lasko
Marvelene C. Moore
Dixie Piver

Wendy Taucher
Susan Thomasson
Judith Thompson-Barthwell

Recording Producers

Buryl Red, Executive Producer

Rick Baitz
Rick Bassett
Bill and Charlene James
Joseph Joubert
Bryan Louiselle
Tom Moore
J. Douglas Pummill

Michael Rafter
Mick Rossi
Buddy Skipper
Robert Spivak
Jeanine Tesori
Linda Twine

CONTENTS

The Business of Music

Careers in the Music Industry

WORLD MUSIC MIX

World Popular Styles and Performers

Music Through Time

Historical Contexts and Styles

DRUMS AND BEYOND

Playing in Percussion Ensembles

KEYS and CHORDS

Playing Keyboard Chords and Progressions

POWER STRUMMING

**Playing Guitar Chords,
Progressions, and Strums**

Let Your Voice Be Heard

Singing in Unison and Parts

Sounds and Symbols

Music Theory and Fundamentals

Performance Anthology

The Business of Music

Careers in the Music Industry

MOVIE MUSIC AND SOUND FX

▲ Sound Lab at Experience Music Project

▲ Film composer Danny Elfman

◄ Guitarist Pat Metheny

▲ Wigmaker

▲ Propmaker

"Music and composition, in their latest evolution have now incorporated other branches of art and science and the composer of the future may well be a combination physicist-mathematician, architect-electronic engineer-musician."

—Irwin Bazelon (1922–1995)

MULTIMEDIA MUSIC

There is a commonly held misconception that all computer musicians just write 'blip blop' music. This is simply NOT true!
—Andrew Barnabas

▲ (E3) Electronic Entertainment Exposition in Los Angeles, California

▲ George Sanger, David Govett, Kevin Phelan, and Joe McDermott on the back cover of *Zhadnost* video game.

How does music come into your life? Radio? Television? Live music?

Having a career in the music industry is not just about playing an instrument or singing. It is about providing music to people in their daily lives.

One popular job for musicians today is creating music for multimedia technologies, like Web pages, video games, and Internet advertising.

Multimedia music may be **linear** or **interactive.** Linear music is used for purposes such as background music for Web pages. Interactive music has sections that may occur in a variety of possible orders, depending on how the listener interacts with the computer. In a video game, for example, one music selection plays if you win; another selection plays if you lose.

Sounds Interactive

Listen to selections from a composition for interactive multimedia. They are from the video game *The 7th Guest.* **Describe** why the composition would sound correct in any order.

🎧 **Themes from The 7th Guest**

by George Alistair Sanger

1-1   *The 7th Guest* game is a series of puzzles that must be solved to discover the name of the seventh guest. Each puzzle has its own musical composition.

Put ·gether a te that would you. Check out ; for more music :hoices.

---

linear music Music that is always played in the same order, as specified by the composer.

interactive music Music with sections that may play in different orders, depending on the actions of the listener.

Music in Gaming

Create an imaginary video game with a partner or small group. Decide whether it will be a puzzle game, an adventure game, or a battle game. Make up a title for your game and create a series of scenes. Suggestions could include

- an opening scene to set the stage.
- an indoor scene with dialogue.
- an outdoor scene with environmental sounds.
- a closing scene to resolve the story.

Analyze and discuss what kind of music would sound best with each scene. Using music you bring in from home, selections from this book, or choices from available music sites, choose compositions to musically illustrate each of the scenes.

You can also plan where in your scenes the music could be interactive. What activities could you include where the music will change with the action?

Put It Together

Make your own multimedia presentation of your favorite board game. Using a game from home, create an opening page for an electronic version that could be played on a gameplayer or computer. How does your music help make the game more interesting? Share your ideas with your classmates.

Note This

Some composers specialize in writing music for video games. What is your favorite video game? Is music used all of the time or only at the end of a level? Does the music influence or reflect the action?

Music $ells

Ask adults to sing the commercial jingle for Oscar Mayer® bologna. Do they remember it? How about Jell-O®? Radio, television, and even sports arenas are loaded with commercials that include music called **jingles.** Companies use the listener's ability to recall music (the jingle) to promote and sell products.

The Jingle Shop

A jingle composer might work independently, for a **jingle shop,** or for an advertising agency. From the biggest ad agency to an individual composer, the goal of a jingle writer is the same— to promote the client's product.

Something Old, Something New

A jingle writer may compose new music or use a well-known piece of music in the jingle. Familiar music helps to catch the audience's attention. Composers who choose existing music that is under **copyright** must pay for the right to use it. Music in the **public domain** may be used freely by anyone. Sometimes a client requests new music that sounds a lot like the style of a well-known song. Because a composer must be careful not to violate another composer's copyright, many jingle shops hire a music expert. The expert listens to the new jingle to make certain there are no infringement issues.

---

jingle A short piece with catchy repetition, used in commercials.

jingle shop A company that specializes in composing, recording, and selling music for jingles.

copyright A legal right granted for exclusive publication, sale, or distribution of a literary, musical, dramatic, or artistic work.

public domain Belonging to the general public.

Music Power!

When a product or idea becomes associated with a catchy tune, buyers think of the product every time they hear the music.

Listen to this jingle for the Radio City Christmas Spectacular® show. What do you think makes it memorable?

Radio City Christmas Spectacular Jingle
by Nancy Coyne and Steve Carmen
1-2 **arranged by Bryan Louiselle**
Each one of the three jingle samples appeals to a different listening audience.

Write Your Own Jingle

Try your hand at jingle writing. Choose a word or phrase you want to remember, such as the date for your next social studies test. Then set the phrase to a familiar melody, your own tune, or a rhythmic rap. Your goal is to help others easily remember the phrase. Here are a few tricks to help your jingle succeed.

- Keep it simple, with a melody and rhythm that is easy to remember. Let the syllables or letters in the word or phrase determine the rhythm.
- Repeat the letters or syllables of the word or phrase to make it memorable.
- Add accents to important syllables or words.
- The word or phrase may suggest a mood or a place. Should the music for your jingle sound happy? Wild? Gentle?
- Choose or **create** an interesting accompaniment.
- Add dance moves or a hand jive to make your jingle easier to remember.
  Play your jingle and see if your classmates can remember it.

Careers JINGLE WRITER
Bryan Louiselle

Bryan Louiselle (born 1966) is a composer, lyricist, arranger, orchestrator, producer, conductor, and vocalist. He has composed music for film documentaries and some of the songs in this book series. His conducting credits include *Dream* and *Buttons on Broadway*. While working on *Dream,* Louiselle was asked to produce a television and radio jingle for that show. Following its success, he was hired for more commercials, including *The Radio City Christmas Spectacular, Into the Woods*, and *42nd Street*. Louiselle notes that one of the challenges of jingle writing is adapting music to the text that will fit 10-, 30- and 60-second commercial spots, and timing the music's dynamics so that any voice-overs can be heard. Louiselle lives in New York City.

Mood Music

Have you ever made a phone call and been put on "hold" in silence? Really irritating, isn't it? Smart businesses know better than to keep customers holding in silence, so they provide music to distract and entertain. Businesses get this music by paying a music service that designs, installs, and selects the music best suited for the company's target customers. A music programmer selects music to match the company's needs. For example, a programmer would likely select pop, rap, or rock tunes if the potential audience was teenagers.

Music for Ups and Downs

You know that music can change your mood, give you energy, and maybe even help you get your homework done. Music has amazing powers. Businesses know this, too. Studies have demonstrated that factory workers get more done with the right music played in the workplace. For example, that sleepy feeling workers (and students) sometimes get just after lunch can be overcome with peppy, high-energy music.

Take It Easy

The next time you go to a restaurant, listen for music playing softly in the background. Background music is inactive. This music creates a relaxing mood, but the listener is not distracted by the words, the rhythm, or the singer. Music in a doctor or dentist's office is usually a soothing sound to comfort the listener.

Airlines try to reduce stress for nervous or bored flyers by providing music that passengers can listen to with headphones. Passengers can choose from many styles of music, news, or even comedy routines.

Careers
MOOD MUSICIAN
ALVIN COLLIS

Alvin Collis (born 1952) started his career with Muzak® Corporation, the environmental music distributor, as a tape editor. As an editor, this punk rocker from Canada sat for four hours at a time just listening for gaps and skips in the recordings. Twelve years later, Collis became chief of audio programming for the corporation. He is responsible for choosing the playlist that editors use to create the tape loops you hear almost everywhere. In the last 15 years, Muzak® has changed its focus from creating instrumental covers of pop songs to incorporating original music choices in its loops for a more authentic music experience. Collis brings his extensive knowledge of all types of music to the song choices that go into the loops.

Action Music

The music you hear while on hold is a type of active music. The company that has you on hold wants to keep you occupied so you won't think too much about the fact that you are waiting.

You can hear another type of active music at an aerobics class and on exercise videos. Adding strong rhythms to a dance track makes exercise fun. You feel less tired with the music moving you along.

Who Are They?

While there are several companies who provide environmental music, the best known is probably a company called Muzak.® Muzak® has been creating environmental music for 65 years. It currently employs 2,000 individuals who select and mix the recorded music provided to offices, restaurants, and telephone service providers. While Muzak® for many years received criticism for bland orchestrated versions of popular music, they now license recordings of original artists, including Herbie Hancock, Will Smith, and Usher for their recorded mixes.

Try This!

Imagine a stressful situation in your life such as an upcoming test. What music would you like to hear that might make you feel more relaxed? **Create** a music mix CD or other recording that helps you stay focused and calm. You're a music programmer!

MOVIE MUSIC AND SOUND FX

4

Sound designers and **Foley artists** use **sound effects (fx),** to make us believe the world we see or hear is real. When we see someone walk, for example, we expect to hear footsteps. If a door opens, it could squeak. The sound designer puts in these squeaks and creaks. Fantasy and science fiction sound designers must create the sounds of worlds that do not exist. For example, no one would know what an alien creature might sound like, so the designer and team must look at the movie version of the alien and create a believable sound for it. In the early days of movies, sound effects were created and recorded with physical objects and actions, such as hitting shoes on the floor to simulate walking. Now many sounds are prerecorded in electronic formats and are available to sound designers and Foley artists to use in their work.

Action!

Every great movie sound track includes three essential elements—**dialogue,** sound effects, and music. The next time you see a movie, watch the credits to see the people involved with the music and sound. The credits will include sound engineer, sound editor, music director, composer, score editor, sound effects artist, and sound designer.

Dialogue conveys the plot and character information that ties the story together. Movie dialogue is usually recorded using boom (overhead) microphones on a sound stage as the actors are filmed. Sometimes the dialogue is recorded in a studio where the actors recreate the timing and emotion of their lines as they watch the film. The sound engineer records the dialogue to make sure it is clear.

Foley artist A person who creates sound effects; named after Jack Foley, one of the original Hollywood technicians.

sound effects (fx) Sounds added to a movie soundtrack or other performance to make it more believable.

dialogue The spoken portion of a movie soundtrack.

Getting the Music Made

Composition of a music score is done in postproduction, after the movie is completely filmed and in the editing process. A composer watches the movie, perhaps several times, to get a sense of what music is needed for each of the scenes. The composer usually has anywhere from four to 12 weeks to write an entire movie score. In a big-budget movie, there are generally three musicians working on the score: a composer, an orchestrator, and a copyist. These three professionals work in sequence, so that all of the music can be prepared well and on time.

Setting the Mood

Background music helps increase the emotional impact of a film. A **film score** can also have musical themes we associate with certain characters. Darth Vader's theme from *Star Wars* is a well-known example. Music in a film can remind the viewer of previous scenes and can link them together.

After dialogue, sound effects, and music are recorded, they can be synchronized and edited to fit each scene. Sound levels are mixed in a studio. The movie is previewed in a theater and changes are made for the final mix.

Make a Mood

Choose a video from your home collection and **create** a score for one of the scenes. With a few of your classmates, review the scene and make a list of what sound effects you will need to include. Do people walk across a wooden floor, carpet, or a cement sidewalk? Does a car door slam? Is there traffic passing by in the background? Use your imagination to help you decide how to make each of the sounds you need. You can also choose background music that matches the mood of the scene to play underneath your sound effects.

Careers
FOLEY ARTIST
TOM KEITH

Sound effects are frequently created because many sounds simply do not record well. For example, recorded footsteps tend to sound muffled. Foley artist **Tom Keith** (born 1946) uses vocal gymnastics combined with props such as doors and kitchen utensils to create a realistic backdrop for the popular weekend radio show *A Prairie Home Companion.* Keith, a St. Paul, Minnesota native and cohost of The Morning Show on Minnesota Public Radio, is known for his memorable sound effects. Some favorites include his impressions of helicopters flying low over trees, explosions, and animal sounds.

---

film score All of the music contained in a movie, including background music and featured songs.

Music from the Movies

Listen to *Main Titles from Edward Scissorhands*. **Identify** Edward's theme every time you hear it. The theme is notated below. Follow the map and timings as you listen.

Edward Scissorhands
LISTENING MAP

Intro.

:31 Voices (Edward's theme)

:58 Voices (variation)

1:25 Interlude

2:04 Voices

2:32 Coda

Main Titles from Edward Scissorhands
by Danny Elfman

1-3

A main title in a movie score is the background music for the opening of the film, the main character, and usually the closing credits.

Describe the timbre of the instruments you hear. What instruments accompany Edward's theme? What do you hear at the other times?

FILM SCORE COMPOSER
DANNY ELFMAN

Danny Elfman (born 1953), the two-time Academy Award winner, is best known for his film scores for movies such as *Batman, The Nightmare Before Christmas, Men in Black,* and *Edward Scissorhands.*

Elfman was born in Texas to a schoolteacher and a novelist. He began his film scoring career by composing music for a film directed by his brother, Richard Elfman. A member of the band Oingo Boingo, Elfman's big break came when he met filmmaker Tim Burton at a concert. The Burton-Elfman partnership has become one of the film industry's most successful collaborations.

FILM SCORE COMPOSER
TAN DUN

Composer/conductor **Tan Dun** [tahn duhn] (born 1957) won the Academy Award in 2001 for his film score to *Crouching Tiger, Hidden Dragon.* Well known for creating music that merges Eastern and Western cultures, Dun has also received classical music's most prestigious honor, the Grawemeyer Award, for his opera, *Marco Polo.*

Originally from the Hunan province in mainland China, Tan Dun was educated both in China and the United States. He began his career with the Peking Opera and has gone on to perform with leading orchestras and ensembles around the world. Dun has collaborated with celebrated cellist Yo-Yo Ma. Ma's work is featured prominently in *Crouching Tiger, Hidden Dragon.*

Crouching Tiger, Hidden Dragon

by Tan Dun

1-4   **as performed by Yo-Yo Ma, cello, and the Shanghai Symphony Orchestra, conducted by Tan Dun**

This score combines traditional Chinese instruments with modern Western orchestration.

5

Composer and Arranger

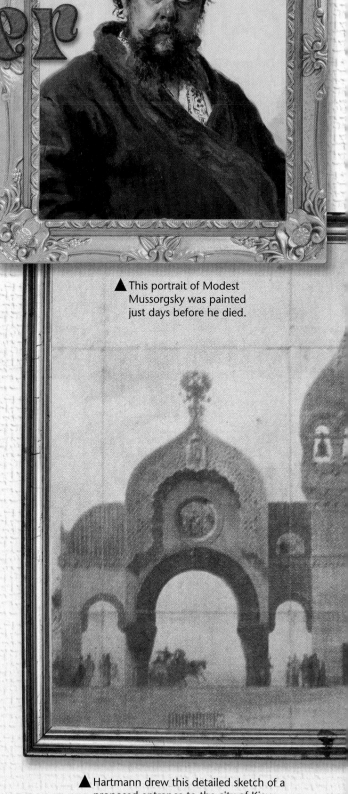

Composers often use music to describe an event, an object, or a scene. While visiting an exhibition, Russian composer Modest Mussorgsky (1839–1881) saw the drawings and watercolors of the Russian artist and architect, Victor Hartmann. They inspired Mussorgsky to create a work for piano called *Pictures at an Exhibition*. It consists of ten movements, each one a musical description of Hartmann's work. The gate of Kiev was one of Hartmann's sketches.

Listen to Mussorgsky's *The Great Gate of Kiev*.

The Great Gate of Kiev

1-5
from *Pictures at an Exhibition*
by Modest Mussorgsky
as performed by Vladimir Horowitz
"The Great Gate of Kiev" is the last movement in *Pictures at an Exhibition*.

Orchestrated Pictures

Maurice Ravel was one of many musicians to arrange *Pictures at an Exhibition*. Ravel chose different instruments to play various parts of the music. **Listen** for the different instrument timbres Ravel chose.

The Great Gate of Kiev

1-6
from *Pictures at an Exhibition*
by Modest Mussorgsky, arranged by Maurice Ravel
as performed by the Chicago Symphony
This movement features the brass section of the orchestra.

What's the Difference?

Now **analyze** both versions of the same composition.

- What decisions did the arranger make?
- What makes the two recordings seem similar?
- In what ways are the recordings different from one another?
- Which version do you prefer? Why?

▲ This portrait of Modest Mussorgsky was painted just days before he died.

▲ Hartmann drew this detailed sketch of a proposed entrance to the city of Kiev.

Music MAKERS
Maurice Ravel

French composer **Maurice Ravel** (1875–1937) is considered by many to be one of the most original and sophisticated composers of the early twentieth century. Although Ravel devoted most of his musical career to composing, he was an exceptional arranger—one of the great orchestrators of modern times. The composer Igor Stravinsky called him a "connoisseur of instrumental jewelry." Ravel arranged music written by other composers, including that of Mussorgsky, Schumann, Chopin, Satie, and Debussy.

When World War I broke out, the 40-year-old Ravel volunteered in the French Air Force as an ambulance driver. After the war, Ravel became known internationally and was considered the foremost composer in France.

In 1928, Ravel traveled to the United States for a four-month concert tour. He conducted his music in twenty-five different cities, and visited Harlem with American composer George Gershwin, where he experienced jazz for the first time. While on tour, he earned about $27,000, enough money to keep him financially secure for life.

Look and Listen

Look at these parts of *The Great Gate of Kiev* as arranged by Ravel.
Listen to the recording again. Which instrument plays the melody?

Arrange with MIDI

Arrange your own version of *The Great Gate of Kiev*. Locate the melody track on the MIDI file and assign an instrument. Assign other instruments to all tracks. Then choose a tempo. When you are satisfied with your arrangement, save your version. Then play it for the class and discuss your choices.

Music MAKERS Isao Tomita

Japanese composer **Isao Tomita** (born 1932) was one of the pioneers of electronic composition with his brilliant interpretations of classical masterpieces. Tomita was classically trained in theory, composition, and art history. Beginning his career as a composer for film, television, and theater in the 1960s, Tomita was soon considered one of Japan's best composers. This success allowed him the freedom to experiment with the potential of electronic instruments. He has arranged works such as Stravinsky's *Firebird Suite*, Ravel's *Bolero*, and John Williams' theme to *Star Wars*. His successes have earned him many Grammy® nominations and an international reputation.

A Rearrangement!

Listen to another version of *The Great Gate of Kiev*. How does this version differ from the two selections you have already heard?

The Great Gate of Kiev
by Modest Mussorgsky
1-7   **arranged by Isao Tomita**
This version is performed on a Moog 3 synthesizer.

Tomita's electronic arrangements stood out from those before him because he took great stylistic liberties in adapting the music to electronic instruments.

A New Take

Listen to a MIDI recording of the song "Bye Bye Love." Then listen to the completed arrangement as found on page F-9 in Power Strumming. What instrumental and vocal timbres did you hear in the second recording? How did the choices affect your understanding of the style and mood of the song? What other timbre choices might you make?

Bye Bye Love
by Felice Bryant and Boudleaux Bryant
1-8   The Everly Brothers made this tune a hit in 1957.

Try Your Hand

Read through the song notation for "America, the Beautiful" found on page I-4 in Performance Anthology. What stylistic choices might you make to **arrange** it? Using MIDI file 18, **create** an arrangement of the song. Consider these choices.

- style and character
- tempo
- register
- timbre
- changing rhythm

Using the list above, or an idea of your own, **arrange** the song. Then play back the file for your classmates.

If no software is available, your teacher can help you notate the song, incorporating your ideas into the song notation. Then play back your arrangement on the instrument of your choice. You may also arrange the song for several instruments and play it with some of your classmates.

6

Spotlight on Performance

Making a living as a musical performer is a demanding career. Professional musicians and professional athletes have a lot in common. Both have to begin training at a fairly early age, work diligently with very few days off, and constantly compete with others. There's an old joke that asks, "How do I get to **Carnegie Hall?**" The answer is, "Practice, practice, practice." The joke sums up the life of professional performers. These are the sounds and stories of a few of today's top professional musicians.

Careers
INSTRUMENTAL PERFORMER
Yo-Yo Ma

Yo-Yo Ma (born 1955) is the most widely acclaimed cellist in the world today. Ma performs as a classical concert artist and collaborates with musicians of many different styles. Born in Paris, Ma began playing the cello at age four, taking lessons with his father. His family later moved to New York, where Ma studied at the Juilliard School. At Harvard University in Boston, Ma studied humanities, rather than music. In 1991, Harvard gave him an honorary doctorate in music.

Ma has recorded 75 albums and won 14 Grammy Awards. In 2001, he was awarded the National Medal of the Arts. He collaborated with a variety of artists from other fields in the multimedia project *Inspired by Bach,* a series of six films. The series featured the reactions of a landscape designer, a film director, a choreographer, a Kabuki actor, an artist/architect, and a pair of ice dancers, to Ma's performance of the *Suites for Cello* by Johann Sebastian Bach.

Ice dancers Torville and Dean ▶

Carnegie Hall One of the most famous concert halls in the world, located on 57th St. and 7th Ave. in New York City.

A Dynamite Team!

Although best known as a classical musician, Yo-Yo Ma also enjoys "crossing over" to different styles of music. Alison Krauss, who collaborates with Ma in the following selection, is also a "crossover" artist. She began classical violin lessons at age five. By age eight, she knew that bluegrass fiddling was her style. Today she is also famous for her great voice.

Listen to Alison Krauss and Yo-Yo Ma's recording of a well-known song. What instruments do you hear?

Simple Gifts

1-9   traditional Shaker melody
as performed by Alison Krauss and Yo-Yo Ma
Notice the key change that occurs with Krauss' entrance.

A Simple Song

Listen to another version of "Simple Gifts." **Compare** it to the version you just heard. How is it different?

▲ Alison Krauss

CD 1-10

Simple Gifts

'Tis the gift to be sim-ple 'Tis the gift to be free, 'Tis the gift to come down
where we ought to be. And when we find our-selves __ in the place just __ right, 'Twill __
be in the val-ley of love and de-light. When true sim-pli-ci-ty is gained, To bow and to bend we __
shan't be a-shamed, To turn, turn will be our de-light, 'Till by turn-ing turn-ing we come 'round right.

Take It to the Net For more information on Yo-Yo Ma, go to *www.sfsuccessnet.com.*

Which Comes First?

Some performers are songwriters first. **John Hiatt** is a singer/songwriter whose songs have been recorded by numerous other musicians, including Bonnie Raitt, Don Henley, Bob Dylan, The Everly Brothers and Jewel. Hiatt's songwriting gift is his ability to write songs that so many musicians are able to perform well.

Hiatt has written in many styles over his long career, including folk, pop, and blues.

Listen to *Have a Little Faith in Me*. What qualities of music make this easy to perform?

▲ John Hiatt

Have a Little Faith in Me

by John Hiatt
1-12 **as performed by Kenny Rogers**
This rendition is performed in a country style.

Breaking with Tradition

Pat Metheny's grandfather, father, and brother were trumpet players, so he began trumpet lessons at age eight. At twelve, he decided the trumpet was not for him and switched to guitar. By the time he was fifteen, he was playing with the top jazz groups in his hometown of Kansas City. At age eighteen, Metheny became the youngest teacher ever at the University of Miami, and at nineteen, the youngest teacher at the Berklee College of Music.

Listen to *April Joy*.

April Joy

by Pat Metheny
1-13 **as performed by the Pat Metheny Group**
This selection displays Metheny's outstanding melodic style and technical ability.

◀ Pat Metheny

Note This

Besides performing, Metheny has developed several new types of guitars, including one with 42 strings!

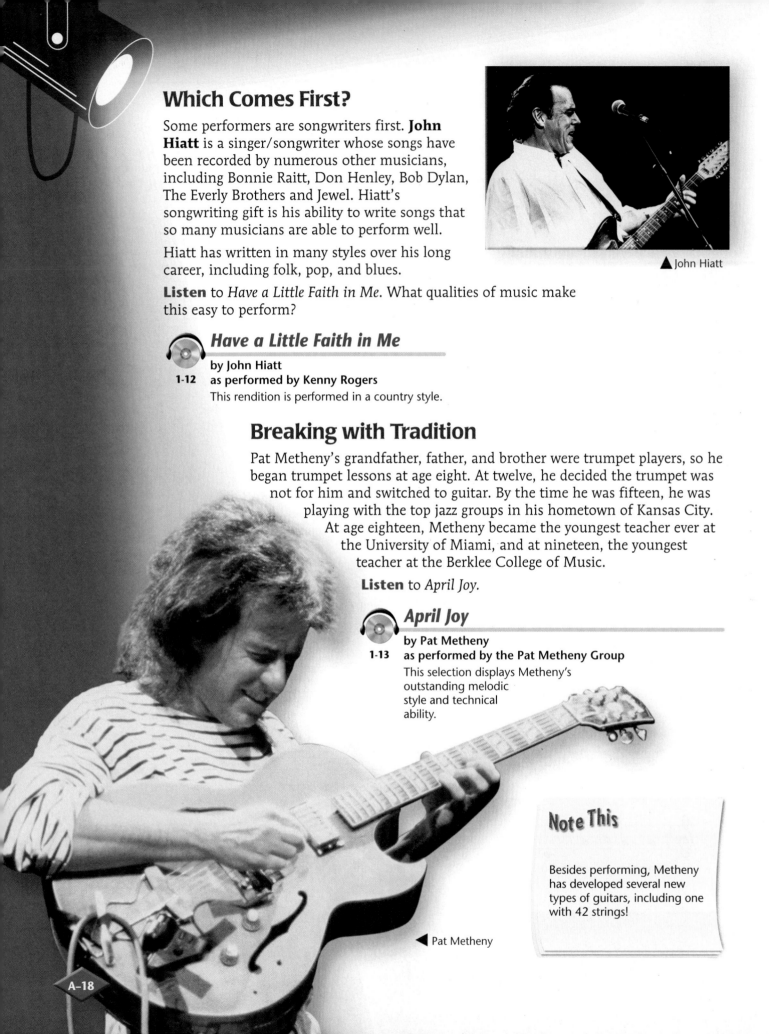

Checkpoint

Listen to recordings of young performing artists. Make a list of the skills, instruments, styles, and other attributes that you think contribute to their musical success. **Compare** answers with your classmates.

Solo de concours

by Andre Messager

1-14 **as performed by Julian Bliss and Ashley Wass**

This composition for clarinet and piano was written in 1899.

Brace Yourself

written and performed by Howie Day

1-15 Day's signature style includes playing each song differently each time he performs it.

Bairagi

by Ravi Shankar

1-16 **as performed by Anoushka Shankar**

This composition for *sitar* describes the Earth as mother.

◀ Born in St. Alban's, England, in 1989, Julian Bliss is the youngest person ever to complete an Artists' Diploma in Music at Indiana University.

Anoushka Shankar began studying *sitar* with her father, world-famous sitarist Ravi Shankar, when she was very young. ▶

◀ A native of Bangor, Maine, Howie Day played piano as a child and took up the guitar at age 14.

BEHIND THE SCENES

What does it take to put on a Broadway show? You need performers and a pit orchestra. You also need many, many people whose work makes a Broadway show come to life.

A Broadway Veteran

Jeanine Tesori is a composer, musical director, conductor, and pianist for musicals on Broadway in New York City. **Listen** to this live interview with Tesori and members of the production team from *Thoroughly Modern Millie*. How do they describe their role in a musical theater production? List the responsibilities workers "behind the scenes" have in creating a great show.

Backstage with Jeanine Tesori

1-17 with Michael Mayer, Dick Scanlan, Kristen Caskey, and Rob Ashford

▲ Costume design

▲ Prompters

▲ Makeup artist

▲ Makeup artist

▲ Propmaker

Behind the Scenes

Many more people are involved in a musical theater production than those we see and hear on the stage. Careers in musical theater include the following.

- **producer**—hires and pays cast and crew
- **writer/composer/lyricist**—creates the story, words, and music
- **director**—directs the stage movements of the actors for the performance
- **musical director**—directs the music for the performance
- **choreographer**—designs dance numbers in the show
- **orchestra**—instrumentalists who perform in the orchestra pit
- **conductor**—leads the orchestra
- **vocal coach**—assists actors/singers in learning their songs
- **lighting designer**—designs lighting for the performance
- **sound designer**—creates sound effects
- **rigger**—suspends lighting and sound equipment
- **set designer**—creates ideas for the set
- **carpenter**—builds the set
- **costume designer**—creates ideas for the costumes
- **costumer**—makes and cares for costumes
- **stage manager**—oversees all aspects of the performance, including props, entrances, costumes, and lighting

▲ Wigmaker

▲ Set crew and carpenter

On with the Show

"Seasons of Love" is from the Broadway show *Rent*.
Sing "Seasons of Love." What mood does the song convey?

Seasons of Love

Words and Music by Jonathan Larson

Five hun-dred twen-ty five thou-sand six hun-dred min - utes, five hun-dred twen-ty five thou-sand

mo-ments so __ dear. __
jour-neys to __ plan. __
five hun-dred twen-ty five thou-sand six hun-dred min - utes.

How do you meas-ure, meas-ure a __ year? __ In day-lights, in sun-sets, in mid-nights, in cups __ of cof-fee,

in inch-es, in miles, in laugh-ter, in __ strife, __ in five hun-dred twen-ty five thou-sand

six hun-dred min - utes How do you meas-ure a year in __ the life. __ How a-bout

love? __ How a-bout love? __

How a-bout love? __ Meas-ure in love.

Sea-sons of love, __ sea-sons of love. __

It's Show Time!

Collaborate with a team of class members to create or adapt a story or dramatize the words of a song, a book, or a movie. List production ideas for your show including

- set appearance
- use of dance
- lighting
- musical style
- costumes

Each team member should pick a different career and perform the tasks required of that professional for the production.

Rent, opening of the second act ▼

ON YOUR OWN

After rehearsing your production, take your show on the road. Perform it at several places in your community.

six hun-dred min - utes. How do you meas-ure the life of a wom-an or __ a man? __ in truth that __ she learned or in times that __ he cried, __ in bridg - es __ he burned or the way that she died. ___ it's time now to sing out, though the sto - ry nev - er ends. ___ Let's cel - e - brate, re - mem - ber a year in the life of ___ friends. _ Re-mem-ber the

WINNER!
THE MOST TONY AWARDS® EVER
INCLUDING
BEST MUSICAL

716

NATHAN LANE   MATTHEW BRODERICK

THE PRODUCERS
the new
MEL BROOKS
musical

direction and
choreography by
SUSAN STROMAN

BOOK BY
MEL BROOKS & THOMAS MEEHAN   MUSIC & LYRICS BY MEL BROOKS
and by special arrangement with StudioCanal

ST. JAMES THEATRE
246 W. 44th ST.

▲ Bill board for a Broadway musical

Producers work in many different media. Movies, television shows, theatre productions, and radio broadcasts all require a producer to oversee the creation of the performance. While each of the productions requires some different skills, there are similar responsibilities involved.

Producers supervise and sometimes finance all aspects of a concert or musical production. They plan the budget, find the **venue**, hire employees, supervise advertising, and do many other tasks necessary to put on a show. Good organization and leadership skills, plus plenty of advance planning, help a producer present a successful event. The producer needs an overall vision of the event and the ability to work well with people.

Producer Hal Prince with composer Stephen Sondheim ▶

---

venue The location where an event takes place.

Planning Ahead

Most producers work with a control sheet, a "to-do" list for the event. The control sheet begins with a simple daily plan and rehearsal schedule. As the event approaches, it grows into a detailed schedule listing activities for every minute of the performance day. Lighting, sound support, and visual effects are scheduled down to the split second. The control sheet lets everyone know the sequence of events for the show.

The Main Event

Producers help select the performers who will best fit the location and the preferences of the targeted crowd. The producer must have an eye for talent and a feel for the timing of events. A big-name artist or band usually prefers to have another act begin an evening's performance. The goal of this warm-up act is to help the crowd get into the mood for the star's appearance.

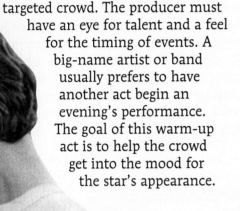

Supporting Roles

Producers cannot put on a show alone. They need a staff of skilled people to manage each detail of the show. A stage director makes sure the performers are in the right place at the right time. A lighting director presets the lights and lighting effects to create a pleasing visual image. A sound engineer tests all sound equipment. The stage crew raises the curtain, moves props, changes scenes, connects cables and wiring, and helps with any emergencies. All of this happens out of sight, so the performance is all that the audience sees.

Attention!

Every producer wants an SRO (Standing Room Only) crowd. Producers often use a **publicist** as part of the production process. Publicists know how to "create a buzz" for a performance. They use press kits, Web sites, e-mail, and personal telephone calls to provide stories to the media.

The Money Trail

Lighting, rehearsal space, venue rental, publicists, staff and talent salaries, advertising, printing tickets and programs, and security generate expenses long before the first ticket is sold. The producer recruits sponsors to **underwrite** performances and help with the advance costs. Sponsors may include beverage companies, car dealers, or anyone with a product to promote. Sometimes individual investors risk their own money, hoping the event will be successful and make them a profit.

It's Your Turn

Be a producer. Choose a simple scene from a favorite movie or play, or write your own. Determine how you would produce the scene. Consider lighting, actors, props and costumes, and advertising. Put together a control sheet of rehearsals and deadlines. Then **compare** your control sheet with your classmates and share ideas on making the production successful.

publicist Someone who advertises or attracts attention to an event.
underwrite To finance an event, usually in return for advertising, or in the hope of making a profit.

9

Music Helps People

If you enjoy music and working with people, music therapy might be a career choice for you. Music therapy helps people improve their lives when an injury or illness has made it difficult for them to function. Therapists can choose from a variety of musical activities to help their clients, such as listening to music, moving with music, or making music. If a problem has affected one portion of the brain and limited its function, music can help create new neural pathways. Clinical studies suggest that music involves the entire brain, not just one specific part.

Treat Body and Mind

People tend to have routines for doing things, which become patterns in their brains. When the brain suffers an illness or injury, these patterns may become interrupted. Music therapy can help to stimulate the brain and restore some of the lost function. Music can also motivate people. Playing songs from their youth for senior citizens may

encourage them to exercise. Playing instruments and singing songs with developmentally disabled children may help them learn.

Therapists often use music to get patients involved. The therapist might set a beat that matches the speed of the client's movements. The therapist can speed up or slow down the tempo to help the client move at a different speed or move more evenly. Rhythm can be used to retrain patients in tasks such as reaching for an object, or to help a stutterer smooth speech patterns. Therapists may use listening to and participating in music to improve memory.

Clive Robbins and Paul Nordoff working with Matti ▼

Careers MUSIC THERAPIST Dr. Paul Nordoff

Dr. Paul Nordoff (1910–1977) was a pioneer of music therapy. Trained as a composer and pianist, Nordoff began his work with disabled children in 1958. He and his teammate, Dr. Clive Robbins, brought their work from Great Britain to the United States in 1961, working with autistic and otherwise disabled children.

Nordoff's use of piano and vocal improvisation made him a leader in his field. After his death,

Dr. and Mrs. Robbins continued Nordoff's work, eventually creating the Nordoff-Robbins Center for Music Therapy at New York University. Nordoff's work continues at the Center, providing outpatient music therapy, training future therapists, and directing research, library resources, and seminars.

—Plato

Teachers Shape the Future

Teaching is another great career for people who love music and working with people. You can teach music to people of all ages, from infants to senior citizens. Some music teachers specialize in group instruction in primary and secondary schools, colleges, church choirs and orchestras, or community music groups. Other music teachers specialize in individual instruction—teaching one person at a time how to sing or play an instrument.

A Rewarding Career

The process of teaching music is ever-changing. There are centuries worth of music to study, and new music is being written every day. Music teachers never run out of new material. From the first time a student sees a piece of music until the day of performance, there are fun and exciting discoveries and rewards.

Analyze this music teaching chart. How many of these steps do you recognize from your own experience with learning music? Notice that each step uses repetition as a key to success.

Arts Connection

▲ *The Piano Lesson* by Romare Bearden, 1984

Step 1: The teacher presents the basics of music performance and helps the student select music.

Step 2: The teacher regularly listens to the student's tone, rhythm, and pitch on the assigned music.

Step 3: The teacher notes the student's progress, then helps the student decide what needs to improve.

Step 4: The teacher gives suggestions to improve the performance.

Step 5: The student practices music with the teacher's suggestions until mastery is achieved.

Step 6: Return to Step 1, with more challenging music.

You're the Teacher

Select a short piece of vocal or instrumental music to teach to some of your classmates. Plan which parts of the music you want to improve. For example, you can have your group repeat the beginning of the music until everyone starts together. You can make suggestions on how to pronounce words while singing, or point out pitches that are out of tune. You can make sure every student is watching you and ready before you start conducting. Notice how your thoughtful suggestions improve the performance.

10

Paul McGill inserting frets on the neck of a steel-string guitar ▼

Careers
LUTHIER
Paul McGill

Paul McGill (born 1958) of Nashville has been building high quality classical, steel-string, and resonator guitars for the past 25 years. A wide variety of famous guitarists choose his instruments for recording and live performance. Performers who have used McGill's instruments include country guitarist Chet Atkins, jazz guitarist Earl Klugh, fingerstyle and classical guitarist Muriel Anderson, and Brazilian guitar duo *Los Indios Tabajaras*.

Paul McGill prepared for his guitar building career by beginning lutherie school when he was 18 years old. When he finished school, he honed his abilities by building and selling a few guitars a year while working in a guitar restoration shop. As he restored valuable collector guitars, he "got to see how things held up, what things worked, what things didn't." Soon McGill was so busy building guitars that he stopped restoring them and devoted all his time to building new instruments.

McGill considers himself part of a new breed of guitar builders, based in tradition, but constantly trying to go beyond old boundaries to build the best instruments possible.

Great Instrument Makers

Most of us buy instruments without giving much thought to who actually built them. Many of the instruments we buy have been built in factories. But today elite craftsmen are building one-of-a-kind instruments far superior to mass-produced instruments. In the guitar world, some people even call today the "golden age of **lutherie.**"

lutherie The art of building string instruments.

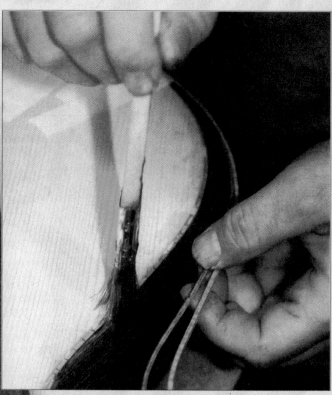

▲ McGill fits binding along the edge of the guitar body.

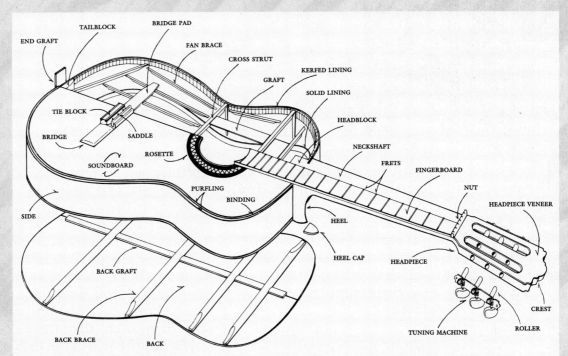

Secrets of a Great Guitar-Maker

According to Paul McGill, acoustic guitar construction is rather simple. Basically, guitars have two parts.

- a box to amplify the sound generated by vibrating strings
- a fretted neck attached to the box that allows the player to change pitches

The trick is to build a box that can both make beautiful sounds and withstand string tension of many thousands of pounds.

Build Your Own Instrument

You can design and construct your own string instrument to illustrate the principles of guitar building. Instrument bodies can be made from metal cookie tins. Scrap lumber is good for an instrument neck. A screw with an eye from your local hardware store can be used for an instrument tuning knob. Nylon fishing line works well for strings. What other materials could you use?

Hear a McGill Guitar

Guitarist Muriel Anderson performs throughout the world. Originally from Illinois, she studied classical guitar with Christopher Parkening and fingerstyle guitar with country great Chet Atkins. **Listen** to Muriel Anderson's performance of "Linus and Lucy" on her signature model Paul McGill classic guitar.

Linus and Lucy

by Vincent Guaraldi
1-20 **arranged and performed by Muriel Anderson**
Anderson's arrangement of this piece treats the guitar like three separate instruments.

On Your Own

Folk-instrument retailers feature complete kits for building mountain dulcimers, banjos, and harps. Order one of these kits to assemble a good quality instrument without the demands of expensive tools and equipment. Share your finished project with the class.

11 Fun- Not Profit

Most people love music of one style or another, but not everyone wants to make a career in music. For many people music becomes an **avocation.** The difference between professional musicians and hobbyists is not always talent. Pursuing music as a career requires great dedication, and some people simply don't want to spend their whole lives focused on music. Avocational musicians enjoy music purely for the love of it.

There is no age limit for enjoying music. Babies, grandparents, and people in between have their favorite musical sounds and can participate in music in many ways. With practice and patience, anyone can develop musical talent.

Music for Life

Today most people have busy, complicated lives. What inspires music lovers to practice in their spare time, outside of jobs and school, even when tired? People have diverse reasons for pursuing music for fun. Members of community choruses and garage bands enjoy the sense of accomplishment they feel when practicing or performing.

A pianist with a stressful "day job" plays for relaxation. A rapper expresses emotions and relates a story about life, which helps others understand a particular point of view. A community band stirs patriotic feelings in its audience by playing "America, the Beautiful." A guitarist builds short-term memory skills by carefully practicing repetitions of chords. An organ restorer brings back beautiful sounds to a hundred-year-old organ. In all of these examples, music plays a positive role in the lives of its performers and listeners.

Giving Something Back

Think of all the places where amateur musicians perform. Does a community band play holiday music in your town? Does a church in your community have a volunteer choir? Is there a community theater? Hospitals, senior centers, and retirement communities are often happy to have volunteer musicians visit. All of these volunteers make themselves and others happy with their music performances.

---

avocation Something a person does for enjoyment, but not to make a living; a hobby.

A Little Extra Cash

In between the people who make a living exclusively through music and those who are strictly volunteers, there are avocational musicians who earn extra income through music. A teacher, doctor, and truck driver can form a country and western band that earns money by playing for dances. A businessperson who is also a talented pianist may offer piano lessons on weekends. A police officer might also play the trumpet and perform for Sunday church services. Avocational musicians have the potential to earn thousands of dollars per year outside of their regular jobs.

How Do They Do It?

The best way to learn about music as an avocation is to talk to someone with experience. Interview someone who plays an instrument or sings for fun. Use the five questions below as a starting point for your interview.

- When did you first learn music?
- What has been the best musical experience in your life?
- Have you ever made money with your music?
- What inspires you to practice?
- Why should someone keep studying music?

Share your findings in a report to your class.

▼ Avon Lake, Ohio, Community Band

CREATE A CAREER

What are your interests? How do you like to spend your time? You can combine subjects you are interested in and things you enjoy doing to create your own career. Here are a few examples.

Physics
Microphone Designer
Music

Computers
Multimedia Designer
Art
Music

Health Sciences
Music Therapist
Music
Psychology

Writing
Copyright Lawyer
Music
Research

Math
Royalties Accountant
Music

Religion
Church Musician
Music

Flexible Careers

The world of music and media is constantly developing and changing. People develop and change, too. Many musicians start in one type of job but later try other jobs. Someone who began as a choir director might become a college music professor, and then a music textbook author. A professional musician could later be an elementary music teacher and then land a job in music marketing. A rock musician could go from performer to recording engineer to record producer, composer, or conductor. A video game tester could become a video game programmer and end up as a multimedia producer. The possibilities are endless!

Careers
MULTIMEDIA MUSICIAN
ANDREA WEATHERHEAD

Andrea Weatherhead (born 1960) combined several interests and abilities to create a very flexible career in music. She majored in English at Stanford University in California, and played guitar in a rock band. Next, she worked as a sound engineer, recording live concerts and studio sessions as well as producing records. Weatherhead earned a master's degree in audio engineering, acoustics, and production from American University in Washington, D.C.; then she taught there. She combined her recording experience with her love of visual arts when she worked for Microsoft, programming an interactive Web project featuring a virtual recording studio. Later, Weatherhead used her knowledge of rock music, performance, MIDI, programming, art, and multimedia to design the Sound Lab in Seattle. Now she is co-owner of her own company, Weatherhead Design, that specializes in creating interactive multimedia projects for museums.

▲ Experience Music Project (E.M.P.), designed by Frank Gehry to represent musical form

◄ Sound Lab at E.M.P.

Please Touch the Exhibits!

The Sound Lab at the Experience Music Project in Seattle, Washington, is an interactive display that includes instruments, computers, a stage, and soundproof rooms. And it's all hands-on! The giant "Jam-O-Drum" has lights that respond to what you play. In "On Stage," you and your friends can perform for an audience in your own rock band without a single lesson. All the pitches are programmed into the system. The "Trios" exhibit teaches you to play *Louie Louie.* "DJ Hallway" lets you become a turntable-scratching DJ.

The Business of Music

Review and Assess

Throughout The Business of Music, you have

- learned about different people in the music industry whose job descriptions range from performing artist to sales person.
- discovered how many occupations there are that deal with creating, performing, recording, selling, and disseminating music.
- experimented with the career choices in this module.

One of the best ways to develop your understanding of music careers is to explain your ideas verbally and in writing. Here are three projects that will help you show what you've learned in this module.

Review What You Learned

In small groups, choose three different occupations related to music. You may also choose related occupations not discussed in the module.

Arrange in-person or telephone interviews with one person in each of the three occupations you selected. Before you go, compose a list of questions that you will ask all three of your professionals. Your questions should focus not only on the details of their jobs, like hours, income, and responsibilities, but also on the reasons they had for selecting the occupations they're in, what they like most about their jobs, and what a typical day is like.

If you have recording equipment available, you may ask your interview subjects whether you could record the interviews. If you receive permission, listen to the interviews afterwards to take notes and recall what was discussed. Consider editing your tape to make a concise presentation that summarizes the most interesting and important information that you learned.

Write a brief report that describes each of the professions you investigated and explains the similarities and differences among them.

In small groups of three to four students, discuss the findings. Make sure that everyone in the group understands the observations made by each presenter.

Experience the Life of a Music Professional

Arrange to spend several hours with a music professional at work.

Rather than asking questions, try to observe the person doing the job.

- If your subject is a performing musician, for example, arrange to watch a rehearsal or practice session.
- If your subject is a costume designer, arrange to follow a typical day, either at the office or on site.
- If your subject is a music teacher or music therapist, arrange to see a session with students and clients.
- If your subject works in music sales, arrange to see interaction with customers and processing paperwork associated with music commerce (e.g., inventory, marketing, invoicing).

After your visit, prepare an oral presentation or write a brief paper that describes your experiences. Answer these questions in your summary.

1. What did I learn from observing?
2. How did my preconceptions about the job change after watching someone at work for several hours?
3. Did the job seem like something that I would enjoy doing every day?

Share What You Know

Help others understand the many roles of those involved in music. From among the professions you've been learning about, select one that seems particularly interesting to you. Prepare a presentation for a class of younger children or your peers that illustrates what you've learned about that profession. Your presentation may be placed on poster board, on overhead transparencies, or on slides created with presentation software.

Include in your presentation basic facts about the life of the professional—e.g., job title, responsibilities, daily routine—and descriptions of a person or persons that you observed working at this job. Compose a list of questions to ask after your presentation that covers the facts you presented.

Allow time for your audience to ask questions of you as well. Talk to your teacher about how to prepare for this part of your presentation.

WORLD MUSIC MIX

World Popular Styles and Performers

"In a world such as ours, in this world of cruelty and exploitation in which the tawdry and the mediocre are proliferated endlessly for the sake of financial profit, it is necessary to understand why a madrigal by Gesualdo or a Bach passion, a sitar melody from India or a song from Africa, Berg's Wozzeck or Britten's War Requiem, a Balinese gamelan or a Cantonese opera, or a symphony by Mozart, Beethoven, or Mahler, may be profoundly necessary for human survival."

—John Blacking, ethnomusicologist
(1928–1990)

▲ Irish fiddler

▼ Alpha Yaya Diallo

◀ Andean dancers

Ganbaatar Khongorzul ▶

B–1

1

ROOTS TO POP

Just as each person prefers certain types of food and styles of clothing, people prefer certain kinds of music. Our musical tastes change as we mature and have new experiences. What kind of music did you enjoy when you were younger? Do you still like it now? How have your tastes changed?

Hearing unfamiliar music is like tasting a new food for the first time. Take a chance and you'll find new things to enjoy in food and music. New tastes and sounds can grow on you.

The sounds of world music may be a brand new type of music for you. If you keep your mind and your ears open, you are almost certain to find some styles that suit your taste. As you listen, you may

- Make connections with your "old" favorite styles.
- Discover new favorite artists.
- Open up an entire world of possibilities.

Ready to listen? Let's go!

ON YOUR OWN

Interview family members or friends who are at least ten years older than you about how their taste in music has changed over the years. Are there any groups or styles they have always enjoyed? If their taste has changed, ask them how and why the changes happened.

A Musical Family Tree

Just as you are related to your ancestors, music of today is related to music that came before it. And it helps to know which musical roots or cultures have influenced the music you listen to.

African Ancestors

From the 1600s through the 1800s, millions of Africans were brought to the Americas through the slave trade. Africans brought their rich musical traditions with them. Even though they did not have their own instruments and were often kept from performing their traditional music, their musical structures and styles endured. These musical traditions had a tremendous influence on North and South American as well as Caribbean music. In the United States, African influences can be heard in blues, jazz, gospel, and rock. In the Caribbean Islands, everything from reggae to Afro-Cuban music has African roots. In turn, music from the Americas has traveled back to Africa and influenced the pop scene there.

African Roots to Pop Styles

Listen to these musical examples from Nigeria, Puerto Rico, and South Africa. Use the diagram to **identify** the connections you hear between traditional and contemporary sounds.

Ajaja
African Roots Style

ostinatos
layers
percussion
cross rhythms
call and response

Bomba te traigo yo
Bomba Style

vocals
harmony
cuatro
bass guitar
percussion

Nyamphemphe
Afro-pop Style

vocals
electric guitars
drum set
percussion

Ajaja

2-1 written and performed by Babatunde Olatunji

Ajaja is a song in call-and-response style, which is commonly found in traditional West African music.

Bomba te traigo yo

2-2 by José González as performed by *José González y Banda Criolla*

This Puerto Rican song is in a style called *bomba*. This style of party music incorporates African-influenced rhythms.

Nyamphemphe

2-3 by Marube Jagome and Marks Mankwane as performed by Mahlathini and the Mahotella Queens

This South African highlife song features ultra-bass male solos with all-female harmony singing.

Ostinatos Unite!

The music of every culture has characteristics that make it unique. Even so, diverse cultures that are independent of each other sometimes develop music with strikingly similar characteristics. For example, **ostinatos** are found in cultures throughout the world. Musicians everywhere use ostinatos because repetition appeals to listeners and can give music a great groove!

Listen to *Ostinatos Around the World*, which includes music from a variety of cultures. **Describe** how the ostinato is used in each selection.

Ostinatos Around the World

2-4 *Sabhayatâ*
2-5 *Yolele*
2-6 *Over and Under a Theme of Mark Isham's*

The first selection is performed by Karmix, a fusion band that incorporates European, Algerian, Indian, and Brazilian music styles. The second selection is by Papa Wemba, a popular performer from the Congo. The third selection is by Terry Bozzio, a drummer from the United States who plays the theme, using African and Asian percussion techniques.

ostinatos Short rhythm or melody patterns in music that repeat.

▼ The Peatbog Faeries

▼ Papa Wemba

Get in the Groove

When multiple ostinatos are layered and performed together, they can establish a rhythmic groove that gets your toes tapping. **Listen** to the layered ostinatos in the percussion accompaniment of the Celtic pop song *Faerie Stories*. Then choose an instrument from the arrangement and **play** along.

Faerie Stories

by P. Morrison

2-7 **as performed by the Peatbog Faeries**

This selection opens with live and electronic drums. When the bagpipes enter, they take the lead role.

Note This

The music of the Peatbog Faeries, a popular band from Scotland, combines traditional Celtic sounds with styles from the Americas, including jazz, hip-hop, and reggae.

An Ear for Color

When you listen to a recording, you cannot see the instruments that are playing. The only way to recognize them is by their sound, also known as tone color, or **timbre.** Timbre is like a musical fingerprint—it is unique to each instrument and voice type. Training your ear to spot different timbres can help you identify

- Each instrumental or voice part in the music.
- The regional origin of the music.
- The style of the music.

---

timbre The unique sound of a musical instrument or voice.

Percussion Rocks the World

In American popular music, the rhythm section—drum set, bass, and keyboard or guitar—often establishes the groove. Many world cultures, however, use different kinds of percussion instruments in various combinations to lay a musical foundation.

Listen to *World Percussion Sounds.* **Describe** the timbres of the instruments. From what region of the world does each selection come? How are the selections similar? How are they different?

◀ *Balaphon* player (Ghana, West Africa)

World Percussion Sounds

2-8 *Rain*
2-9 *Wandenza*
2-10 *A Quality of Seven*
2-11 *Rhythms of the Cook Islands*

These selections feature percussion instruments from Egypt, Uganda, India, and the Cook Islands.

◀ *Tabla* players (India): Alla Rakha (left) and Zakir Hussain ▶

Strings Attached

The unique sounds and timbres of string instruments can be heard all over the world. Some string-instrument musicians can play both solos and accompaniments. Traditionally, string instruments are **acoustic** instruments. When plugged into amplifiers and effects processors, their timbres change. String instruments can also sound different when used in world pop styles.

Listen to *World String Sounds* and **identify** the string instrument you hear in each selection.

World String Sounds

2-12 *Calliope House*
2-13 *Puente de los alunados*
2-14 *Bebiendo al alba*
2-15 *Drift*
2-16 *Duniya*

These selections feature the sounds of the Irish fiddle, *flamenco* guitar, *cuatro*, *ud*, violin, lute, and harp.

▲ *Flamenco* guitarist

▲ *Pipa* player

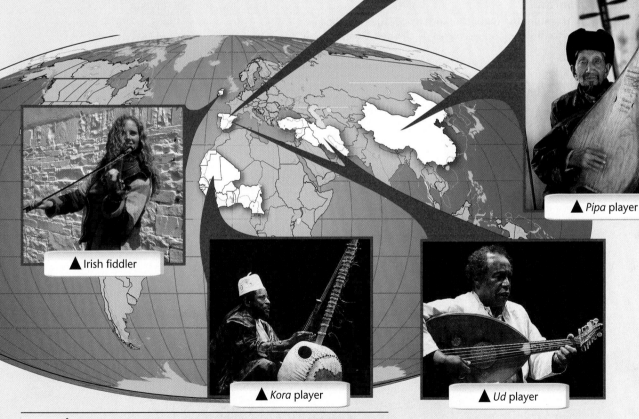
▲ Irish fiddler

▲ *Kora* player

▲ *Ud* player

acoustic Term for an instrument that is not electronically amplified; for example, an *acoustic* guitar.

Worldwide Winds

Woodwind and brass instruments add spice to pop music. Wind instruments do not appear in every piece, but when they do, they are hard to miss! Woodwinds—flutes and reed instruments—have somewhat different designs and timbres, depending on the culture in which they were developed. Brass instruments—especially trumpets and trombones—are typically included in Latin musical styles, particularly *salsa*. They really help make music saucy! Winds and brass liven up *klezmer* music too.

Listen to *World Winds* for examples of woodwinds and brass in popular music. **Describe** the timbre of the instruments. **Identify** the instruments you hear and the musical style.

World Winds

2-17 *Tribute to Peadar O'Donnell*
2-18 *Through My Eyes*
2-19 *Tema de maimara*
2-20 *Gimpel the Fool*

These selections feature the timbres of Irish and Native American flutes, panpipes from Peru, and *klezmer*-style clarinet, trumpet, and trombone.

▲ *Klezmer* clarinet player

▲ Irish flute player

▲ Panpipe player

▲ Native American flute player

Sounds Like . . .

Now is the time to test your world music ears. **Listen** closely to the instruments played in *World Instrument Families*. For each selection, first **identify** the instrument family, or families. Then look for a photo below that corresponds to each timbre you hear. Finally, match the listening selection with the name of a country.

ON YOUR OWN

Research the history of one of these instruments or another you find interesting. Why and how did the instrument develop? Report your discoveries in class.

 World Instrument Families

2-21 *The Waves of the Gola*
2-22 *Chang on the Jew's Harp*
2-23 *Toei khong*
2-24 *Inongo*

These selections, representing various cultures, feature instruments from the string, wind, and percussion families.

AFRICA   LAOS   Ireland   Pakistan

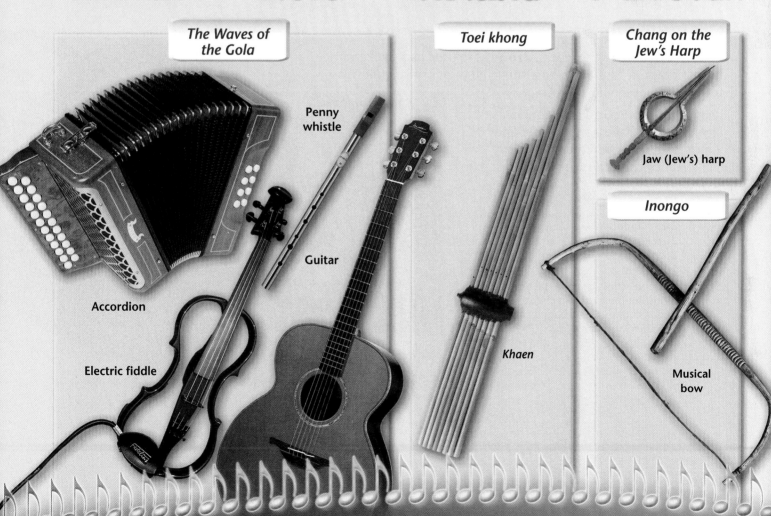

The Waves of the Gola

Penny whistle

Guitar

Accordion

Electric fiddle

Toei khong

Khaen

Chang on the Jew's Harp

Jaw (Jew's) harp

Inongo

Musical bow

Drones and *Scales*

3

While there are many different styles, methods, and reasons for making music, people sing and play instruments all over the world. People have made music in virtually every culture throughout the history of humankind.

Pitch is a common element in the music of many cultures. The relationship, or "space," between two pitches is called an interval. You can learn more about intervals in Sounds and Symbols on page H-7. Three specific intervals tend to appear in music all over the world—the fourth, the fifth, and the octave. Use the diagram on the right to find examples of these intervals on a keyboard. Listen for these intervals in the music in this lesson.

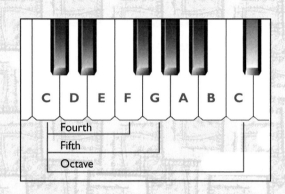

C D E F G A B C
Fourth
Fifth
Octave

Ground Sound

In many regions of the world, **drones** are used as a background for melodies. A drone can be a single pitch or an interval of a fourth, fifth, or even an octave.

Listen for drones in *Planet Drone*. Notice which have a single note and which combine two notes. **Describe** the effect of the drone in the music.

Planet Drone

2-25 *Bairagi*
2-26 *Khöömei*
2-27 *Eanáir*
2-28 *Gapu*

These selections include the droning sounds of the Indian *tanpura,* Tuvan throat singing, Celtic bagpipes, and the Australian aboriginal *yidaki* (*didjeridu*).

▲ Throat singer from the Republic of Tuva

▲ Celtic bagpipes

pitch Another word for a musical note, pitch is how high or low a note sounds. In science, pitch is known as frequency.

drone A continuous, unvarying musical sound, used to accompany melodies.

Tales of Scales

Although almost every culture uses fourths, fifths, and octaves, that is where pitch similarity ends. Most American and European music uses 12 "half steps" or divisions per octave. Some cultures use fewer, and some use many more. It may be hard to believe, but humans are capable of hearing about 120 variations in pitch per octave.

▲ Performers featured in *Singing Scales*

Every culture has specific **scales** on which its music is based, and there are hundreds of scales in the world.

One of the most common scales, the pentatonic scale, is made up of five pitches. Many pentatonic scales have no half steps. You can easily play this type of scale on the keyboard. Start on the black key for F♯, play five black keys going up, and you have it! Versions of this pentatonic scale are used in several Asian cultures, in folk music from the Appalachian region of the United States, and in other regions worldwide.

Indian and Arabic cultures use pitches called *microtones*—tiny variations in pitch that are smaller than those familiar in Western music. As early as six months of age, humans develop sensitivity to the scales used in their own cultures. You may need to stretch your ears to appreciate the different scales used in music from around the world.

Listen to *Singing Scales*, which includes music based on scale systems from a variety of cultures. Write down words that describe what you hear.

 Singing Scales

2-29 *Vaka atua*
2-30 *The Face of Love*
2-31 *Neend koyi*
2-32 *Mayingo*

These songs include examples of Polynesian, Pakistani, and Persian singing, as well as singing from the West African nation of Gabon.

Note This

Without a melody over it, a drone could be incredibly monotonous. The term *drone* is also used to describe a boring speaker.

---

scale The arrangement of pitches from lower to higher, according to a specific pattern of intervals.

World Voices

The voice is an amazing instrument. Like a fingerprint, each person's voice is unique. Its capabilities depend both on the singer's physical makeup and cultural background.

When you hear a song, you might notice whether the singer is male or female and the **range** of the song. Is the range wide or narrow? **Listen** to these recordings. **Describe** the quality and range of each performer's voice.

Shumba

written and performed by Thomas Mapfumo

2-33 Mapfumo, who is from Zimbabwe, has a rich voice, and his singing seems to merge spoken phrases with lyrical melodies.

She Is Like the Swallow

Folk song from Ireland

2-34 **as performed by Karan Casey**

Casey's clear vocal quality and her melodic phrasing are typical of many Irish singers.

From Solo to Group

Songs with contrasting vocal textures can be more interesting to the listener. Using more than one singer also changes the timbre and intensity of a song. **Listen** to these recordings. **Describe** the voices you hear and **analyze** how the texture or timbre changes when more voices are added.

Tihore mai

by Hirini Melbourne

2-35 **as performed by Moena and the Moahunters**

This is a song from the Maori people of New Zealand.

Vonjeo

written and performed by Rajery

2-36 Rajery is known as the "Prince of the *valiha*" (African tube zither) in his native Madagascar.

▲ Karan Casey

Thomas Mapfumo ▶

---

range A term used to describe the span from the lowest pitch to the highest pitch in a voice or piece of music.

The Ear of the Beholder

People identify with and respond to different qualities in the singing voice. Preferences vary from culture to culture and even within the same culture. **Listen** to two singers with very different voices and **describe** what you hear. Both singers are considered great artists in their cultures.

Allah hoo Allah hoo

by Nusrat Fateh Ali Khan
2-37   This singer was from Pakistan.

The Blower's Daughter

by Damien Rice
2-38   This singer is from Ireland.

Nusrat Fateh Ali Khan ▲

Ornamentation

Singers have many ways to "decorate" their songs. Decoration in music is called *ornamentation*. The type and amount of ornamentation in music varies from culture to culture.

Listen to *Vocal Ornamentations* and **describe** how each singer decorates the melody.

Vocal Ornamentations

2-39 *Hai wedi*
2-40 *Byala stala*
2-41 *Siuil á ruin*
2-42 *Akita kusakari uta*

These vocal selections are sung in Arabic, Bulgarian, English, and Japanese.

▲ Damien Rice

Scottish Melodic Variation

Listen to this version of a traditional chant. **Read** the plain melody and the variation. **Sing** the chant; then **create** your own variation, with or without words.

Melody

Yun - dah   yun - dah   yun - dah   oh dah.

Variation

He-ee oh dun dah, He-ee oh dun dah, He-ee oh dun dah,   oh   dah.

Sealwoman/Yundah

Folk song from Scotland
2-43 **as arranged and performed by Mary McLaughlin**
Yundah is a traditional chant from the Hebrides Islands, off the coast of Scotland.

▲ Mary McLaughlin

Vocal Olympics

Just like Olympic athletes, singers around the world perform physical feats that inspire and amaze us. **Listen** to this example of how long someone can sing on a single breath.

Mongolian Long Song

Mongolian traditional long song
2-44 **as performed by Ganbaatar Khongorzul**
Originally sung on the open plains of Mongolia, the traditional *long song* got its name because of the way very few words are stretched over long musical phrases.

Rap for a Reason

Listen to this pop song, which features *haka*, a rap-like performance style meant to convey messages like "beware," "private property," and "don't interfere with our culture."

Tahi

as performed by Moana and the Moahunters
2-45 *Haka* is a genre of dance and rhythm chant that is popular among the Maori of New Zealand.

▼Ganbaatar Khongorzul

▼Moana and the Moahunters

Go for the Gold

Now, **listen** to *Vocal Olympics*, which includes examples of even more stupendous vocal feats.

Vocal Olympics

2-46 *Round Dance*
2-47 *Cô hàng xóm*
2-48 *Kargyraa-style Song*

These songs are performed by Native American, Vietnamese, and Tuvan singers.

When Cultures Combine

What happens when singers from two distinctively different cultures come together to sing the same song? If they are true artists, with carefully crafted vocal skills, and if they listen perceptively to one another, the results can be masterly!

Listen to the way each singer sings the melody in *The Face of Love*. **Describe** the differences between the two singing styles.

The Face of Love

2-49

by Eddie Vedder
as performed by Nusrat Fateh Ali Khan and Eddie Vedder

Nusrat Fateh Ali Khan (1948–1997) was a renowned singer from Pakistan. Eddie Vedder is the vocalist for the band Pearl Jam.

Your Turn

Play the melody for *The Face of Love* on a keyboard or other melody instrument. Then **create** your own version with another performer.

ON YOUR OWN

Listen to some recordings you have at home. Do your favorite singers use ornamentation? Identify a song in which the melody is ornamented in spots. How does ornamentation affect the music? Share your findings in class.

Eddie Vedder ▶

5

Celebrate!

Celebrations take place when people gather to commemorate an important event, a person, or a holiday. Some celebrations are just for fun. Music is often a very important part of celebrations.

Carnaval in Brazil

The days just before the solemn season of Lent are a time for great celebration in many places around the world. In Brazil, *Carnaval* celebrations are centered in three major cities—Salvador da Bahi, Rio de Janeiro, and Olinda. Hundreds of thousands of people show up for parades, processionals, and parties in these cities. All through the year, drumming practice in the *samba* schools is geared toward preparing for these events, which usually occur in February. Bands dance down the streets or ride on the backs of open trucks. Celebrants wear wild and colorful costumes as they parade down the streets.

Listen to *Malê Debalê*, a song that you might hear at *Carnaval*. **Identify** and **describe** the way percussion instruments are used in the song. Listen again and **improvise** rhythms on drums, tambourines, or maracas.

Malê Debalê

2-50

by E. Pacheco and P. C. Pinheiro
as performed by Lazzo

Malê Debalê is the name of an Afro band from the Brazillian state of Bahia.

◀ *Carnaval* celebrations, Rio de Janeiro

Carnaval in the Caribbean

Carnaval is particularly lively in the Caribbean Islands. From Port-au-Prince, Haiti, to Port of Spain, Trinidad, the islands are full of drumming, dancing, singing, and marching party-goers. **Listen** to this recording from Haiti with a reggae beat. **Move** to the music by stretching to the right for four beats, then to the left for four beats, while nodding your head. Then stand up and move a little more!

Retounen

written and performed by King Posse

2-51 This song begs King Posse's fans not to be upset if the band doesn't show up for *Carnaval!*

Carnaval in Colombia

The sounds of *Carnaval* in Colombia, South America, include the *cumbia*, Colombia's national music. Trumpets, trombones, saxophones, and keyboards blend with percussion and voices for an unmistakable sound. **Listen** to this *cumbia* from Colombia. As you listen, **improvise** a rhythm pattern on percussion.

Mardi Gras!

In New Orleans, Louisiana, *Carnaval* is called *Mardi Gras*, French for "Fat Tuesday." Why do you think they call it "Fat Tuesday"? (Hint: Lent always begins on a Wednesday.) **Listen** to the chord changes in *I Know You Mardi Gras*. Then **identify** the form of the song.

▲ *Carnaval* parade, St. John (U.S. Virgin Islands)

El nuevo caiman

by Ernesto "Fruko" Estrada

2-52 **as performed by** *Fruko y Ses Tesos*

This song, in the highly syncopated *cumbia* style, is about a well-traveled alligator.

I Know You Mardi Gras

written and performed by Eddie Bo

2-53 This song features solos played on a bass trombone.

▲ *Mardi Gras* parade, New Orleans

The Power of Powwows

In Native American culture, gatherings to celebrate life are known as powwows. Most often held in the summer, powwows include speechmaking, giftgiving, feasting, dancing, and much musicmaking. Powwows take place in many places throughout North America and can last anywhere from a single weekend to an entire week. People often travel long distances to attend. Music and dancing are two of the most important elements of a powwow. Participants dressed in traditional tribal attire sing, play, and dance all day and far into the night.

The Black Lodge Singers are popular performers at local and intertribal powwows. **Listen** to them sing this song that they perform at powwows. As you listen, **identify** the melodic contour of each phrase.

▲ Red Earth powwow drummers

Intertribal Song

Powwow song
2-54 **as performed by the Black Lodge Singers**
Most members of the Black Lodge Singers are also members of the Blackfoot Nation.

The Black Lodge Singers ▼

Beyond Tradition

Now **listen** to this recording of *Cherokee Morning Song*. **Identify** the elements that make this traditional song sound more contemporary. **Play** along on the beat, using shakers or a drum.

 ### *Cherokee Morning Song*

Cherokee Song

2-55   **as performed by Walela**

Walela is a group of three Native American women. They sing traditional as well as contemporary songs and add techniques such as harmony and electronics.

ON YOUR OWN

Why and how do people celebrate? How does the music you have heard relate to the music you hear at your celebrations? The next time you attend a celebration in your community, listen carefully to the music. How is it similar to the music in this lesson? How is it different?

Walela ▶

Checkpoint

Review the music you listened to in lessons one through five. Which selections appeal to your ears and your mind? In each of those selections, what musical elements are the most appealing? Describe the elements in terms of rhythm, melody, form, timbre, and texture/harmony.

6

DANCE MUSIC

Dance has been an instinctive form of expression since the beginning of human history. Music inspires people to move. Most cultures have their own styles of dancing and their own type of music for dancing.

Scandinavia

The popular dances in the Scandinavian countries of Norway, Sweden, Finland, and Denmark involve turning and twirling movements. Couples fill the dance floors for such dances as the waltz, polka, *polska*, *pols*, *hambo*, and *springar*.

Listen to the Finnish tune *Bambodansarna*. This dance is called a *polska*. In a *polska*, partners twirl around the room, making a full turn every three beats. **Identify** the instruments you hear.

Bambodansarna

by Olov Johansson
3-1 **as performed by Väsen**
One of the instruments in this recording functions as a drone under the melody.

▲ Scandinavian folk dancers

Ireland

Jigs and reels are the most famous styles of Irish dancing. **Listen** to *Tommy Peoples,* a reel in traditional style.

Tommy Peoples

by Tommy Peoples
3-2 **as performed by Altan**
This reel might be heard at a *feis,* a Gaelic word for an Irish harvest celebration.

Listen again and **play** this pattern with your fingertips on your desktop or on a hand drum laid flat on your lap.

◀ Irish reel dancers

Greece

In Greece, dance music is popular at weddings, family reunions, picnics, in restaurants and clubs, and at other significant events. Greek dance formations include circles, lines, and couples. There are styles where men and women dance separately and together. Public schools in Greece include dance as a major subject, and therefore many Greeks know how to perform the traditional dances easily and beautifully.

Listen for the sound of the *bouzouki* (a long-necked mandolin), drum set, and electric bass in *Stalia, Stalia*. Notice that the music is in duple meter. As you listen, perform the combined rhythm of the drums and bass, using a pat-clap pattern. When you are ready, **sing** along with the melody that is played on the *bouzouki*.

Now **move** to the music, using these dance steps. Begin with your weight on the left foot.

▲ Greek folk dancers

Beat 1, step R	Beat 2, cross L in front
Beat 1, step R	Beat 2, cross L behind
Beat 1, step R	Beat 2, point L
Beat 1, step L	Beat 2, point R

Begin again and continue throughout the music.

 Stalia, Stalia

3-3 **Folk dance from Greece as performed by Alexandros Xenofrontos**

This selection was featured in the film *My Big Fat Greek Wedding*.

Asia

In northeastern Thailand, where Laotian culture is prominent, traditional music has been reinvented, with new instruments and added technology. **Read** the melody of a popular *mawlum* song, *Toei khong*, which is meant to be sung by a young man and woman to express their love for each other.

Now **listen** to *Toei khong* as performed by a contemporary band from Canada.

 Toei khong

3-4 **Traditional music from Thailand as performed by Asza**

Asza is a Canadian fusion band.

◀ Dancers from the Wai Thai classical dance group

ON YOUR OWN

What kind of music do you like for dancing? Which music in this lesson is most similar to your favorite music? Did your parents or other older family members enjoy dancing to the same style of music when they were teens? Ask them what was popular then and compare it to today's dance music.

India in Great Britain

Young people from India living in Great Britain revolutionized Indian music by taking a traditional style of Punjabi dance music, called *bhangra*, and remixing the melodies on top of rhythm tracks. **Listen** to *Saqian da dhol*, a song in this new Indian style. **Perform** this ostinato using body percussion or nonpitched percussion instruments as you listen.

pat   clap   snap-snap   clap   pat   clap   snap-snap   clap

 Saqian da dhol

3-5 **as performed by Saqi**
This recording features the sound of the *dholak*, a double-headed drum.

◀ Singer from the group
Bhangra Jazzi B

The Andes

In the Andes Mountains of South America, dances are lively. Favorite dance-music instruments include wood flutes, panpipes, lutes called *charangos*, shakers made from llama hooves, and *bomba* drums. **Listen** to *Baila caporal*, an example of Andes dance music. **Play** this rhythm on a drum along with the recording.

 Baila caporal

3-6 by Roberto Marquez
as performed by Illapu
Although Andean dances are lively, the music often has rather sad lyrics about lost love.

▲ Andes-Quechoua Indian
dancers (Bolivia)

Caribbean Dancing

In the French Antilles, as in most of the Caribbean islands, many people have ancestors from both Europe and Africa. This Euro-African blend is reflected in the islands' style of music and dancing. A highly energetic type of party music, called *zouk*, has become very popular. **Listen** to *Carrament News*, a song in *zouk* style. Notice and tap along with the repeated patterns played by guitar, bass, and brass.

 **Carrament News**

3-7 as performed by Gazoline
Zouk has now traveled from the Caribbean back to Europe, where it is popular in the Caribbean communities in Paris.

Calypso to *Soca* to *Salsa*

Trinidad is known for its calypso music. People dance to calypso even though the songs often express political views. In recent years drum machines have been added to calypso. Elements of calypso have also fused with soul music to create a whole new style called *soca*. **Listen** to this *soca* from Trinidad. **Move** to the music. Form a line or circle, then step forward for eight beats and back for eight beats, clapping on each weak beat (beats 2, 4, and so on). Then **improvise** eight-beat movement patterns. Think party!

Love You Forever

written and performed by Lord Nelson

3-8 Lord Nelson has appeared on calypso and *soca*-style albums since 1962. He recorded *Love You Forever* in 1988.

We can thank Puerto Ricans and Cubans for the development of the "spicy" style of music and dance called *salsa*. **Listen** to this tune by Puerto Rican *salsa* giant, Eddie Palmieri.

Humpty Dumpty

written and performed by Eddie Palmieri

3-9 You may recognize the lyrics of this song from a well-known nursery rhyme.

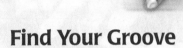

▲ *Salsa* dancers

Find Your Groove

With a partner or small group, **create** a piece using eight-beat patterns that really groove. **Play** your piece on percussion instruments. Then **move** to your music.

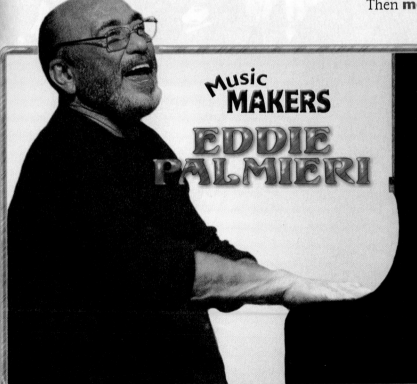

Music MAKERS
EDDIE PALMIERI

Eddie Palmieri (born 1936) is a pianist, composer, arranger, and band leader. He has been a major innovator of *salsa* music since it first hit the dance scene in New York's Puerto Rican community in the 1950s. He was born to Puerto Rican parents in New York City and began playing classical piano at the age of eight. At age eleven he made his debut at Carnegie Hall in New York. After playing in various bands, he formed his own band in the early 1960s, and later received a Grammy award for his contributions to *salsa* music. He has since released more than 32 award-winning albums, seven of which have won Grammy awards.

7

Hear the Band!

One of the best parts of being a musician is playing in a group. When the right combination of musicians gets together, the results can be amazing! **Ensemble** playing requires each player to listen carefully to the others and to adjust as needed to make the music sound best.

Border Music

A popular style of music along the border of Texas and Mexico is *conjunto*, a combination of Spanish-style music from Mexico and German polkas from Texas. Eva Ybarra, an accordion player and one of the few women to achieve recognition in the *conjunto* style, leads an ensemble called *Eva Ybarra y su Conjunto*. Ybarra began playing the accordion when she was four. By the time she was six, she and her brother were playing in restaurants around San Antonio, Texas. **Listen** to some music written and performed by Eva Ybarra. **Identify** the instruments you hear and **describe** how well the players collaborate.

A mi querido Austin

by Eva Ybarra
3-10   **as performed by** *Eva Ybarra y su Conjunto*
This song celebrates Austin, the capital of Texas.

---

ensemble A group united for a single artistic purpose, such as making music.

▲ Eva Ybarra

Klezmer Sounds

Klezmer bands sometimes play concerts and make recordings, but they are best known for playing at parties. Originally found in the Jewish tradition of Eastern Europe, the *klezmer* style includes wind, brass, and string instruments, as well as a singer. *Klezmer* is sometimes fondly referred to as Jewish jazz because of the extensive improvisation performed by band members.

▲ Trombone

▲ Clarinet

Listen to *Slow Hora/Freylekhs*. **Describe** the unique sounds of the clarinet and trombone.

Slow Hora/Freylekhs

3-11

Traditional Yiddish melody
as performed by the Klezmer Conservatory Band
This piece is originally from Romania.

Perform the first theme from the *Slow Hora* section on a melody instrument with the recording.

THEME 1 (simplified)

▲ The Klezmer Conservatory Band

Two Worlds Join Together

Considered one of the hottest world music styles today, *bhangra* began as the music of field workers in the Punjabi region of northern India. The workers sang about working hard and playing hard. When many of them immigrated to Great Britain, traditional *bhangra* was mixed with various styles of pop music, and a whole new style was born.

Bhangra has a unique flavor. Depending on the artist, it may be fused with rhythm and blues, disco, *salsa*, hip-hop, or reggae. *Bhangra* bands usually include a double-headed drum called the *dholak,* a pair of *tabla,* and the harmonium.

▼ Dholak

▲ Tabla

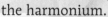
▲ Harmonium

A Dynamic Duo

Listen to *Terian gulabi buliyan* by A.S. Kang, a world-renowned singer of Punjabi and *bhangra* music. The other member of this ensemble is Sukshinder Shinda, a leading producer of *bhangra.* He is a multi-instrumentalist who plays all of the instruments on this recording. Notice the rhythm and blues feel of this music. **Identify** the various instruments you hear. Work in a small group to **create** your own map of the musical events in this piece. Show the instruments used and their relationship to the vocal part.

▲ Sukshinder Shinda

▲ A.S. Kang

Terian gulabi buliyan

by A.S. Kang

3-12   A.S. Kang had his first hit record, *Lut Ke lehgai,* in the early 1970s. He was the first Punjabi artist from Britain to make the hit charts in India.

Polynesian Pop

Te Vaka is a band of eight men and two women from New Zealand that blends Polynesian music with pop.

Listen to *Lua afe (2000)*, written to celebrate the new millennium. It conveys a wish that people of all colors, races, and religions learn to live together without prejudice. Notice the rhythms of traditional Polynesian log drums, as well as the other sounds that add to the rhythmic feel of this music.

Lua afe (2000)

by Opetaia Foa'i
3-13   **as performed by Te Vaka**

Te Vaka's music includes guitar, keyboard, log drums, and other percussion instruments, as well as singing and dancing. Opetaia Foa'i is the leader of the band.

Listen to another song by Te Vaka called *Ki mua*, which means "to the future." **Compare** it with *Lua afe (2000)*. **Sing** along during the last verse.

ga-lu-lue mai ki mu-a nei   ta-ha-hao mai ki mu-a nei
pe-he-pehe mai ki mu-a nei   fa-te-le mai ki mu-a nei

Ki mua

by Opetaia Foa'i
3-14   **as performed by Te Vaka**

Ki mua is a song of gratitude to the composer's parents, who risked a great deal to give their children a better education.

Afro-pop

Many great pop music sounds come out of Africa. The combinations of instruments vary with the region and style. Some bands use instruments associated with cultures outside of Africa, including brass, saxophones, drum set, and guitars. Others include more traditional instruments, such as African drums and xylophones. Most bands use a combination of instruments. Afro-pop establishes a feeling that is distinctly African by using ostinatos, layers of patterns, repetition, and cross-rhythms.

Listen to the song *Badenma* (*Friendship*) by West African artist and multi-instrumentalist, Alpha Yaya Diallo. In this song, Diallo is singing as well as playing the guitar, *djembe,* and *dundun* drums. He is accompanied by the *balafon*, congas, bass guitar, and more drums. **Identify** the sounds of these instruments and the roles they play.

Badenma uses a typical pentatonic scale from Africa. **Listen** for this pattern in the music, then **play** it on the black keys of a keyboard.

▲ Balafon

◀ Djembe

▲ Congas

Badenma (Friendship)

by Alpha Yaya Diallo

3-15   Diallo sings in the Malinke language in this song. The lyrics convey the message that working together in friendship is better than fighting.

▲ Alpha Yaya Diallo

Celtic Near and Far

Celtic bands are some of the most popular to come out of the British Isles. The Celtic people lived for thousands of years in the Scottish Highlands, Ireland, Wales, England, and Cape Breton Island in Canada. Many of their descendents still live in those places. They speak a language called Gaelic. The Celts also left a rich heritage of lively music and dance.

▲ Seamus Egan with Solas

When these people from the British Isles immigrated to the United States, they brought their music with them. Many of them settled in the Appalachian Mountains of the eastern United States. That region is now known for its distinctive musical style as well.

Listen to *The Flowing Bowl* and *Soldier's Joy*. **Compare** the two recordings and **identify** similarities and differences. The instruments used in each piece are listed in the diagram. Notice which instruments are used in both selections.

Discuss the style of playing by each group. Which instrument plays the melody, or lead? How do the lead instruments relate to each other? How do the instruments trade off? Are the rhythms in each piece similar or different?

The Flowing Bowl

Irish flute
bagpipes
bass
accordion

fiddle
guitar

Soldier's Joy

Dobro®
banjo
penny whistle
piano

The Flowing Bowl

3-16

by Seamus [SHAY mus] Egan
as performed by Solas
The Flowing Bowl is composed in Celtic folk style.

Soldier's Joy

3-17

Folk melody from Appalachia
arranged by Mark O'Connor
The melody in *Soldier's Joy* is traded back and forth among the various instruments. Each instrument adds its unique color to the music.

Checkpoint

Work alone or with a partner to research one of the ensembles you have heard in this lesson or another world music ensemble. **Describe** their instruments, music, and style to your class.

Dig-a Dum!

8

Say *dig - a dum.*

Say it fast, slow, once out loud, and once silently. This rhythm is at the heart of musicmaking all around the world. As sure as singers sing, drummers drum, guitarists strum, and fiddlers fiddle, the *dig-a dum* rhythm pattern is imbedded in the music they perform.

The genius of Wolfgang Amadeus Mozart turned *dig-a dum* into musical brilliance in his *Symphony No. 40 in G Minor*. The repeated *dig-a dum* rhythm makes this one of the most catchy tunes of all time. **Listen** to this excerpt of the first movement from *Symphony No. 40*. **Sing** from notation this opening phrase of the theme.

dig - a dum dig - a dum dig - a dum ___ dig - a dum dig - a dum dig - a dum

Symphony No. 40 in G Minor, K. 550

3-18

Movement 1
by W. A. Mozart
as performed by the Chicago Symphony Orchestra
Mozart (1756–1791) wrote this piece in 1788, hoping it would earn him some money and a higher position in the musical life of Vienna.

Planet *Dig-a Dum*

The *dig-a dum* rhythm occurs in many different musical styles, and it is played by all kinds of musical groups around the world. **Listen** to *Imbube* and *Rice Bowl*. **Identify** the instruments playing the *dig-a dum* rhythm and tap it along with the recording.

Imbube (Wimoweh)

3-19

Folk melody from South Africa
adapted and arranged by G. Beggs, S.R. and T. Khemese, and M. Mnguni
as performed by the Soweto String Quartet
You will hear the *dig-a dum* rhythm in the accompaniment.

Rice Bowl

3-20

by ASIABEAT
The members of the jazz-fusion group ASIABEAT are some of the best musicians in Singapore. Their music blends Latin, Chinese, Indian, Malaysian, Japanese, and Western styles.

▼ ASIABEAT

◄ The *jaltarong* plays melodic phrases over the *dig-a dum* rhythm.

Variations on *Dig-a Dum*

Any simple rhythm can sound quite different when performed by musicians from different cultures and traditions. It can be played on different instruments, as a solo or with a group, fast or slow, loud or soft. It can be in the melody, in a background accompaniment, or repeated over and over as an ostinato. The rhythm can be ornamented or varied, and yet we can still recognize it as a part of the texture of the music.

Listen to *Dig-a Dum Variations*, samples of music in which the *dig-a dum* rhythm is varied in different ways. For example, sometimes *dig-a dum* becomes *diggity-dum*. **Describe** how the rhythm is used in each piece. **Improvise** *dig-a dum* rhythms with the recording.

Dig-a Dum Variations

3-21 *Vale do javari*
3-22 *Karaw*
3-23 *Ijexá, Filhos de Gandhi*
3-24 *Wo ba wo ba shue*

These selections are from the Amazon, Mali, Brazil, and Ghana.

Gavioes da Fiel, *samba* percussion school from Brazil ▼

Dig-a Dum Extensions

The versatile *dig-a dum* rhythm can be linked with other rhythms to form an extended rhythmic pattern. Musicians in West Africa enjoy layering a variety of percussion instruments in various rhythm patterns. In this recording, **listen** to the woodblock and **play** its time-keeping pattern. How is the *dig-a dum* rhythm extended?

Ekombi

written and performed by Sowah Mensah

3-25   The percussion instruments featured in this piece are made from wood, metal, and animal skin, which creates an interesting mix of timbres.

Ali Farka Touré, guitarist from Mali ▶

Rap-a Dum

Dig-a dum rhythms can be found in rap music too. **Read** this rhythm, and then rap along with the recording.

dig-a dum dig-a dum dig-a dig-a dig-a dum

Rap Intro

by Speaking in Tongues

3-26 This rap, performed by Gao Hong, is spoken in Chinese.

◀ Gao Hong, from the group Speaking in Tongues, playing a *pipa*

Dig-a Dum Duo

Listen to the recording of an Afghani lute, called a *rabāb*, playing a duo with an Indian *tabla*. Notice the ten-beat melody played on the *rabāb*. Find the *dig-a dum* rhythm in the melody. **Sing** the melody with the recording.

dig-a dig-a dig-a dum dig-a dig-a dum dum dig-a dum

Tabla Solo

by Ustad Mohammad Omar and Zakir Hussain

3-27 Afghani *rabāb* player Ustad Mohammad Omar and Indian *tabla* player Zakir Hussain are both among the top musicians in their respective countries.

◀ Zakir Hussain

Your Turn to *Dig-a Dum*

Now that you have heard the *dig-a dum* rhythm used by musicians around the planet, it is time for you to *dig-a dum*. Work on one or more of these projects.

Nonpitched *Dig-a Dum*

With a group of four or five players, **create** a 16-beat *dig-a dum* piece using nonpitched percussion. Determine

- Whether *dig-a dum* will be played as an ostinato.
- Which instrument(s) will play the *dig-a dum*.
- Whether all instruments will play constantly, or only on certain beats.

Practice the piece. Then **perform** it for your class.

Pitched *Dig-a Dum*

Create a 16-beat *dig-a dum* piece for pitched instruments such as keyboard, xylophones, guitar, recorder, or whatever is available. Include the *dig-a dum* rhythm prominently as a constant sound or as a rhythm that can be heard often. **Perform** it for your class.

Rap *Dig-a Dum*

Compose a vocal rap based on *dig-a dum* rhythms. Think of words that have the same short-short-long pattern, such as *hap-py day*, *best of friends,* and *on-ly you.* Experiment with ideas, write them down, and then link them together. **Create** six lines of four beats each. Use a *dig-a dum* rhythm at least once per line. Vary your rap by emphasizing certain beats, and make some lines louder or softer. Add percussion or body percussion (stamps, pats, claps, snaps) to your rap. **Perform** it for your class.

ON YOUR OWN

Listen to your favorite recordings and find four examples of *dig-a dum* rhythms. Share them in class.

◄ Ustad Mohammad Omar

9 MUSIC FOR DRAMA

▲ Scene from the film *Close Encounters of the Third Kind*

Film and theater producers around the world use music to increase the interest and emotional impact of their films. Music can enhance visual images and motivate us to remember them. The themes from a movie can help us recall the characters, the setting, the plot, and the point of a film. Sometimes, even when we have not seen the movie, we can get a sense of its plot or its atmosphere by listening to its music.

Listen to these recordings of film music. **Describe** the scene you think each musical excerpt might represent. Notice the composer's choice of instruments or voices. Is the music fast or slow? Loud or soft? Is the texture of the music thin or thick? How can you tell from listening to the music which world cultures are represented?

Close Encounters of the Third Kind

3-28

by John Williams
as performed by the City of Prague Philharmonic and the Crouch End Festival Chorus

This music is meant to convey an alien-to-earthling dialogue, using a synthesizer that plays a five-note friendship theme.

Rose

3-29

by James Horner

This selection features the melodic theme from the movie *Titanic*.

▲ Scene from the film *My Big Fat Greek Wedding*

Istanbul Coffee House (Kafe neio)

3-30

written and performed by Daghan Baydur and Richard Thomas

The melody and instruments of this music help establish a Greek cultural atmosphere for a scene in *My Big Fat Greek Wedding*.

Scene from the musical *Bombay Dreams* ▶

Dreams of Bollywood

The movie industry has been very important in India since the early 1900s. The city of Mumbai (formerly Bombay), India, is the film center of India and is called Bollywood (a humorous take-off on America's Hollywood). *Bombay Dreams* is a musical theater production that tells the story of Akaash, a talented young man from the slums of Mumbai, and his adventures on the road to Bollywood stardom. The music is by one of India's most popular film composers, A.R. Rahman. His music is an east-meets-west blend of traditional ragas and contemporary electronic dance music.

The show opens with music and street sounds that set the scene of a Mumbai slum in the midst of demolition. **Listen** to the song *Bombay Dreams*. **Describe** which musical elements sound "Indian" and which sound "urban." How does the music help you to visualize the city scene?

Bombay Dreams

by A.R. Rahman and Don Black

3-31   The many layers of sound in this song include street criers, flutes, drones, electric guitar, bells, men's and women's choruses, and a solo male voice.

Listen to the singers in *Wedding Qawwali* and **identify** melodic phrases that are repeated, slightly varied, and highly ornamented.

Wedding Qawwali

from *Bombay Dreams*

3-32   **by A.R. Rahman and Don Black**

The *qawwali* is one of the most important musical forms of North Indian and Pakistani culture. It is an exuberant song of praise, celebrating spiritual joy and thanksgiving.

A.R. Rahman (born 1966) is India's top film composer and music director, which is quite an honor in a culture that so highly values its films. His father was also a successful film composer. Rahman spent his childhood in Malayalam, on the southwest coast of India. He worked as a keyboard session musician from the age of 13, and he studied both Indian and Western classical music. Rahman played in a rock band and a jazz ensemble, and has also performed *qawwali* music. He says, "I've tried in some of my work to create music that can be appreciated worldwide, without losing out on the 'Indianness' in it."

▲ Scene from the film *Smoke Signals*

Road Trip Movie

In the past, portrayals of Native Americans on film by those from outside their culture have been filled with stereotypes—Indians as secondary characters, equipped with tomahawks and feathers, acting as braves, squaws, and shamans. *Smoke Signals* is a movie about Native Americans made by Native Americans. It is the story of Victor and Thomas, two young modern-day Native American men, on a journey to Phoenix to collect the ashes of Victor's recently deceased father. On their journey, they are exposed to aspects of contemporary life that they have not experienced at home on the reservation. The conflict that Victor and Thomas feel between their old traditions and contemporary lifestyle is highlighted by the music.

Listen to *On Fire Suite*. It is a medley of musical parts sewn together, from the opening rock band segment, to the singing of traditional-style vocables, to the beating of a drum, to the wailing of the guitar over the voices, drums, and rattles. **Evaluate** the effects of this musical mixture. What does it communicate to the listener?

 On Fire Suite

3-33 from *Smoke Signals*
by B.C. Smith and André L. Picard, Jr.
as performed by André L. Picard, Jr. and John Sirois
This music is from an early scene in the movie when the home of Thomas's parents is burning down.

One internal conflict dealt with in this movie is the issue of broken treaties. Treaties are official promises, and when they are broken, there can be hard times and hard feelings. **Listen** for these words in the song *Treaties*.

> *Treaties never remember,*
> *they give and take 'til they fall apart.*
> *Treaties never surrender.*
> *Treaties were made to break this Indian's heart.*

When you hear the response phrase *listen to me*, **sing** along.

 Treaties

3-34 from *Smoke Signals*
by Jim Boyd and Sherman Alexie
as performed by Jim Boyd

The lyrics and music express Victor's feelings about both the Native American history of treaties and his personal history of relationships with family and friends.

ON YOUR OWN

At home, watch a favorite movie. Turn off the sound and watch the images only. Choose a three-minute segment and create a new soundtrack for it.

Careers
FILMMAKER
SHERMAN ALEXIE

Sherman Alexie (born 1966) is an award-winning poet and novelist and a member of the Spokane, Washington, Coeur d'Alene Nation. His books include *The Lone Ranger and Tonto Fistfight in Heaven* and *Reservation Blues.* Alexie's poetry collections include *I Would Steal Horses, Old Shirts and New Skins,* and *First Indian on the Moon.* His role in the production of the film *Smoke Signals* included writing the screenplay, co-producing the movie, and collaborating with a songwriter on four of the songs. Commenting on *Smoke Signals,* Alexie says, "I had completely planned the whole movie... I didn't want music to be an afterthought, but an inherent and organic part of the film... Using songs in the film is a way of telling the story, of adding more layers to the story."

Smoke Signal Songs

Now **listen** to the songs *Reservation Blues* and *John Wayne's Teeth.* What different musical styles do you hear? What do these songs tell you about the film? Tap the beat and **sing** along when you have learned the songs by ear.

Reservation Blues

3-35   from *Smoke Signals*
by Jim Boyd and Sherman Alexie
as performed by Jim Boyd

The lyrics of this song reflect the sense of isolation one might feel living on a reservation.

John Wayne's Teeth

3-36   from *Smoke Signals*
by the Eaglebear Singers and Sherman Alexie
as performed by the Eaglebear Singers

Victor and Thomas sing this song during their bus ride in an attempt to break the monotony of their journey.

◀ Scene from the film *Smoke Signals*; Victor (left) and Thomas (right) on their way to Phoenix

10

When Styles Meet

Musicians are explorers. They journey into new styles by doing what musicians do well—listening. In their travels, they may find something new or exotic that stimulates the creation of new and innovative sounds. They may blend or fuse elements of the various styles into something brand new, or they might allow each style to retain its own character or identity. Regardless of the route taken, new and refreshing ideas emerge simply because of the richness of listening and sharing.

Listen to *Gapu* to hear Yothu Yindi performing ancestral music of the Gumatj and Rirratingu clans of Australia. Then **listen** to Yothu Yindi play a contemporary rock piece called *Dharpa*, which means "tree." Notice the relationship between traditional and contemporary sounds in *Dharpa*. Create your own listening map by drawing a grid with these six headings.

As you listen to *Dharpa*, **identify** the instruments that are playing in each section of the music. Decide whether the music seems traditional, contemporary, or both. Complete the map by filling in the columns with your observations. Review your map as you listen again. Did styles blend and fuse, or did each style hold its own alongside the other?

Gapu
4-1
Aboriginal music from Australia as performed by Yothu Yindi
The *didjeridu* player sometimes makes the sounds of animals with his throat while using circular breathing to keep the drone going.

Dharpa (Tree)
4-2
by M. Yunupingu and S. Kellaway as performed by Yothu Yindi
This song tells the story of a Gumatj warrior who is stalking a red kangaroo.

| INTRODUCTION | VERSE | INTERLUDE | VERSE | INTERLUDE | ENDING |

Music MAKERS Yothu Yindi

Yothu Yindi is a group of aboriginal musicians from northeast Arnhem Land in the Northern Territory of Australia. The members of Yothu Yindi are descendents of people who lived in that region for the last 40,000 years. They have inherited the beliefs and traditions of their ancestors of the Gumatj and Rirratingu clans. Sometimes Yothu Yindi performs only the music that has been around for centuries. They use the *didjeridu* to play a drone and sticks to play rhythms. Beginning in the 1970s, outside influences, including the sounds of rock music, began to permeate the music of their culture. This has inspired the group to make the two contrasting styles— traditional aboriginal music and rock—work together.

Arts Connection

Lambarena by McDavid Henderson. This album cover art represents the merging of music from Gabon and Europe. ▶

African Combinations

Listen to *Bombé/Ruht wohl, ruht wohl, ihr heiligen Gebeine*, a piece that combines music from two very different cultures. One style is a traditional hand-clapping pattern from Gabon in West Africa, and the other is European Baroque music by the great German composer Johann Sebastian Bach. As you listen, **perform** the clapping pattern below with the recording. Listen carefully to discover where the pattern changes. Catch up with it when it comes back. Hang in there!

	Clap																												
Clap																													
Lap																													

Bombé/Ruht wohl, ruht wohl, ihr heiligen Gebeine

4-3

Clapping music from Gabon
from the album *Lambarena*
arranged by Pierre Akendengué/from *St. John Passion* by J.S. Bach

This music was recorded as part of a project to honor Albert Schweitzer, the famous physician, scientist, missionary, and musician who lived in Gabon for many years.

Sometimes musical combinations occur within the work of one person who pulls together many influences. Oliver Mtukudzi, nicknamed "Tuku," creates such music. He is the most famous pop music star in Zimbabwe. People love his lyrics and his sense of humor. Often he sings out about challenging topics such as societal norms and the AIDS epidemic.

Listen to *Mai varamba*. It is a song about Zimbabwean society's tradition of requiring boys to grow up quickly in order to provide for their family. The lyrics express the concern of one mother about these expectations.

Analyze the elements of this song that make it sound like American pop music, and the elements that make it seem African. Compare your findings with those of a classmate and see if the two of you agree or disagree.

Mai varamba

4-4

Written and performed by Oliver Mtukudzi

Mtukudzi has also worked with American singer/songwriter Bonnie Raitt, who wrote the introduction to this recording.

Sound Influences

The sound of Tuvan throat singing is so amazing that musicians all over the world have been inspired to include it in their music. Because very few people can perform the throat-singing technique, recording artists use pre-recorded segments and patch them into their tracks. First, **listen** to *Kargiraa-Style Song*, a traditional recording of throat singing, so that you will be able to recognize its unique sound in other music. Then **listen** to *A Moment So Close* and *Gi pai pa yul chola*, two songs that incorporate throat singing. **Describe** the role throat singing plays in the music. Does it hold its own, or does it blend into the rest of the music? Complete a description of the music using the categories in the boxes for each piece.

Kargiraa-Style Song

4-5

Traditional singing from Tuva as performed by Kongar-ol Ondar

Kargiraa is a style of very low Tuvan singing. Harmonic tones can be heard in this example.

A Moment So Close

4-6

by Béla Fleck and the Flecktones with Kongar-ol Ondar

Tuvan throat singer Ondar begins the song. Then other elements and styles are added, including jazz-influenced pop instrumentals, spoken word, and synthesized vocals.

Béla Fleck ▼

◀ Kongar-ol Ondar

Gi pai pa yul chola

4-7

by Yungchen Lhamo

A throat singer also begins this song. Then the female vocalist sings a traditional-style Tibetan melody.

Yungchen Lhamo ▼

Traditional Throat Singing

Texture:	Two layers; drone/harmonics
Melody:	Harmonics produced from a drone
Timbre:	Raspy voice
Lyrics:	Syllables only
Style:	Traditional

A Moment So Close

Texture:	
Melody:	
Timbre:	
Lyrics:	
Style:	
Role of throat singing:	

?

Gi pai pa yul chola

Texture:	
Melody:	
Timbre:	
Lyrics:	
Style:	
Role of throat singing:	

Major Contrasts Merge

What kind of a groove happens when three brilliant musicians bring three distinctive styles together? **Listen** to *One Fine Mama* by the group Native Ground. Hear how Gordy Ryan on a West African *djembe*, Al Schackman on jazz guitar, and Gary Thomas on a *didjeridu* from Australia bring these three very different instrument sounds together.

Describe what is happening in the performance. Ask yourself these questions.

- What provides unity in this piece?
- What creates variety?
- Do the different styles fuse, hold their own, or both?

Discuss and compare your findings with a classmate.

One Fine Mama

4-8

by Gordy Ryan, Al Schackman, and Gary Thomas
as performed by Native Ground

These three musicians work individually as well as with other groups to promote music that celebrates world cultures.

◄ Didjeridu

▼ West African djembe

Jazz guitar ►

Bring the World Home

With a few classmates, compose a short piece that incorporates the ideas of world music that you have heard in this lesson. Plan to mirror some of those ideas: use of a drone, percussion rhythms, and a melody with chords. Layer your piece in ways that allow the parts to move in and out of the foreground and background. Decide what instruments will provide the interest and contrast you need. Then **play** your composition for the rest of the class.

11

When Styles Fuse

Sometimes musicians from different regions and cultures meet and play music together. As they play, they influence each other and something new emerges from the blending of styles. The resulting music takes on the sounds of the various styles. When distinct musical styles blend, the music is called *fusion.* In the world pop scene, musicians fuse roots-style music from their own cultures with the sounds of hip-hop, rock 'n' roll, and the music of other cultures.

Ancient Routes to Today's Music

Nearly 1,500 years ago, traders traveled the Silk Road to bring goods from China to Persia. This cultural interaction influenced the music we hear today. The Silk Road traders brought instruments and music with them, spreading instrument types and styles of music from Asia to India, the Middle East, the Mediterranean, and Europe. **Listen** to *Mido Mountain* and *Avaz-e dashti,* traditional pieces from opposite ends of the Silk Road—China and Persia. Then listen to *Drift,* a contemporary selection that fuses Chinese traditional music with other styles. **Describe** similarities and differences between the sounds and styles of all three selections.

Yo-Yo Ma (left) and the Silk Road Ensemble ▼

Mido Mountain

4-9
Traditional Music from China
as performed by Yo-Yo Ma and the Silk Road Ensemble
In this selection listen for the *sheng,* a Chinese wind instrument.

Avaz-e dashti

4-10
Traditional Music from Persia
as performed by members of the Silk Road Ensemble
In this selection the featured instruments are the *setar* (lute), *santur* (zither), and *ney* (bamboo flute).

Drift

4-11
by Qui Xia He
as performed by Asza
A Chinese-style pentatonic melody played on a *pipa* (four-string lute) is combined with African rhythms played on a *djembe.*

From the 700s to the 1400s, the Islamic empire spread from Persia to Spain, merging the rich traditions and sounds of Muslim, Jewish, and Spanish styles. This period is called *Al-Andalus.* **Listen** for elements of the three cultures in *Maitreem.*

Maitreem

4-12
by Tarik and Julia Banzi and R. Krishnar
as performed by Al-Andalus
The Sanskrit lyrics of this song are a prayer for world peace.

Asian Fusion

Contemporary forms of Asian-influenced popular music can be heard throughout Europe and beyond. These forms come about when young people rediscover the traditional music of their culture and fuse it with contemporary styles such as hip-hop, rock, and electronica. **Listen** to two different selections that combine various traditions with exciting new sounds and grooves. **Identify** timbres and musical ideas represented in both pieces and make a list for each. What are the similarities and differences?

Sabhyatâ (Civilization)

4-13   **by Mohamed Bellal and J. Mahtani**
as performed by Karmix

Sabhyatâ is a mix of percussion, sound effects, Hindi singing, Algerian-style violin playing, hip-hop bass lines, and DJ techniques.

Neend koyi

4-14   **by Najma Akhtar**
British born Najma Akhtar sings in the Indian *ghazal* tradition. She is accompanied by *tabla* and *santoor,* as well as violin, saxophone, bass, and keyboards.

Najma Akhtar ▶

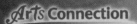

Map of Silk Road through Asia ▼

When Celtic Goes Electric

Celtic bands typically include singers, bagpipes, fiddles, flutes, guitar, and drums. Today, many Celtic bands are pushing the edge of their traditional style by adding electric basses, synthesizers, and other electronic devices that are common in rock 'n' roll music. **Listen** to Capercaillie, a Celtic fusion band from Scotland. **Analyze** the way the electronic sounds impact the music. What characterisitics are traditional to the style of Celtic music and what seems new?

Alasdair mhic cholla ghasda

4-15 Gaelic *waulking* song from the Outer Hebrides Islands (Scotland) as performed by Capercaillie

Waulking songs were sung to establish a rhythm for wool workers as they pulled and beat the cloth.

▼ Capercaillie

▲ Eilean Donan Castle, Scotland

Bringing It Home

Listen to Béla Fleck and the Flecktones play their own arrangement of Aaron Copland's *Hoedown*. Béla Fleck's arrangement is a fusion of many different styles of music, including jazz, country, bluegrass, electric rock, Celtic, and others. List the styles in the order they occur in the music. Hint—some styles occur more than once. What instruments help you to identify a style?

Hoedown

from *Rodeo*
4-16   by Aaron Copland
as arranged and performed by Béla Fleck and the Flecktones
Copland wrote this music for his ballet *Rodeo*. It was originally performed by a symphony orchestra.

ON YOUR OWN

Visit the World Music section of your record store and listen to some selections. Find a group that is fusing various styles and sounds. Describe the instruments, styles, and cultures that the group combines to identify it as a fusion group. Research that group to find out what influences its music making. Share your findings.

CD-ROM Play a melody into *Band-in-a-Box*. Select "loop" so the melody will play over and over. Create an accompaniment that changes styles several times. Change the rhythm and the instrumentation to create the feeling of different styles. Play your piece for classmates. Ask them to describe the ways you changed the style.

Béla Fleck and the Flecktones ▼

Review and Assess

Summary

In World Music Mix you've listened to music from all over the world. You've learned about

- typical instrument choices.

- music from different cultures.

- various music styles that constitute world music.

- various performance styles.

- how a particular culture's traditions shape its music experiences.

You can better understand what you've learned by formulating descriptions of the music you've heard. Consider the following common musical elements.

- **timbre**—tone color (sound) of an instrument or voice.

- **melody, rhythm, harmony, dynamics, and tempo**—compositional elements.

- **form**—compositional elements.

- **dynamics**—the degrees of loudness and softness of a sound.

- **expression**—emotional effect on the listener.

- **cultural function**—when and where it is used.

One of the best ways to develop your understanding of music (or any subject, for that matter) is to explain your ideas verbally and in writing. Here are five projects that will help you show what you've learned in this module.

Review What You Learned

Review three varied listening selections in this module. In small groups, discuss what elements in each selection makes it distinct to its country or culture. Refer to the corresponding lessons for more information and reinforcement.

What Do You Hear? 1

4-17

Listen to the following excerpts. Each one demonstrates a different style of American music. Make five observations about each of the selections to help you determine the style.

- instrumentation

- rhythm

- harmony
- cultural influence
- emotion conveyed

Which of these elements helped you determine the style of the excerpts?

Share What You Know

With your classmates, choose three very different pieces from the module. Listen to each one again. As you listen, write down a sentence that describes

- title and performance media.

- musical texture.

- instruments and voices used.

- form - how the music is organized.

- rhythm choices.

- expression: dynamics, mood, tempo and how they affect the music.

- where this music would likely be performed or listened to.

Repeat for the second and third pieces.

In small groups, discuss each others' ideas and discover why different members of the group might come to different conclusions. Everyone need not agree at the end of the discussion, but everyone should be able to explain his or her own point of view.

What to Listen For

Regardless of its country of origin, most music is intended to tell a story or to express some kind of idea—an emotion or a visual image, for example. Music can remind you of an experience in your past, or create an image in your mind. How does music convey emotions and images through sound alone?

Listen to the following excerpts of music from the module. After hearing each one, explain how it is distinct from other selections. What elements are different from other songs you already know?

What elements are similar? Consider choices of instrumentation, timbre, electronic media, vocal styles, rhythmic elements, and so on to explain what you hear.

Nyamphemphe page B-3

Tihore mai page B-12

Tommy Peoples page B-20

Terian gulabi buliyan page B-26

Treaties page B-36

Sabhyatâ page B-43

Share What You Know

Select one piece from the module that is your personal favorite. Prepare a presentation for the class or another person that will help them understand the selection and why you like the music. You should begin your presentation with basic facts about the piece including title, composer, culture, and whether it is contemporary or traditional.

Explain how you think the elements convey the composer's intentions—the mood, the emotion, the picture, the musical idea, or cultural function. Include the elements of music listed on page B-46 in your description.

Your presentation may be placed on poster board, on overhead transparencies, or on slides created with presentation software. Play excerpts from the piece to illustrate your points.

Create a list of questions that might direct the listener's understanding of music to the ideas you have about the music. Compare it to other songs your audience might already know and share your observations.

Music Through Time

Historical Contexts and Styles

◀ Gerald Finley as Papageno and Danielle de Niese as Papagena

Shofar ▶

▲ The Grand March from Verdi's Aida

▲ Clara and Robert Schumann

"Why speak of time travel? We have a tried and proven method with us. Music moves us across centuries and continents without ever leaving our chairs."

—Pam Brown (born 1928)

Ages of Music

Musicians throughout history and across cultures have created music for many purposes. Music is sung and played. Music has been used for ceremonies and festivals. Music is used to accompany drama and dancing. Some music is simply meant to be enjoyed as an art form.

Music changes with the time and place. Music created in one century sounds different from music of another century. Musicians from different parts of the world make music in unique ways. Our musical journey through the history of Western art music will take some pathways to many musical adventures.

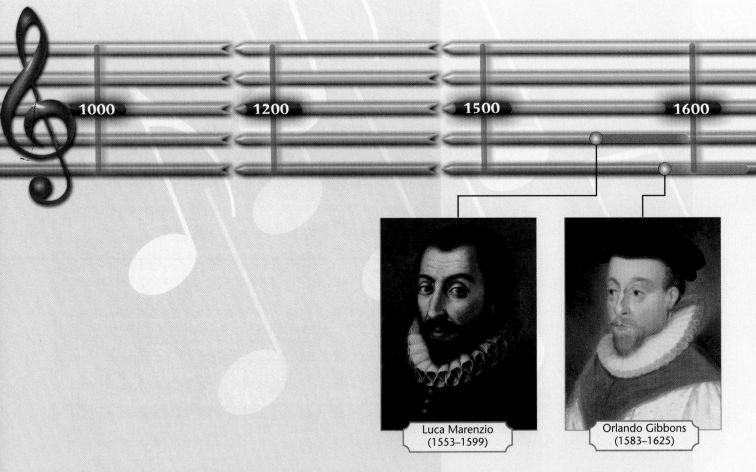

1000   1200   1500   1600

Luca Marenzio
(1553–1599)

Orlando Gibbons
(1583–1625)

Medieval
(1100–1450)

Renaissance
(1450–1600)

Listen to these excerpts of music by the composers and performers you see pictured here. Match the musicians and the music. What qualities of the music give you clues about the answers?

George Frideric Handel
(1685–1759)

Clara Schumann
(1819–1896)

Maurice Ravel
(1875–1937)

Cindy McTee
(born 1953)

1700

1800

1900

2000

Wolfgang Amadeus Mozart
(1756–1791)

Heitor Villa-Lobos
(1887–1959)

Duke Ellington
(1899–1974)

Baroque
(1600–1750)

CLASSICAL
(1750–1830)

Romantic
(1830–1900)

MODERN
(1900–Present)

Oldies but Goodies

Picture this: A knight in armor rides off to battle. Next to his heart he carries the handkerchief of his lady love. Before leaving, he has written her a love poem and has just sung it beneath her window. Will he return and marry her? No, she is probably from a higher class of society and promised to another. But to the knight she is the "ideal woman" whom he will love and serve but never win. The concept of courtly love was found in France and Germany in medieval times.

Love, Medieval Style

In southern France in the 1200s, there were traveling singer/poets who composed and sang many songs about courtly love. They were called *troubadours*. One troubadour song is *Ahi! Amours*, written in the time of the Crusades. In this song, a knight is going off to war. Read the English meaning of the text. Then **listen** to this old love song.

> *Alas, Love, how hard it is to part*
> *A better lady never was loved or served*
> *May God bring me back to her in his sweetness*
> *inasmuch as I depart in pain.*
> *Alas! What have I said? I will not leave her:*
> *even as my body goes to serve our Lord,*
> *my heart remains completely in her service.*

Arts Connection

Scenes of courtly love ▶ often appeared on armor like this wooden Medieval kite shield from the 1400s.

Ahi! Amours

4-30 by Conon de Bethune
as performed by the Early Music Consort of London, conducted by David Munrow
The language of this song is Medieval French.

Medieval rhythm was organized in **modes.** The next Medieval song you will hear is based on this simple rhythm: ♩ ♪

modes Small rhythmic ideas based on groupings of 3 used in Medieval music.

Listen to *O tocius Asie*. The vocal parts weave in and out independently. **Describe** what the accompanying instrument parts do.

O tocius Asie (Oh, Glory of All Asia)

4-31 Anonymous
as performed by the Early Music Consort of London, conducted by David Munrow
This song was composed by an unknown musician during the time of the Crusades.

Take It to the Net To learn more about Medieval and Renaissance music, visit www.sfsuccessnet.com.

Folger Consort, with guest artists Trefoil (vocal trio) performing at the Folger Shakespeare Library in Washington D.C. ▶

Madrigals—
Popular Hits of the Renaissance

The outstanding **secular** vocal music of the 1500s was the **madrigal**. In some phrases, the voice parts move together in **homophonic** texture. In other phrases, the voice parts move independently, creating **polyphonic** texture.

Listen to *Ombrose e care selve, in* which the composer, Luca Marenzio writes about the beauty of nature and how it compares to Amaryllis and Thirsis' love. **Listen** for musical elements that create a mood of longing in this song.

Luca Marenzio

🎧 *Ombrose e care selve*

4-32
by Luca Marenzio
as performed by the Folger Consort
Love songs like this one were popular in the Renaissance Era.

English Madrigals

The madrigal next caught on in England. Follow the lyrics as you **listen** to *The Silver Swan*. The poetry expresses the composer's reflections on death, and the virtue of silence.

> *The silver swan, who living had no note,*
> *When death approached unlocked her silent*
> *throat.*
> *Leaning her breast against the reedy shore,*
> *Thus sang her first and last and sang no more.*
> *Farewell, all joys, oh death come close mine eyes.*
> *More geese than swans now live, more fools*
> *than wise.*

Orlando Gibbons

🎧 *The Silver Swan*

4-33
by Orlando Gibbons
as performed by the Hilliard Ensemble
Orlando Gibbons wrote the words and the music for this madrigal.

English madrigals could also be lighthearted. **Listen** for the *fa la la* refrains in *Sing We and Chant It*.

🎧 *Sing We and Chant It*

4-34
by Thomas Morley
as performed by the Folger Consort
The original version of this lighthearted song was composed by Giovanni Gastoldi and published in 1591.

secular Nonreligious in nature.
madrigal An unaccompanied song for four to six voices with poetic text that was developed in Italy.
homophonic Melody supported by harmony.
polyphonic Music consisting of two or more independent melodies sung or played together.

◀ Composer Francesco Landini in an illumination, or an elaborately designed sheet of music, from the "*Squarcialupi Codex.*"

What About Instruments?

In medieval times, secular music could be sung or performed with any combination of instruments. **Listen** to this troubadour song played by instruments of the time. Note the alternation between verse and refrain. How can you tell the difference?

Domna, pos vos ay chausida (Lady, for You)

Anonymous

5-1 as performed by Ensemble Unicorn

In this selection, the bagpipe plays the introduction, then is joined by the *shawm* and drums.

Medieval books and music scores were made by hand. Most of them have disappeared. One way to find out what medieval instruments looked like is to examine Medieval visual art. Paintings and other art works show the instruments played then.

The *estampie* [es-tom-PEE] was an early kind of music intended for instruments only and may have been used for dancing. It consists of short phrases that are repeated, with first and second endings that are like a refrain.

Now **listen** to *La tierce estampie real*. **Identify** the two alternating endings for each phrase.

The *crumhorn* is a curved double-reed instrument that sounds like a kazoo. ▶

Courtesy of Firenze, Biblioteca Medicea Laurenziana/Ministry for Cultural Affairs/Med. Palat. 87, c. 121v.

ON YOUR OWN

Look at concert listings in your local newspaper to see if there are performances of Medieval and Renaissance music. Look up the composers listed to see if they are from these eras. Attend one concert and write about the performance.

La tierche estampie real

Anonymous

5-2 as performed by the Early Music Consort of London

Scholars are undecided as to whether this music was played for dancing or just for listening.

◀ The *sackbut* is a brass instrument with a slide that is the ancestor of the trombone.

◀ The *regal* is a small organ that can be carried.

Instruments in the Renaissance

Tylman Susato (c. 1500–1561) was a Renaissance instrumentalist, composer, and publisher who lived in Antwerp, Belgium. Today he is remembered for *Danserye*, a collection of dances published in 1551. This collection serves as a valuable record because little music from that time was written down. Renaissance musicians usually played from memory or improvised. **Listen** to *Ronde* by Susato, and **conduct** in duple meter.

Ronde

from *Danserye*
5-3   **by Tylman Susato**
as performed by the Early Music Consort of London
This music is played by *crumhorns*, a *regal*, and *sackbuts*.

Dueling Brass

During the Renaissance, some churches allowed instrumental music and some did not. A few churches featured it. In Venice, Italy, the composer Giovanni Gabrieli (c. 1557–1612) wrote brass music for the great Cathedral of St. Mark. Gabrieli took advantage of the expansive size and acoustical possibilities of the cathedral by writing **antiphonal** music. As you **listen** to this *canzon,* imagine sitting between two groups of musicians located on opposite sides of a huge space with the sound meeting and mingling around your head.

Canzon in Echo Duodecimi Toni a 10

5-4   **by Giovanni Gabrieli**
as performed by the London Symphony Orchestra Brass
This *canzon* may be performed with twenty people: two groups of ten players.

---

antiphonal Singing or playing that involves one group echoing or answering the other.
canzon Italian word for a song.

Baroque Style

Select one word from each of the following pairs to help you **describe** the art work at right.

simple	ornamented
flamboyant	understated
crowded	empty

This work represents the period in art history known as the Baroque Era (in music, about 1600 to 1750). One of the most outstanding Baroque composers was George Frideric Handel. Handel wrote many kinds of music, including around 30 **oratorios.** The Handel oratorio most frequently heard today is *Messiah*.

Listen to the "Hallelujah!" chorus from *Messiah*. **Identify** the changes from homophonic texture to polyphonic texture.

Hallelujah!

5-5
from *Messiah*
by George Frideric Handel
as performed by the Toronto Symphony and Mendelssohn Choir
In 1743, King George II of England began the custom of standing during this chorus of the *Messiah* which is still done at most performances today.

Listen to the **recitative,** *Behold I Tell You a Mystery*. **Describe** the rhythm of this recitative. Then **listen** to *The Trumpet Shall Sound*. It is a **da capo aria.**

Behold, I Tell You a Mystery

5-6
from *Messiah*
by George Frideric Handel
as performed by Samuel Ramey, bass
This music prepares the audience for the next selection.

The Trumpet Shall Sound

5-7
from *Messiah*
by George Frideric Handel
as performed by Samuel Ramey
This *aria* features the singer and the trumpet.

Arts Connection

▲ A painting of the Thames River in 17th century London entitled *London, England* by Jan Griffier (1652-1718)

oratorio An extended work for orchestra, chorus, and solo voices based on religious, mythological, or poetic literature.

recitative In a vocal work with a story, this movement moves the story along, giving information. It is sung by a soloist in free rhythm.

aria A song for solo voice and accompaniment, which often includes a solo instrument.

da capo aria An *aria* in ABA form.

Note This

Beethoven called Handel ". . . the greatest and ablest of all composers." Haydn had this to say about Handel, "He is the master of us all."

Baroque Boat Party Music

Handel's best-known instrumental works are for orchestra. Especially famous is the *Water Music*, a **suite** of pieces composed as a surprise for King George I of England around 1717. A newspaper reporter of the time wrote this description of the boat party:

> About eight in the evening the King repaired to his barge . . . Next to the King's barge was that of the musicians, about 50 in number, who played on all kinds of instruments . . . trumpets, horns, oboes, bassoons, flutes, violins and basses . . . The music had been composed specially by the famous Handel . . . His Majesty approved of it so greatly that he caused it to be repeated three times in all . . . boats filled with people desirous of hearing was beyond counting.

Listen to the "Hornpipe" from Handel's *Water Music*. **Describe** how Handel creates contrast between different sections of the music.

Hornpipe

from *Water Music*
5-8 by George Frideric Handel
as performed by the Los Angeles Chamber Orchestra

Follow the ABABAB form in this music.

Music MAKERS *George Frideric Handel*

George Frideric Handel (1685–1759) was born and raised in northern Germany. His father wanted him to study law. When Handel was twelve his father died, but he did begin law study at age 18 at the University of Halle. Soon he changed to studying music. His first jobs were in Hamburg, playing in the opera orchestra and composing his first operas. Since Italy was the place for opera at that time, Handel went there in 1706; he stayed for five years and became known as a talented composer. For a brief period he was director of music for the royal family of Hanover in northern Germany. He was attracted to the opportunities in England, however, and after 1711 he moved there permanently.

Handel became internationally famous as a composer during his lifetime. Dramatic works were his primary interest—first operas, and then the English oratorio, which he invented.

Although today Baroque composer Johann Sebastian Bach is equally or perhaps more famous, apparently Handel was unaware of Bach's music. Bach's fame developed much later.

---

suite A type of musical composition with several short parts or movements of varying character. Frequently these parts are written in dance forms.

5

Music MAKERS
Wolfgang Amadeus Mozart

Wolfgang Amadeus Mozart (1756–1791) is one of the most famous musicians of all time. Born in Salzburg, Austria, his childhood and youth were busy with traveling, composing, and performing. As a young child he composed minuets and could play violin and harpsichord. His musically gifted father, Leopold, recognized that Mozart and his sister, Maria Anna (Nannerl), were very talented. Leopold encouraged their abilities. The children played concerts all over Europe. Before his teenage years were over, Mozart had composed operas, symphonies, string quartets, piano music, and more.

As an adult, Mozart settled in Vienna, Austria, where he continued composing, performing, and teaching. He wrote about 15 operas, 41 symphonies, and many other kinds of music. Although he received an income from wealthy patrons for his music, he did not manage money well and died very poor. He was buried in an unmarked grave somewhere in Vienna.

Magnificent Mozart

He began his first concert tour of Europe when he was seven years old and composed his first symphony at age nine. By age fifteen he was an internationally famous performer and composer. Who was he? Wolfgang Amadeus Mozart!

Mozart was a child prodigy. He entertained royalty in the capitals of Europe with his precocious personality and his performances on violin and harpsichord. Later he would write down music composed by others—after hearing it only once or twice. He composed just by thinking about the music, then writing it down, with few changes.

Mozart wrote beautiful melodies, as in the **concerto** you are about to hear. **Listen** to the melody in his *Concerto for Flute and Harp in C Major.* **Analyze** what you hear. Make a chart to show when you hear flute, harp, orchestra, or all three at once.

Concerto for Flute and Harp in C Major

5-9 Movement 2
by Wolfgang Amadeus Mozart as performed by James Galway, flute, and Marisa Robles, harp, with the London Symphony

Mozart wrote this piece in 1778. The tempo, or speed, of this movement, is *Andantino*, a leisurely walking pace.

ON YOUR OWN

Visit your local library or record store. Find the section of Mozart's recordings. Make a list of all the different kinds of recordings of his music, including multiple recordings of the same piece. Make a chart that shows your findings and post it on a classroom bulletin board.

concerto A composition written for orchestra and one or more solo instruments.

"He is . . . the greatest composer known to me in person or by name; he has taste and, what is more, the greatest knowledge of composition."

—*Franz Joseph Haydn, speaking to Mozart's father, Leopold*

Concertos for a Friend

Mozart had many musician friends in Salzburg and Vienna. He wrote four concertos for a good friend who played the French horn. Mozart was a practical joker. To confuse his friend, he wrote the music in red, blue, green, and black ink. Mozart wrote teasing messages and even drew a picture of him in the music!

Mozart and other composers of the Classical Era in Europe often composed the last movement of a concerto in **rondo** form.

Sing or **play** these three melodies.

Theme A (first phrase)

Theme B (first phrase)

Theme C (first phrase)

▲ Natural horn and crooks for changing keys

Note This

In Mozart's time, horn players used "natural horns," which had no valves, because valves had not yet been invented.

Listen to this movement in rondo form from a concerto by Mozart. **Identify** each theme as you hear it, and make a chart that shows the order of the themes.

Concerto No. 4 in E-flat Major for French Horn

Movement 3
5-10 **by Wolfgang Amadeus Mozart**
as performed by Dennis Brain
Mozart wrote four horn concertos between 1783 and 1787.

rondo A musical form in which the A section repeats between two or more contrasting sections, such as ABACABA.

What's in a Form

In the summer of 1788, Mozart wrote three symphonies in six weeks! They were his last three symphonies, and only one of them, *Symphony No. 40*, was performed before he died in 1791.

In the Classical Era, composers refined **sonata form.** Mozart and his fellow composers wrote symphonies, concertos, string quartets, and solo pieces in which at least one movement is in sonata form. **Sing** or **play** these themes from one of Mozart's symphonies. Then **read** the chart to learn the parts of sonata form. Follow the chart and **identify** the themes and form of Mozart's *Symphony No. 40, Mvt 1.*

Theme 1

Theme 2

Sonata Form

Exposition	Development	Recapitulation
Theme 1	A composer can develop a theme by	Back to the home key
Theme 2 in a different key	• changing the key	Theme 1
The themes in the exposition are repeated.	• using small parts of the theme as motives	Theme 2
	• writing motives or phrases in a different order	**coda**
	• using part of the theme in **melodic sequence**	
	• changing the dynamics	

 ### Symphony No. 40 in G Minor

Movement 1
5-11 **by Wolfgang Amadeus Mozart**
as performed by The English Baroque Soloists,
John Eliot Gardiner, conductor

Mozart didn't include clarinets when he first wrote Symphony No. 40. He added clarinets to his score later (for the first performance).

---

sonata form A musical selection consisting of three main parts: the exposition, in which the themes are introduced; the development that contains theme parts in changing keys; and the recapitulation in which the original themes are heard again in the home key.

melodic sequence The repetition of a melodic pattern at a higher or lower pitch level.

coda Italian for tail; a short section added to the end of a piece.

Dynamic Duets

Mozart wrote both serious and comic operas. Sometimes his operas mix serious moments or even horror with comedy. Mozart's *Don Giovanni* is a good example. Don Giovanni is a noble who has too many girlfriends. The comic part of the opera involves cloaks used as disguises, mistaken identities, and unusual situations. The horror involves a duel in which the Don kills the irate father of a girl he mistreated. Later in the opera, a statue on the grave of the girl's father comes to life and is invited by the Don to a dinner party where it gets revenge. For this reason, the opera is sometimes called *The Stone Guest*.

Listen to this duet from *Don Giovanni*. **Read** the first part of the music as you listen. The Don is trying to persuade Zerlina, a girl in the village, to go away with him. What clue lets you know that Zerlina might give in?

▲ Rebecca Evans as Zerlina and Dmitri Hvorostovsky as Don Giovanni

Don Giovanni

Là ci da - rem la ma - no,
Give me your hand, my beau - ty,

là mi di - rai di sí;
Then you'll say "yes" to me,

ve - di, non è lon - ta - no,
There, in my house, we'll mar - ry,

par - tiam, ben mio, da qui.
Come, now, my love, we must flee.

Lá ci darem la mano (Give Me Your Hand)

5-12

from *Don Giovanni*
by Wolfgang Amadeus Mozart
as performed by the Vienna State Opera Choir and the Vienna Philharmonic with Cesare Siepi and Elisabeth Grümmer
Mozart wrote *Don Giovanni* in 1787. It is still performed often.

In 1791, the last year of his life, Mozart wrote *Die Zauberflöte* (*The Magic Flute*). The story involves Tamino, a prince, and a magic flute that he uses to rescue Pamina, the daughter of the Queen of the Night. Tamino has the help of his friend Sarastro, a magician, and Papageno, a bird catcher. During the opera, many magical things happen. When Tamino and Pamina are finally united, Papageno the bird catcher meets his true love, Papagena. They sing this duet.

Listen to this duet performed by Papageno and Papagena. What qualities of the music make it sound humorous?

Pa-pa-pa-pa-pa-pa-pagena

5-13

from *Die Zauberflöte* (*The Magic Flute*)
by Wolfgang Amadeus Mozart
as performed by Vienna State Opera, Christian Boesch, Ileana Cotrubas
Mozart wrote the story of *Die Zauberflöte,* along with theater director Emanuel Schikaneder.

▲ Gerald Finley as Papageno and Danielle de Niese as Papagena

6

BRASS FEVER

Brass instruments have a long, colorful, and cross-cultural history. Today, brass instruments can be heard everywhere—in marching bands, jazz bands, and symphony orchestras. In Europe, Africa, Asia, and the Americas, many different types of "horns" have long been used for ritual, military, and signaling purposes.

The first horns were just that—horns from animals. **Listen** to this performance of music from Uganda played on animal horns.

Rwakanembe

Anonymous
5-14 **as performed by the Abanyabyata Royal Horn Band**
The horns the royal band members are playing are similar to those their ancestors have played over thousands of years.

As centuries passed and people learned to work with metal, they used the shape of animal horns as a basis for creating instruments from metal. Gold and silver were used to make instruments, but most were made from mixtures of copper, zinc, or nickel. At first the instruments were used more for communication than for music—a sort of ancient cell phone. Later, what we now call French horns were used by hunters to signal each other. Trumpets were used to announce the arrival of royalty.

During the Renaissance in Western Europe, brass instruments became important for playing in parades, at holiday events, and for religious purposes. From the late Renaissance through the Baroque era, brass ensembles formed to play music, and the trumpet became a leading virtuosic instrument.

Listen to this recording and **move** your hands to show the rise and fall of the melody played by the trumpet.

Galliard Battaglia

by Samuel Scheidt
5-15 **as performed by the St. Louis Brass**
Galliard Battaglia is music for a dance depicting a battle.

The *shofar* [sho-far] is made from a ram's horn. *Shofars* have been played for thousands of years in special Jewish religious services. ▶

▲ From left to right: *natural trumpet, cornetto,* serpent

Symphonic Brass

By the 1700s, brass instruments were being added to the European orchestra. The invention of valves, around 1815, enabled trumpet, French horn, and tuba players to play all the notes of the chromatic scale. Valves also allowed composers to write more complex brass parts. Since the 1800s, brass instruments have played an important role in orchestral music, sometimes playing solo melodies.

Sing or **play** this melody slowly, in a stately manner.

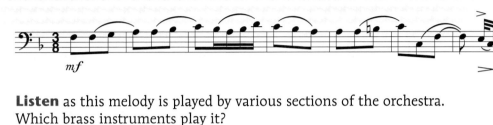

Listen as this melody is played by various sections of the orchestra. Which brass instruments play it?

Minuetto

5-16
from *Pulcinella Suite*
by Igor Stravinsky
as performed by the Saint Paul Chamber Orchestra
Stravinsky arranged his *Pulcinella* ballet, composed in 1920, into an orchestral suite in 1922. Each movement features different solo instruments.

Contemporary composers use the bright and dark sounds of brass instruments to color their music. **Listen** to this performance of *Sensemaya* by Silvestre Revueltas. **Identify** each entrance of each brass instrument you hear. List these instruments.

Sensemaya

5-17
by Silvestre Revueltas
as performed by the New Philharmonia Orchestra
Silvestre Revueltas (1899–1940) composed *Sensemaya* in 1938, in his native Mexico.

ON YOUR OWN

Scan the radio for the sound of brass instruments. In what styles of music do you hear brass instruments? What recordings do you own that feature brass instruments? Look for recordings of brass music in your library or a record store. Compile a list of brass instruments and the styles of music you heard them play.

The brass instruments of a modern orchestra or band

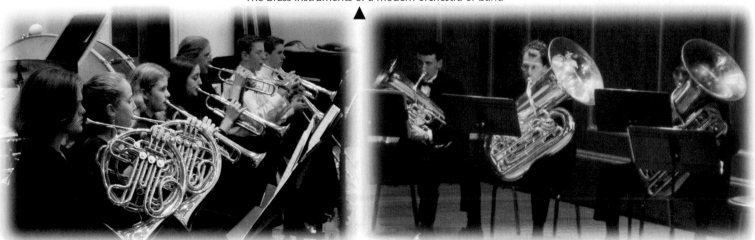

7

A Revolutionary Work

In the early 1800s Ludwig van Beethoven (1770–1827) was a man caught in a difficult dilemma. Members of the ruling class supported him financially, but he did not believe in their values. He sided with poor and working-class people. One of the greatest pianists and improvisers of his time, he was going deaf. He could no longer support himself by performing. Wealthy sponsors, for whom he had little respect, were his only hope for making a living.

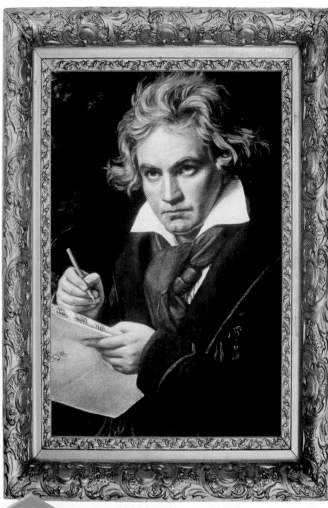

Some of Beethoven's struggles are reflected in his renowned *Symphony No. 3 in E-flat Major,* which he composed from 1803–1804. Beethoven was disgusted with the decadence of European society. He admired the promise of democracy that had emerged from the American Revolution. He considered Napoleon Bonaparte a revolutionary hero and hoped that Napoleon would bring democracy to Europe. When Napoleon crowned himself emperor instead, Beethoven's hopes for a democratic form of government in Europe were crushed. He felt his hero was not a hero after all.

Originally, Beethoven had named the symphony *Bonaparte,* for Napoleon, but he changed that title and renamed it *Eroica.* As its name suggests, *Symphony No. 3* contains heroic qualities. It is a powerful and energetic piece with many memorable themes.

Arts Connection

◄ *Beethoven, while composing the Missa Solemnis* by Joseph Karl Stielere (1781–1858)

Arts **Connection**

▲ *Reunion of Artists in Studio of Jean-Baptiste Isabey,* by Louis Leopold Boilly (1761–1845)

Arts **Connection**

▲ *Scéne de cabaret,* by Louis Leopold Boilly

Heroic Themes

The first movement of the *Eroica Symphony* has themes that establish a sense of the heroic. **Play** the opening theme below on a keyboard instrument.

Listen to Beethoven's work and follow the theme. **Identify** the instruments in the orchestra that play this theme. As you listen, count the number of times you hear the theme in this excerpt.

Symphony No. 3 in E-flat Major

5-18   Movement 1
by Ludwig van Beethoven
as performed by the Cleveland Orchestra, conducted by George Szell

The tempo for the first movement of *Symphony No. 3* is *allegro con brio,* which means "joyful and quick, with energy."

Listen to the movement a second time, and think about these questions.

• What makes this music sound heroic?
• What contrasting moods do you hear in the music?

A Heroic Memorial

In the second movement of *Symphony No. 3,* Beethoven uses techniques from funeral marches, such as this **motive** that suggests a drum roll.

Listen for the drum roll in this part of Beethoven's funeral march. **Identify** which terms in each pair apply to the music you are hearing.

major key	minor key
very slow	moderate tempo
repetitive	not repetitive
loud	quiet
even rhythms	uneven rhythm

Symphony No. 3 in E-flat Major

5-19   Movement 2
by Ludwig van Beethoven
as performed by the Cleveland Orchestra, conducted by George Szell

Eroica was the first of Beethoven's symphonies to break from classical tradition.

Take It to the Net To learn more about Ludwig van Beethoven, go to *www.sfsuccessnet.com.*

---

motive A rhythmic or melodic fragment that can serve as the basic element from which a more complex musical structure can be created.

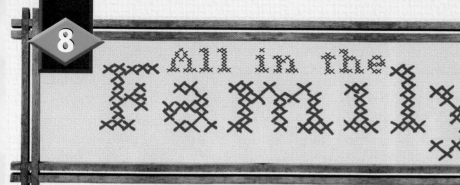

8

All in the Family

Families of talented musicians have always been part of music history. Johann Sebastian Bach (1685–1750) was the most famous musician in his family, but the Bachs produced seven generations of well-known musicians. In popular music, Judy Garland performed with her daughters, Liza Minnelli and Lorna Luft. Naomi Judd and her daughter, Wynona Judd, have performed country music.

Historically, women musicians did not often have the same opportunities as their brothers, fathers, and husbands. Women learned to play instruments and sing, but they were often excluded from the business of music. They had little chance to perform, even less to conduct, and their compositions were not often performed or published. It is hard to judge what women might have been able to accomplish, since they were simply not given the same opportunities as men. As you will see, however, there were some exceptions.

The Mendelssohns

Fanny Mendelssohn (1805–1847) was a pianist and composer. She was also the older sister of pianist, conductor, and composer Felix Mendelssohn. Fanny Mendelssohn composed piano pieces, including a suite titled *Das Jahr* [DAHS YAHR] (The Year).

Listen to *Mai* (May) from *Das Jahr*. **Describe** how Mendelssohn used musical elements to give an impression of springtime.

▲ Naomi Judd performing with her daughter, Wynona

◀ The Bach family musicians in the early 1700s

▲ Judy Garland performs with her daughter, Liza Minnelli.

 Mai

from *Das Jahr*
5-20   by Fanny Mendelssohn
as performed by Jennifer Eley

Mai is the fifth movement in this suite, which includes a movement for each month of the year.

Felix Mendelssohn (1809–1847) composed many different kinds of pieces, including a famous violin concerto. **Listen** to an excerpt of Mendelssohn's *Violin Concerto in E Minor*. **Describe** what makes this a concerto.

 Violin Concerto in E Minor, Op. 64

Movement 1
5-21   by Felix Mendelssohn
as performed by Isaac Stern and the Philadelphia Orchestra

Mendelssohn's *Violin Concerto in E Minor* is one of the most famous works for violin; it is studied and performed by all serious violinists.

The Schumanns

Clara Wieck (1819–1896) was an extraordinary pianist who made her concert debut at age nine. She became Clara Schumann when she married composer Robert Schumann (1810–1856). Clara Schumann introduced many of her husband's compositions to the public by performing them in concerts. Besides being a star pianist, Clara was also a composer.

Listen to this piano trio by Clara Schumann. What instruments play the melody?

Piano Trio in G Minor, Op. 17

5-22

Movement 1
by Clara Wieck Schumann
as performed by the Darlington Piano Trio
This work was written for violin, piano, and cello. The violin has the melody first, then the piano.

Robert Schumann was famous both for writing music and for writing commentary about music. Some of Clara's compositions bear a strong resemblance to Robert's, but the reverse is also true. This is not surprising, since they spent many hours a day hearing each others' music and talking about music together.

Listen to this excerpt of Robert Schumann's *Quintet for Piano and Strings in E-flat Major.* **Describe** how it is similar or different from Clara Schumann's trio.

Quintet for Piano and Strings in E-flat Major

5-23

Movement 1
by Robert Schumann
as performed by the Beaux Arts Trio and Friends
Both this piece and the piano trio by Clara Schumann are examples of **chamber music.** This piano quintet is for string quartet plus piano.

---

chamber music Music written for a small group often having only one voice or instrument for each part, and no conductor.

Clara and Robert Schumann kept a weekly diary in which they took turns writing. What do you learn about the Schumanns and their times from reading these entries from their diary?

▲ Clara and Robert Schumann

Saturday . . . Mendelssohn played—as only Mendelssohn can play. I heard a trio by Beethoven in E-flat for the first time; as one gets older, "first times" become rarer; it was a festive occasion for body and soul.

—Robert Schumann

Today, Monday, Robert pretty well completed his symphony; it seems to have arisen mostly during the night—my poor Robert has already spent several sleepless nights because of it. He calls it "Spring Symphony"—tender and poetic, as all his musical ideas are!

—Clara Schumann

ON YOUR OWN

Investigate a music-making family from any musical style: classical, folk, rock, or whatever interests you. Write a short essay about this family and why you think more than one generation chose music as a career.

Take It to the Net For information on the Mendelssohn and Schumann musical families, go to *www.sfsuccessnet.com.*

9

Brilliantly Brahms

Johannes Brahms (1833–1897) did not come from a musical family. He had to work hard to establish his own reputation since his career began in Beethoven's shadow. Brahms wrote many different kinds of music, such as the *Academic Festival Overture* you will soon hear.

Brahms Goes Back to School

Brahms dedicated *Academic Festival Overture* to the University of Breslau in Poland. He included German student songs as themes in the overture.

Sing these three German folk songs. **Listen** for them in the *Academic Festival Overture.*

 Academic Festival Overture

6-1 **by Johannes Brahms**
as performed by the London Symphony Orchestra
In 1879, a Polish university gave Brahms an honorary degree. In turn, Brahms wrote this piece and dedicated it to the university.

▲ Johannes Brahms

 CD 6-2

Gaudeamus Igitur

(Hail to Youth and Hail to Love)

College Song from Germany

Gau - de - a - mus   i - gi - tur,   Ju - ve - nes   dum   su - mus;
Hail   to youth   and   hail   to love!   Hail   to life   so   won - der - ful!

Post   ju - cun - dam   ju - ven - tu - tem,   Post   mo - les - tam   se - nec - tu - tem,
We   will toss   a - side   all   care, ___   And   with all   our   com - rades   share ___

Nos   ha - be - bit ___   hu - mus,   Nos   ha - be - bit ___   hu - mus.
One   long round   of ___   mer - ri - ment,   One   long round   of ___   mer - ri - ment.

 Take It to the Net To learn more about Johannes Brahms, visit *www.sfsuccessnet.com.*

Was kommt dort von der Höh?
(What Comes There O'er the Hill?)

College Song from Germany

1. Was kommt dort von der Höh'? Was kommt dort von der Höh'? Was
1. What comes there o'er the hill? What comes there o'er the hill? What
2. Es ist ein Pos - till - ion, Es ist ein Pos - till - ion, Es
2. It is the post - man, sure, It is the post - man, sure, It

kommt dort von der leder-nen Höh'? ça, ça, leder-nen Höh', Was kommt dort von der Höh'?
comes there ov - er yon-der hill, yes, sir, yon-der hill, What comes there o'er the hill?
ist ein leder-nen Pos - till - ion, ça, ça, Pos - till - ion, Es ist ein Pos - till - ion.
is the post-man yon-der sure, yes, sir, yon-der sure, It is the post-man sure.

3. Was bringt der Postillion? . . .
   Was bringt der ledernen Postillion, . . .

3. What does the postman bring? . . .
   What does the postman yonder bring, . . .

4. Er bringt 'nen Fuchsen mit, . . .
   Er bringt 'nen ledernen Fuchsen mit, . . .

4. He brings a fox with him, . . .
   He brings a little fox with him, . . .

Wir hatten gebauet
(The Stately House)

College Song from Germany
German Words by Daniel August von Binzer

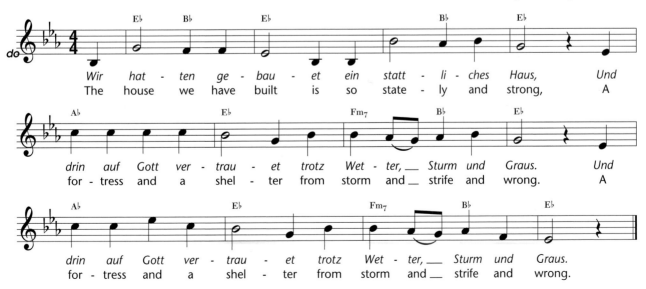

Wir hat - ten ge - bau - et ein statt - li - ches Haus, Und
The house we have built is so state - ly and strong, A

drin auf Gott ver - trau - et trotz Wet - ter, __ Sturm und Graus. Und
for - tress and a shel - ter from storm and __ strife and wrong. A

drin auf Gott ver - trau - et trotz Wet - ter, __ Sturm und Graus.
for - tress and a shel - ter from storm and __ strife and wrong.

10

Myths and Music

▲ A mask worn by actors in ancient Greek dramas

Imagine setting your favorite story to music, then putting it on stage. What kinds of music would you compose? What kind of staging and costumes would you create?

Long before the invention of film or television, people throughout the world combined music with dance and drama to create a sense of mystery and excitement in the telling of dramatic stories. Actors wore costumes and masks. Music was almost always a part of the drama.

Richard Wagner

One of the most famous composers of **opera** was Richard Wagner [REEK-ahrd VAHG-nr] (1813–1883). Wagner was from Germany and grew up loving the plays of Shakespeare. During his early days as a composer, he combined those plays with his music. Later in his career, he developed a vision for large-scale "music dramas" based on various European myths.

Wagner wrote an opera based on the story of Lohengrin [LOW-en-grin], the Swan Knight, son of

opera A theatrical production combining drama, vocal and orchestral music, costumes, scenery, and sometimes dance.

Arts Connection

◀ A painting of Richard Wagner in his study in "Villa Wahnfried" in Bayreuth by W. Beckmann (1880)

Parsifal, The Lord of the Holy Grail. In this story, Lohengrin uses his magical sword to defeat Telramund who wants to harm Elsa. Lohengrin marries Elsa instead, but she is forbidden to ask his name or where he has come from. When she breaks this pledge, Lohengrin disappears, and Elsa is left alone.

Listen to "Prelude to Act III" from the opera *Lohengrin*. **Describe** the musical characteristics of each section in the ABA form. Which section might represent your image of Lohengrin? Which section might represent Elsa?

Prelude to Act III

6-14

from *Lohengrin*
by Richard Wagner
as performed by the New York Philharmonic

Wagner composed *Lohengrin* between 1845 and 1848. It premiered in Weimar, Germany, in 1850, with Franz Liszt conducting.

▲ Placido Domingo in the title role in Wagner's *Lohengrin*

ON YOUR OWN

Research the making of the film, *Lord of the Rings,* based on the books by J.R.R. Tolkien. Find out how the special effects were created. How does music contribute to the sense of drama? What resources are available to the filmmakers that Wagner did not have available to him? What resources are similar?

Music Drama on a Large Scale

Wagner may be best known for his longest work, called *The Ring of the Nibelung,* or simply, *The Ring.* Its **libretto** is a cycle of four operas based on the story of the mythic hero, Siegfried. Siegfried must return the cursed treasure of the Nibelung dwarfs—a ring of gold. Along the way, he falls in love and has many adventures. During one adventure, he encounters the Valkyries. The Valkyries are mythical, immortal women who take the souls of brave men killed in battle to Valhalla, the great hall of the god Odin.

Staging these operas requires unusual facilities. Wagner wanted all kinds of special effects, such as Valkyries flying into the sky, Rhine maidens immersed in water, horses galloping across the stage, and fire devouring the hero and heroine. To hold all of this, Wagner drew the designs for a large theater to be built in Bayreuth [BI-royt], Germany. Wagner's works are still performed there.

Listen to the opening section of *The Ride of the Valkyries.* Imagine valkyries flying around the stage and soldiers being swept upward to Valhalla. **Describe** what Wagner did in the music to create this illusion. Describe the melodic contour of the main theme.

The Ride of the Valkyries

6-15

from *Die Walküre (The Valkyries)*
by Richard Wagner
as performed by the New York Philharmonic

Wagner wrote a prose outline for his "Ring Cycle" of operas, including *Die Walküre* in 1848.

Note This

It takes about fifteen hours to perform all four operas in the "Ring Cycle," so they are sometimes performed one per day for four days.

---

libretto The text of an opera or oratorio; from the Italian word meaning "little book."

A Grand Scene

Although operas mostly feature vocal solos and pieces for small groups of singers, they also include songs for chorus. Some operas include sections for the orchestra alone. The following example contains sections for both chorus and orchestra.

In Giuseppe Verdi's opera *Aida*, the setting is ancient Egypt. The people of Thebes are singing the praises of their king and their gods, and they are welcoming Prince Rhadames (RAH-da-mes) back from his recent victory in battle with the Ethiopians. Then, to the sound of the orchestra,

the Egyptian soldiers file past, leading Ethiopian prisoners. It is a grand scene, which sometimes even includes real animals such as elephants and horses! The music features a famous theme written for long, straight trumpets that are played onstage by musicians in costume. **Listen** for chorus with orchestra and for orchestra alone in the "Grand March" from *Aida*.

Grand March "Gloria all 'egitto"

from *Aida*
6-16 by Giuseppe Verdi
as performed by the Chicago Symphony and Chorus
Like Verdi's other operas, *Aida* is sung in Italian.

▼The Grand March from the second act of the Metropolitan Opera production of Verdi's *Aida*

Peking Opera

Various regions of China have longstanding traditions of musical drama. The tradition belonging to the Beijing (formerly known as Peking) area became the most prominent and was dubbed "opera" by European visitors. The stories are from ancient legends, and characters wear costumes and face paint to take on the identity of a character. Performing with singing actors are acrobats and musicians. There is almost no staging—only a few props. In the orchestra, a fiddle or flute—or both—leads the singing, percussion and sonas highlight battle scenes, and sonas announce the entrance of officials.

A Warrior Princess

In the Peking opera *The Princess Hundred Flowers,* the king is plagued by villains and bandits who are hungry for power. His daughter is a brave warrior named *Baihua* (Hundred Flowers). After many complicated political turns, in the scene "Falling in the Trap," the princess warrior wins her fight and the enemies retreat. Then a messenger brings news that her father has been killed, the kingdom has fallen, and nobody has seen her beloved. In the final scene, "The Disparition of a Flower," her beloved comes to help her fight an evil commander, but he is killed. The princess then kills the evil commander. Just like many Western operas, there is a tragic ending—the princess warrior stabs herself with a sabre.

Listen to "Falling in the Trap" from *The Princess Hundred Flowers.* **Identify** music that may represent the battle scene and music that might represent the messenger's announcement and the response of the princess.

▲ Li Ping in *The Princess Hundred Flowers*

Falling in the Trap

from *The Princess Hundred Flowers*
6-17 Anonymous
as performed by Li Ping and the Dalian Troupe
Operas like this one are honored in China where there is a national "Peking Opera Month."

Checkpoint

Choose two compositions you have heard in other lessons in this module. **Listen** to both compositions. Then listen to the Peking Opera selection again. **Analyze** and **compare** the musical characteristics of all three selections. Make a chart that shows your analysis or write a short essay comparing the three pieces.

11

The French Connection

▲ Visitors in Paris (1900) traveling to the International Exposition in bath-chairs pushed by porters

In Paris, France, the late nineteenth and early twentieth century was a wonderfully exciting time for creative people. Musicians, artists, and writers from all over the world met there, studied each other's works, and shared ideas. Painters borrowed ideas from writers, musicians borrowed ideas from painters, and so on. Many of these brilliant innovators were multitalented. Some of the great composers drew and painted. Some of the visual artists studied music, too. Paris was alive and vibrant with creativity.

Tradition Goes Out the Window!

These artists, writers, and musicians wanted to break with tradition. They had new and original ideas—they did not want to paint, write, or compose music as it had been done before. In their search for new ideas, some artists created paintings with less attention to detail. These artists wanted more attention paid to light, color, and the "impression" one received by glancing at a scene for just a moment. This artistic movement is called **Impressionism.** The term probably came from an 1872 painting by Claude Monet, entitled *Impression: Soleil levant* (Impression: Sunrise).

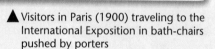

Arts Connection

▲ *Impression: Soleil levant,* (1870) by French painter Claude Monet (1840–1926), may have given the "impressionist" movement in art and music its name

Impressionism A style of painting in late nineteenth-century France that attempted to give an "impression" of a scene at one given moment in time, as opposed to an exact representation of it. The style is also found in music, literature, and sculpture.

Impressionism in Music

Some composers of the late nineteenth century borrowed ideas from Monet and other impressionist artists. These musicians also became known as impressionists. The composer most associated with Impressionism is Claude Debussy (1862–1918). One new idea he used was composing with **whole-tone scales.** Unlike major and minor scales, which are made up of some half and some whole steps, the whole-tone scale is created entirely of whole steps. The six tones per **octave** of the whole-tone scale create a vague, hazy feeling in the music.

Play the whole-tone scale, shown in the illustration above, which is used in Debussy's *Doctor Gradus ad Parnassum.*

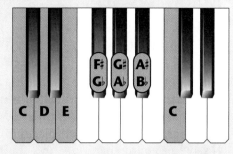

▲ C whole-tone scale

Delightful Debussy

Listen to *Doctor Gradus ad Parnassum*, a piano piece based on whole tone scales that imitates finger exercises for pianists.

Doctor Gradus ad Parnassum

6-18

from *Children's Corner Suite*
by Claude Debussy
as performed by William Kapell

Debussy dedicated his *Children's Corner Suite,* written in 1908, to his daughter Claude-Emma, nicknamed Chouchou, who was born in 1905.

Impression of the Sea

Listen to *"Dialogue du vent et de mer"* ("Dialogue of the Wind and the Sea") from a piece for orchestra by Claude Debussy entitled *La mer* (*The Sea*). As you listen, **analyze** the techniques Debussy used to make his music give the impression of the wind and the sea.

Dialogue du vent et de mer

6-19

from *La mer*
by Claude Debussy
as performed by the Philharmonia Orchestra; Pierre Boulez, conductor

One of Debussy's most famous pieces, *La mer,* written in 1905, was inspired by paintings of Claude Monet and of English painter J.M.W. Turner.

 **Connection**

▼ *Jeunes filles au piano* (Girls at the Piano) by Pierre-Auguste Renoir (1841–1919)

---

whole-tone scale A consecutive succession of six tones, each a whole step apart.

octave The distance between one pitch and the next higher or lower pitch that has the same name.

Maurice Ravel

Another composer who experimented with Impressionism was Maurice Ravel (1875–1937). Even though some people accused him of imitating Debussy, today Ravel is considered a wonderfully inventive and brilliant composer and **orchestrator.** He orchestrated music by composers Robert Schumann, Claude Debussy, and Modest Mussorgsky. He also orchestrated his own piano music, including a suite titled *Le tombeau de Couperin* (*The Tomb of Couperin*).

Listen to this piano version of "Prelude" from *Le tombeau de Couperin.* Think about how you might assign instruments to play the various melodies. List your ideas. For example, what instrument or instruments might play this melody?

Prelude

6-20

from *Le tombeau de Couperin* (piano version)
by Maurice Ravel
as performed by Robert Casadesus

In *Le tombeau de Couperin,* written in 1917, Ravel was paying homage to Baroque composer François Couperin, as well as other musicians of the past. He also honored friends who had died in World War I by writing their names over each movement in the piano score.

Now **listen** to Ravel's orchestration of "Prelude" from *Le tombeau de Couperin.* **Compare** the piano and orchestral versions. Which instrument or instruments do you hear in the opening theme? How does Ravel's orchestration compare with your ideas? What does the orchestration add to the piece?

Prelude

6-21

from *Le tombeau de Couperin* (orchestral version)
by Maurice Ravel
as performed by the Philadelphia Orchestra, Eugene Ormandy, conductor

This work highlights the woodwinds in almost every movement.

---

orchestrator A person who takes a piece of music in its original form and arranges it as a version to be played by a different combination of instruments.

Maurice Ravel

Perfectly Poulenc

Francis Poulenc [POO-lenk] (1899–1963) belonged to a group of early twentieth-century French composers called *Les six* (The six). Like the impressionist composers, *Les six* also wanted to see a change in the way music was written. They thought music should be simple and witty—a dramatic difference from the weighty, complex music of the nineteenth century. Their ideas influenced music and composers throughout the twentieth century.

Listen to an excerpt from *Sextet* for piano, flute, oboe, clarinet, bassoon, and French horn by Francis Poulenc. Think of words that describe the music. Notice the special technique called **flutter tonguing** used by the flute. Consider how six players stay together without a conductor.

---

flutter tonguing A technique for wind instruments in which the player makes an *r-r-r-r-r* sound with the tongue against the front teeth or in the back of the throat while playing.

 ## Sextet

6-22

for piano, flute, oboe, clarinet, bassoon, and French horn
Movement 1
by Francis Poulenc
as performed by Pascal Rogé, piano; Patrick Gallois, flute; Maurice Bourgue, oboe; Michel Portal, clarinet; Amaury Wallez, bassoon; and André Cazalet, French horn

The five wind instruments in Poulenc's *Sextet* are those found in a traditional woodwind quintet.

Mainly Milhaud

Another member of *Les six*, Darius Milhaud [mee-YOH] was influenced by the music he heard during his travels, including trips to the United States and Brazil. **Listen** to an excerpt from "Brasiliera," the third movement of a piece called *Scaramouche*. **Identify** the instrument(s) that are playing.

 ### *Brasiliera*

6-23

from *Scaramouche*
by Darius Milhaud
as performed by Stephen Coombs and Artur Pizarro

Milhaud composed *Scaramouche* in 1939.

ON YOUR OWN

Find out more about one of the composers of *Les six*. Visit a public library to find a recording by one of these composers. Listen to the recording. Write about what you hear. If possible, bring the recording to class and play an excerpt. Tell others in your class what you learned about the composer and his or her music.

◄ The composers in *Les six*, with writer/filmmaker Jean Cocteau (1889–1963) (at piano) as their spokesman, were Darius Milhaud (1892–1974), Georges Auric (1899–1983), Arthur Honegger (1892–1955), Germaine Tailleferre (1892–1983), Francis Poulenc (1899–1963), and Louis Durey (1888–1979).

Take It to the Net For more information on Debussy, Ravel, and Impressionism, visit *www.sfsuccessnet.com*.

12

The Magical Worlds of STRAVINSKY

Igor Fyodorovich Stravinsky (1882–1971) was born in Russia but lived in France for some time. Later he became a United States citizen and lived there until his death. Stravinsky's works for ballet, orchestra, and chamber groups are widely performed.

In 1909, ballet producer Serge Diaghilev commissioned Stravinsky to write ballet music for the first time. Stravinsky composed *The Firebird*, based on a magical Russian folktale. It was a huge success.

Listen to "Finale" from *The Firebird* as you follow the listening map. Describe how Stravinsky used timbre, rhythm, and articulation to transform the melody.

Finale

6-24

**from *The Firebird*
by Igor Stravinsky
as performed by the Philharmonic Symphony-Orchestra of New York, conducted by Igor Stravinsky**

This performance gives us a clear idea of how the composer wanted the music to sound because he is conducting the orchestra.

The Rite of Spring

Once Stravinsky began writing ballets, he found them fascinating, and he wrote ballets for an entire decade. Stravinsky was part of a stunning trio that included Sergei Diaghilev, who was the producer of the *Ballets Russes*, and its **choreographer,** Vaslav Nijinsky. These three were also privileged to be working with some of the most famous dancers in the history of ballet. Stravinsky wrote *The Rite of Spring* ballet for the *Ballets Russes*.

Listen to "Dance of the Youths and Maidens" from *The Rite of Spring*. **Conduct** as you use rhythm syllables to **read** this rhythm of the strings.

Dance of the Youths and Maidens

6-25

**from *The Rite of Spring*
by Igor Stravinsky
as performed by the New York Philharmonic,
conducted by Igor Stravinsky**

After his big successes with *The Firebird* and another popular ballet, *Petrouchka*, Stravinsky's ballet for the *Ballets Russes*, *The Rite of Spring*, should have been no problem. Its premiere in 1913 caused a riot in the audience. The piece was considered barbaric and shocking, and the press reviews were poisonous.

choreographer A person who designs the movements for a dance.

▲ Igor Stravinsky

◀ **Maria Tallchief
in a production
of Stravinsky's
*Firebird***

"Finale" from *The Firebird*   LISTENING MAP

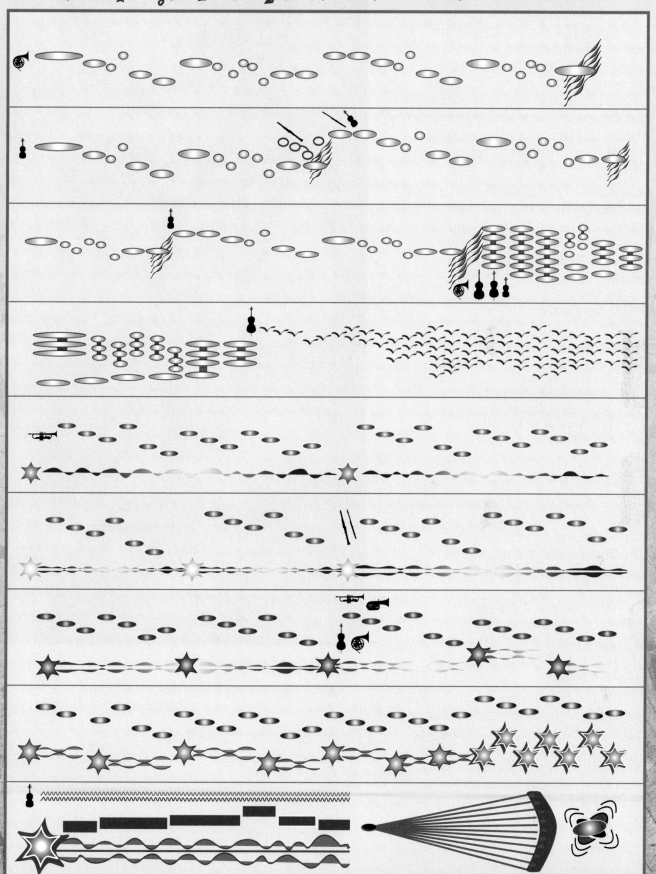

Stravinsky Straightens Up

Only a few years after *The Rite of Spring* caused a riot, Stravinsky was writing new music in a style that sounded old. The style came to be known as *neoclassical*, or "based on classical." He used the same forms that composers such as Haydn and Mozart had used in the late 1700s, but his instrumental tone colors were twentieth century.

Stravinsky's 1920 ballet *Pulcinella* is in neoclassical style. **Listen** to these excerpts. Does the music sound like it comes from the 1700s or the 1900s? **Describe** how the term *neoclassical* fits this music.

Serenata

6-26 from *Pulcinella*
by Igor Stravinsky
as performed by the New York Philharmonic,
conducted by Pierre Boulez

Pulcinella is based on a piece by Giovanni Battista Pergolesi (1710–1736).

The Nightingale

One of Stravinsky's most memorable works is *The Nightingale*. Stravinsky started writing music for Hans Christian Andersen's tale of the Chinese Emperor's two nightingales in 1908. He stopped working on *The Nightingale* to compose *The Firebird*, *Petrouchka*, and *The Rite of Spring*. He began working on *The Nightingale* again in 1913 and made it into an opera.

In Andersen's story, one of the Emperor's nightingales is a miraculous real bird whose voice can bring joy to all who listen. **Listen** to Stravinsky's music for the real nightingale. How does Stravinsky create the impression of a bird with music?

Arts Connection

▲ *"The Nightingale"* by Esteban Fekete (born 1924)

Song of the Nightingale

6-27 from *The Nightingale*
by Igor Stravinsky
as performed by the Columbia Symphony, conducted by Robert Craft

Stravinsky wrote the music for this part of *The Nightingale* in 1908.

The Rest of the Nightingale Story

When the Chinese Emperor receives a mechanical nightingale as a gift, he becomes entranced with its sound and banishes the real bird from his kingdom. Only when the Emperor falls ill and begs for the song of a real nightingale to heal him does the nightingale return to offer his melodious song. **Listen** to Stravinsky's music for the mechanical nightingale. **Compare** the music he wrote for these two different birds.

Game of the Mechanical Nightingale

6-28
from *The Nightingale*
by Igor Stravinsky
as performed by the Columbia Symphony, conducted by Robert Craft
Stravinsky wrote the music for the mechanical nightingale in 1913.

The Young Stravinsky

Igor Stravinsky was born into a musical family. His mother, Anna, was a singer and pianist. His father, Fyodor, was an accomplished bass-baritone who had a long career in opera. The Stravinsky home was filled with the comings-and-goings of great composers such as Rimsky-Korsakov, Borodin, and Mussorgsky. He had access to his mother and father's music, and like most young people of his middle-class upbringing, studied piano from an early age. He studied law in college before settling on a musical career.

Listen to this interview with Stravinsky, in which he talks about the *"Berceuse"* from *The Firebird*.

Interview with Stravinsky

6-29
with *"Berceuse"* from *The Firebird*
Stravinsky conducted the performance within this interview.

Survey family members, friends or teachers to learn more about their early musical life. Find out what role music played in their childhoods and whether a family member was influential to them. Draw conclusions on how having a "musical" family affects a person's interest in music both as a child and as an adult. Share your findings with the class.

Natalia Makarova and Anthony Dowell perform *Le Rossignol*, a dance set to Stravinsky's music. ▼

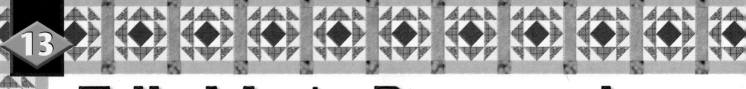

Folk Music Preserved

"The best way to get to knowing any bunch of people is to go and listen to their music."

—Woody Guthrie (1912-1967)

Folk songs and instrumental folk music belong to everyone in a community or culture because many different people contribute to them. The music changes as people perform it. Dance music, songs of celebration and of grieving, work songs, love songs, children's songs, and **ballads** reflect the daily life of the people who sing them. Because much folk music has an oral tradition, some musicians in the 1900s recognized that folk music might disappear. To keep this from happening, they began a campaign to collect, preserve, record, notate, arrange, and teach folk melodies.

John Lomax, his son Alan, and daughter Bess recorded singers and their songs in New England and the southern United States as early as the 1920s. The Seeger family, including musicologist Charles Seeger, his wife Ruth Crawford Seeger, and children Pete, Mike, and Peggy, also captured and preserved American folk songs.

Listen to this recording of *John Henry*, one of the many folk songs that Ruth Crawford Seeger helped to preserve.

Pete Seeger entertaining at the opening of the Washington Labor Canteen in Washington, D.C. in 1944 ▼

🎧 *John Henry*

Folk song from North Carolina
7-1   as performed by Mike and Peggy Seeger

Mike and Peggy Seeger perform together in this recording.

Ruth Crawford Seeger used melodies and textures of American folk music in her compositions. **Listen** for them in her *Suite for Wind Quintet.*

🎧 *Suite for Wind Quintet*

Movement 1
7-2   by Ruth Crawford Seeger
as performed by the Lark Quintet

Ruth Crawford Seeger composed this piece for woodwind quintet, which includes flute, oboe, clarinet, bassoon, and French horn, in 1952.

---

ballad A song that tells a story.

A Tribute to Bach

Villa-Lobos greatly admired the music of Johann Sebastian Bach. His most famous pieces are called *Bachianas Brasileiras*. This music combines the rhythms of Brazilian music with some of the structures of Bach's music. **Listen** to this *aria* which is the first movement of *Bachianas Brasileiras No. 5*, originally written for soprano soloist and an ensemble of eight cellos. What is the language of the *aria*?

▲ Renée Fleming

Aria

7-4
from *Bachianas Brasileiras No. 5*
by Heitor Villa-Lobos
as performed by Renée Fleming

Villa-Lobos wrote this piece in 1938. He composed nine works called *Bachianas Brasileiras*.

Aztec Inspiration

Listen to Carlos Chavez talk about his love of music and his interest in the music of the Mexican people.

Interview with Carlos Chavez

7-5
Besides composing music, Chavez was well known in Mexico and internationally as a conductor and music educator.

Discuss the following questions with your classmates.

- Why does Chavez feel music is important? Are his reasons valid for you?
- Why did Chavez choose music as a career?
- Do you have some ideas about careers you would enjoy? What factors have influenced your career ideas?

The Flower Prince

In his interview, Carlos Chavez talks about his composition *Xochipilli*, an imagined re-creation of Aztec music. *Xochipilli* is the Flower Prince of Aztec lore, patron of music, games, dancing, and love.

As you **listen, identify** three sections in the music. Notice the changes in instruments, flow, and energy as the music shifts from one section to the next. **Describe** how the changes affect the music. What images does this music bring to mind?

Xochipilli

7-6
by Carlos Chavez
as performed by Eduardo Mata and La Camerata Tambuco

Originally Chavez used traditional early Mexican instruments—drums, flutes, and whistles—in this piece, but the recording you will hear substitutes modern orchestral instruments.

Section A	Section B	Section C
Ceremonial Dancing	**Poetic Images**	**Ceremonial Dancing**
flutes, rattles, whistle (piccolo), wooden drums	clarinet, bells, flute, rattles, whistle (piccolo), wooden drums	bass drum, bells, clarinet, conch shell (trombone), rasp, rattles, whistle (piccolo), wooden drums

MARCHING THROUGH HISTORY

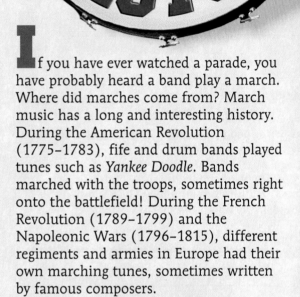

▼ *The Spirit of '76* (circa 1875), by A.M. Williard (1836–1875)

If you have ever watched a parade, you have probably heard a band play a march. Where did marches come from? March music has a long and interesting history. During the American Revolution (1775–1783), fife and drum bands played tunes such as *Yankee Doodle.* Bands marched with the troops, sometimes right onto the battlefield! During the French Revolution (1789–1799) and the Napoleonic Wars (1796–1815), different regiments and armies in Europe had their own marching tunes, sometimes written by famous composers.

Make Music, Not War

By the time of the Civil War in the United States (1861–1865), military bands no longer accompanied the troops into battle. They still played concerts and marched in parades, though, and their music was based on popular melodies of the day.

Listen to this march from the Civil War Era. Tap the beat and **conduct** to show the meter in 2. Do you recognize the melody? **Analyze** the music as you **listen** to discover the form. Then **identify** the brass instruments that you hear.

Glory Hallelujah Grand March

7-7 by W. K. Batchelder
as performed by the Americus Brass Band
Most concert bands include woodwind instruments, but this band includes only brass instruments.

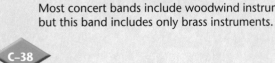

The Marines' Hymn—The President's Band

Each branch of the U.S. military has its own special march music. **Listen** to *The Marines' Hymn*, the official march of the United States Marines. **Read** the notation for the "The Marines' Hymn" as you listen. **Identify** the form of the song's phrases.

The Marines' Hymn

Traditional

7-8 as performed by "The President's Own" U.S. Marine Band

The Marines' Hymn has been the official music for the United States Marine Corps since 1929. Its melody was derived from a theme in the opera *Genevieve de Brabant,* by French composer Jacques Offenbach.

Sing "The Marines' Hymn." This recording features only men's voices, but all branches of the United States military include women too, so everyone sing!

CD 7-9

THE MARINES' HYMN

Traditional

Guitar: capo 3

From the halls of Mon-te-zu - ma To the shores of Trip-o-li; _____

We _ fight our coun-try's bat - tles In the air, on land, and sea. _____

First to fight for right and free - dom And to keep our hon-or clean, _____

We are proud to claim the ti - tle of U-nit-ed States Ma - rine. _____

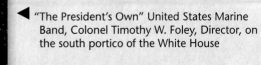

► "The President's Own" United States Marine Band, Colonel Timothy W. Foley, Director, on the south portico of the White House

A Band in Every Town

The late nineteenth and early twentieth centuries represent the "golden age" of the town band in the United States. During this period, John Philip Sousa, America's "March King," composed many of the marches that are still played by bands today.

Listen to *The Washington Post* march by Sousa. **Conduct** the meter in 2 as you listen. **Compare** the instruments and the form of this march to *Glory Hallelujah Grand March*. What is similar in the two marches? What is different?

The Washington Post

by John Philip Sousa

7-11   **as performed by the Philip Jones Ensemble, conducted by Elgar Howarth**

This march was named after *The Washington Post*, a major newspaper in Washington, D.C.

Music MAKERS

JOHN PHILIP SOUSA

John Philip Sousa (1854–1932), was born in Washington, D.C. When he threatened to run away and join the circus at age 13, his father immediately signed him up as an apprentice in the U.S. Marine Band. After seven years, he left the band to play violin and conduct theater orchestras. Sousa returned to the U.S. Marine Band as its conductor in 1880, and under his leadership the Marine Band became one of the best bands in the country. Today it is known as the "The President's Own" U.S. Marine Band. In 1892, Sousa formed his own band and toured in the United States and throughout the world. The "Sousaphone," a marching version of the tuba, was named after Sousa. In addition to composing marches, Sousa arranged orchestra music for bands and composed operettas, the best-known of which is *El Capitan*. His most famous march, *The Stars and Stripes Forever*, is the official march of the United States.

▲ A traditional tuba

▲ Notice what is different about the design of the sousaphone.

From Tuba to Sousaphone

Look at these pictures. Why do you suppose the tuba was modified to create the sousaphone?

Take It to the Net To read more about marching bands, band instruments, and John Philip Sousa, visit *www.sfsuccessnet.com*.

Checkpoint

Choose two compositions you have heard in this unit: one composition from this lesson and one from another lesson. Listen to both compositions and **analyze** them. When and where were they written? What are the musical characteristics of the compositions? Show your analysis of each composition in a chart. Then, compare the two compositions using the information from your charts. In what ways are the compositions similar? In what ways are they different? Write a short essay comparing the two works.

16

The "Duke" –

"My band is my instrument."
—*Duke Ellington*

Edward Kennedy "Duke" Ellington is one of the all-time greats of jazz music. As a bandleader, composer, arranger, pianist, and advocate for African American history and culture, he toured the world and helped to establish jazz as a serious creative art form.

Duke Ellington's band played at the famous Cotton Club in Harlem. It included three "reeds," or woodwind players (clarinets, saxophones), five brass players (trumpets and trombones), and four rhythm players (bass, piano, percussion, and guitar). Ellington directed the music from his spot at the piano. He featured individual musicians in the music he composed, and his musicians tended to remain with the band for a long time.

In 1939, Billy Strayhorn joined Ellington's band to work with him on composing and arranging. Strayhorn is credited with writing *Take the "A" Train*, which became the Ellington Band's "signature tune." **Listen** to *Take the "A" Train*. **Analyze** as you **listen** to find the aaba form of this music.

"We're not worried about writing for posterity. We just want it to sound good right now!"
—*Duke Ellington*

Take the "A" Train

by Billy Strayhorn
7-12 **as performed by Duke Ellington and his Orchestra**
The A train is one of the subways in New York City.

Note This

Most of Duke Ellington's songs and arrangements are almost exactly three minutes long. They were recorded on 78 RPM discs which could hold just that amount of music on each side.

Take It to the Net To learn more about African American Music: Jazz and Blues, go to *www.sfsuccessnet.com.*

Headin' to Harlem

Sometimes *Take the "A" Train* is performed with lyrics that tell how to get to Ellington's home in Sugar Hill in Harlem, a neighborhood in New York City. Here are the words Ella Fitzgerald sang in a 1957 recording. **Sing** them along with the "A Train" melody.

> You must take the A train to go to Sugar Hill way up in Harlem.
>
> If you miss the A train, you'll find you missed the quickest trip to Harlem.
>
> Hurry, get on board, it's coming, listen to those rails a-thrumming—
>
> All aboard! Get on the A train, soon you will be on Sugar Hill in Harlem.

Duke Ellington, at the piano, and his band ▼

A Jazz Legend

Here's a tune by the Duke with a very simple theme. The title refers to the key of this composition—C. **Play** or **sing** the theme. Then **listen** for the same theme in *C-Jam Blues*.

Theme   *3 times*

C-Jam Blues

7-13

by Edward Kennedy "Duke" Ellington
as performed by Duke Ellington

This recording of a live performance at the Whitney Museum in New York City features Ellington at the piano, accompanied by bass and drums.

Music MAKERS
Edward Kennedy "Duke" Ellington

Edward Kennedy Ellington (1899–1974) was born in Washington, D.C. Legend has it that Edward had a high school friend who wanted him to have a classier name—"Duke." The name stuck with him his entire life. Ellington took piano lessons from an early age and started his own band at age 19. The band played at clubs and parties in Washington and then went to New York in 1927 to perform at the Cotton Club in Harlem. Later, the band toured nationally and internationally, played radio broadcasts, and recorded music by Ellington and others.

Ellington composed more than 6,000 pieces of music, many of them collaborations with other musicians. He put together stage revues and created music for films. In addition, he helped set up an annual series of jazz concerts at Carnegie Hall in New York, which ran from 1943–1955. In the 1960s, he turned to writing jazz-style "Sacred Concerts" based on Christian themes. These were performed at large cathedrals in various parts of the world, including San Francisco, New York, Paris, Barcelona, and London. He felt strongly about leaving many compositions as his final legacy.

17

Talent and HIGH ENERGY

These words can be used to describe American conductor, composer, and educator, Leonard Bernstein (1918–1990). He was famous for his spectacular array of musical talents, as well as his highly energetic style. In 1943, 25-year old Bernstein was catapulted into international stardom when he conducted a radio broadcast of the New York Philharmonic on only one day's notice! The concert was a huge success, and Bernstein was a hero. Whether composing, conducting, or telling young people about music, Bernstein did so with great passion and enthusiasm.

▼ Leonard Bernstein

A Man of Many Styles

Bernstein's compositions reflect many styles of American music. His works contain musical ideas from a variety of sources, including hymns, Latin styles, blues, and rock. With lyricist Stephen Sondheim, Bernstein wrote a modern, musical version of Shakespeare's famous play *Romeo and Juliet*. Set on New York City's West Side, the **musical** is called *West Side Story*. In *West Side Story*, Tony and Maria, a young man and woman from rival gangs, fall in love. As in *Romeo and Juliet*, their romance ends in tragedy.

Listen to the duet *Somewhere*. Tony and Maria express their hopes for their relationship. **Describe** how the music shows their relationship. What qualities in the music create a sense of foreboding about things to come?

Somewhere

from *West Side Story*
7-14   by Leonard Bernstein and Stephen Sondheim
as performed by Peter Hofman and Deborah Sasson, Michael Tilson Thomas, conductor

West Side Story opened at Broadway's Winter Garden Theatre on September 26, 1957. Choreographer Jerome Robbins first proposed the idea for the musical to Leonard Bernstein in 1949.

▲ Natalie Wood and Richard Beymer as Maria and Tony in the film *West Side Story*

musical Also known as musical theater, a play that includes singing and dancing.

◀ Dancers perform the school dance scene in the film *West Side Story*

Music for an Important Opening Night

Leonard Bernstein was invited to write the music for the opening of the Kennedy Center in Washington, D.C., on September 8, 1971. He decided to write a huge piece called *Mass*. "Mass" is the name for a Catholic church service. Many composers had written music for church services before, but never a composition like this! Bernstein's *Mass* is subtitled "A Theater Piece for Singers, Players, and Dancers," and requires a large orchestra, two adult choruses, a boys' choir, a gospel choir, a large cast of actors, a ballet company, a marching band, a rock band, and folk guitar, reflecting the diversity of music in the United States.

One of the most famous dance scenes in *West Side Story* features Puerto Rican gang members in a song about moving to America. They dance to a Latin rhythm that alternates between groups of two and three. **Play** this rhythm by tapping it on your desk. Then **listen** to *America*, and **identify** the rhythm in the music.

After an exciting and wild opening number, the actor playing the "celebrant" of *Mass* appears alone in front of the curtain and sings *A Simple Song*. **Listen** to this music and describe why this song is called simple.

America
from *West Side Story*
7-15 by Leonard Bernstein and Stephen Sondheim
as performed by Betty Ward, George Chakiris, and the cast, conducted by Johnny Green, conductor
In 1961, *West Side Story* was made into a movie, starring Natalie Wood as Maria. It won that year's Oscar for Best Picture.

A Simple Song
from *Mass*
7-16 by Leonard Bernstein
as performed by Alan Titus, Leonard Bernstein conducting
Bernstein's *Mass* combines many different styles, from classical to blues to rock and roll.

"Music . . . can name the unnamable and communicate the unknowable."
—*Leonard Bernstein*

18

COMPOSERS TODAY

Composers of the past wrote music for special events, in memory of people they admired, and to express their own ideas. Sometimes they received **commissions** for their works. Sometimes they composed for reasons all their own. What is it like to be a composer today? What inspires today's composers to write music?

Friends Inspire Composers

John Corigliano was born in 1938 in New York City and studied composition at Columbia University. He has written many kinds of music, including music for films and an electric rock opera. His first symphony, completed in 1989, has been played by over 100 orchestras all around the world. He received a commission from the Metropolitan Opera and with it wrote a work called *The Ghost of Versailles*.

Corigliano dedicated a suite of piano pieces called *Gazebo Dances* to some friends who play the piano. **Listen** to *Tarantella*, a composition for two pianists. **Identify** the changes in dynamics and the accents in this music.

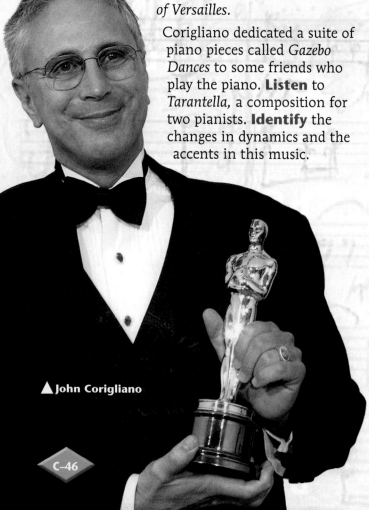
▲ John Corigliano

Tarantella

8-1
from *Gazebo Dances*
by John Corigliano
as performed by John and Richard Contiguglia

This dance is a *tarantella*, a lively dance in compound duple meter, originally from Italy. It is named for the Italian town of Taranto.

Corigliano used the interval of a second and its inversion, a seventh, to build the themes for his *Sonata for Violin and Piano*. **Analyze** the notation below to identify the seconds and sevenths. **Listen** for these intervals in the melody of this work.

Allegro

8-2
from *Sonata for Violin and Piano*
by John Corigliano
as performed by John Corigliano, Sr.

John Corigliano's father plays violin in this recording. He was concert master, or first chair violin, in the New York Philharmonic from 1943–1966.

Play these intervals on a keyboard instrument. Corigliano had these intervals and the motion of a pianist's hands in mind when he wrote *Fifths to Thirds*. **Listen** to this music for piano. What does Corigliano do to make the piece interesting?

Fifths to Thirds

8-3
from *Etude Fantasy for Piano*
by John Corigliano
as performed by Stephen Hough, piano

Corigliano marked one section of this music "slithery." Listen for this section.

commission A fee paid to a composer to write a piece of music for a certain person, group, or occasion.

Visual Art Inspires Composers

Analyze this painting by artist Paul Klee. What do you notice about the movement of its lines, shapes, and colors? American composer Cindy McTee was fascinated by this painting and wrote a composition for orchestra called *The Twittering Machine*. In 1993, she wrote a wind ensemble arrangement of it.

As you **listen** to McTee's music, think about the musical qualities that seem to link to Paul Klee's painting.

California Counterpoint: The Twittering Machine

by Cindy McTee

8-4 **as performed by the University of North Texas Wind Symphony**

McTee added "California Counterpoint" to her title in honor of Mitchell Fennell, a California conductor who commissioned her to write the music.

A Fantastic Fanfare

What instruments would you expect to hear in a fanfare? Composer Cindy McTee wrote a fanfare that has both traditional and unusual elements. **Listen** to *Fanfare*, and **identify** the instruments you hear.

Fanfare

from *Soundings*

8-5 **by Cindy McTee**
as performed by the University of North Texas Wind Symphony

Cindy McTee's *Soundings* was commissioned by the "Big Eight" Band Directors' Association.

What motivates composers to continue creating music? The short answer is that people have a need to express themselves, and one means of expression is writing music. Where do composers get their ideas? From lots of places—friends, other works of art, special events, and sometimes even from music itself.

ON YOUR OWN

For whom or what would you like to write music? On your own or with a friend, compose a piece of music and record it or perform it for your class. Write a paragraph describing how you composed the piece and where you found your ideas.

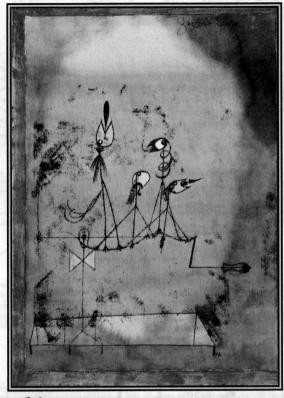

Arts Connection

▲ *The Twittering Machine* by Paul Klee (born 1922)

American composer Cindy McTee (born 1953) has received many commissions to compose music for orchestras, bands, and wind ensembles. She uses both acoustic and electronic sound sources in her works. McTee is a professor of composition at the University of North Texas. ▼

Music Through Time

Review and Assess

Summary

In Music Through Time you've listened to

- music from many different cultures.
- music of the past and present
- music of many styles
- music to serve different functions

Understanding music from all time periods and cultures is easy when you think about what you hear when you play a recording. These are common elements in all compositions.

- **timbre**—tone color (sound) of an instrument or voice
- **melody, rhythm, harmony, and tempo**—compositional elements
- **form**—how the piece is organized
- **dynamics**—the degrees of loudness and softness of a sound
- **expression**—emotional effect on the listener
- **cultural function**—when and where is it used?

Review What You Learned

Look at the timeline on pages C-2 and C-3. This time line depicts periods in the history of Western culture—the culture of Western Europe and North and South America. Note that each period spans over one hundred years of history. The lines indicate arbitrary points in time. Historians chose these breaks in the timelines based roughly on changes in the musical styles and the culture. One thing is certain: music has changed and continues to change over time.

Choose any three listening selections from Music Through Time. As you listen, think about where they might fall in the timeline and why.

What Do You Hear? 2

Listen to the following pairs of excerpts. The two excerpts in each pair are from different periods in the history of Western music. Decide which piece was written first. Explain your answer by describing two features of each piece that place it in an earlier or later time period. Consider the following in formulating your explanations.

- Instrumentation
- Melody
- Harmony
- Rhythm

Exercise 1

Was excerpt A written earlier or later than excerpt B?

How did you decide?

Exercise 2

Was excerpt A written earlier or later than excerpt B?

How did you decide?

Exercise 3

Was excerpt A written earlier or later than excerpt B?

How did you decide?

Show What You Know

One of the best ways to develop understanding is to explain ideas verbally or in writing. As you listen to your selections, write down two sentences that describe each of the musical and expressive elements listed below.

- **timbre** What instruments and voices do you hear?
- **compositional elements** How fast is the tempo? How can you describe the rhythm? What does the harmony sound like?
- **dynamics** How are dynamics used?
- **form** How is the music organized? Are musical ideas repeated?

- **expression** What emotion does the music make you feel?
- **cultural function** When would you likely hear this music? Where would you expect this music to be performed? Does it have a public function, like a parade, or is it more personal?

In small groups, discuss each others' ideas and try to figure out why different members of the group came to different conclusions. The group need not agree, but the members should be able to explain their points of view.

What to Listen For

Most music tells a story or expresses some kind of idea, such as an emotion or a visual image. The sounds of music can make you feel energetic or sad, can trigger a memory, or paint a picture in your imagination. Think about how all of these emotions and images are conveyed through sound alone. How does music do this?

Listen to these selections from Music Through Time. After hearing each one, explain what you think the composer intended to convey, and how the composer communicated his or her ideas,

using the list on page C-48. For example, if a march sounds "triumphant," what in the music creates this sound? If a piece is intended for dancing, how do the elements change?

Share What You Know

Select one piece from the module that is your personal favorite. Prepare a presentation for a class or another person that will help them understand the music itself and why you like the music. You should include in your presentation basic facts about the piece including title, composer, and composition date.

Explain how you think the elements convey the composer's intentions—mood, emotion, a picture, or an idea. Include the elements of music description listed on page C-48.

Your presentation may be placed on poster board, overhead transparencies, or on slides created with presentation software. Play excerpts from the piece during your presentation to illustrate your points.

Create a list of questions that might direct the listener's understanding of the music. For example, a descriptive title such as Tarantella might make them think of a tarantula.

DRUMS AND BEYOND

Playing in Percussion Ensembles

"In the beginning was noise.
And noise begat rhythm.
And rhythm begat everything else.
This is the kind of cosmology a
drummer can live with."
—*Mickey Hart and Jay Stevens (1990)*

◀ Yup'ik dancer

◀ Cloud-chamber Bowls

▲ Richard Cooke

◀ Nigerian udus

1 SLIT DRUMS TO UDU POTS

Many instruments are made of materials found in nature. For example, the cultures in regions where bamboo grows typically have instruments made of bamboo. The people of the islands in the Pacific Ocean share many percussion instruments made of natural materials. These include drums made from hollow logs and instruments made from gourd and bamboo. One of the most interesting Pacific island musical groups is the slit drum ensemble. Slit drums are made from logs that have been hollowed out through a slit, or narrow opening. Large slit drums are placed on the ground and struck with sticks. Smaller slit drums are sometimes hit against each other.

Slit drums are found in parts of the world where large trees are abundant. Drums may be beautifully carved to resemble animals, people, or mythical figures. Large slit drums make a sound loud enough to be heard from a great distance. In some regions they are used for communication.

The Slit Drum Sound

Listen to this performance by a slit drum ensemble. **Identify** the instruments other than slit drums used in this piece.

Ue ue

8-12 **Traditional music from Bora Bora as performed by the Drummers of Bora Bora** In this recording, the leader announces the ensemble and introduces the first rhythm by playing it. Then the other musicians begin to play.

Slit drums from Cameroon ▲

Man playing slit-gong drum ▲

Play Slit Drums

Play the "Bora Bora Boom Ensemble," which is modeled after some of the rhythms used in traditional Polynesian slit drumming. Place woodblocks on carpet and play each with two mallets. Learn Ⓐ first, then Ⓑ. Practice playing Ⓐ three times followed by Ⓑ. Then repeat the cycle—Ⓐ Ⓐ Ⓐ Ⓑ Ⓐ Ⓐ Ⓐ Ⓑ—until the ensemble sounds smooth. Use Ⓒ as a *coda* to end the piece.

Bora Bora Boom Ensemble

Music by Jeff Bush

◀ Slit drum from Sudan

Slit drum from Zaire ▶

▲ Aztec slit drum

Note This

The woodblock, found in the percussion section of a band or orchestra, is actually a small slit drum.

Take It to the Net The Maori people of New Zealand share many cultural similarities with the people of the Polynesian islands. Find out more about Maori music at *www.sfsuccessnet.com.*

Build Slit Drums

Build your own slit drums using PVC tubing. The length of the tube will determine the pitch of the drum. Make low drums out of 4-inch diameter tubing in 6-foot, 5-foot, 4-foot, and 3-foot lengths. These can be laid horizontally on a piece of styrofoam and played with dowels or snare drum sticks. Make several sets of smaller slit drums out of 2-inch diameter PVC tubing in 12-inch and 24-inch lengths. These can also be laid horizontally on styrofoam and played with a dowel. Substitute the large PVC slit drums for the medium and low woodblock, and the small PVC slit drums for the high woodblock parts in the "Bora Bora Boom Ensemble."

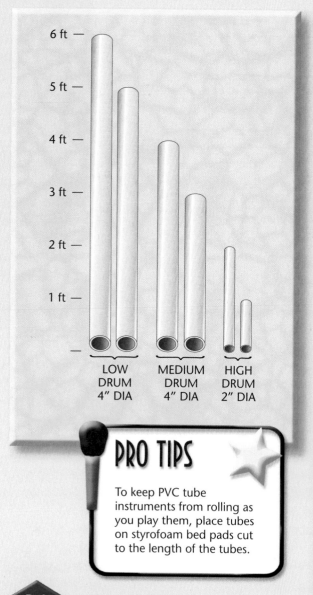

6 ft —
5 ft —
4 ft —
3 ft —
2 ft —
1 ft —

LOW DRUM 4" DIA   MEDIUM DRUM 4" DIA   HIGH DRUM 2" DIA

PRO TIPS

To keep PVC tube instruments from rolling as you play them, place tubes on styrofoam bed pads cut to the length of the tubes.

Clay Gourd Music

The gourd is another natural material that is used to make percussion instruments. Traditionally, gourds have been used to store food, to hold water, and to make music. The *udu* is a gourd-shaped instrument made of clay. Originally from Nigeria, the *udu* is played by slapping the sides and the bottom of the gourd. The player can also place a hand over the top hole of the *udu*. While striking it with one hand, the player can open and close the top hole of the *udu* to create different sounds. Members of the Hausa and Ibo tribes in Nigeria believed that the sound of the *udu* was the voice of their ancestors speaking to them. Originally a water jug played by Nigerian women during ceremonies, the *udu* is now used in many styles of popular and traditional music around the world.

Listen to the variety of sounds produced on the *udu* in *Udu Pot* by Gavin Bates.

Udu Pot

by Gavin Bates

8-13 This music was composed as the soundtrack for a Web site that sells *udu* drums and other African instruments.

Simple *udu* ▶

Nigerian *udu* ▶

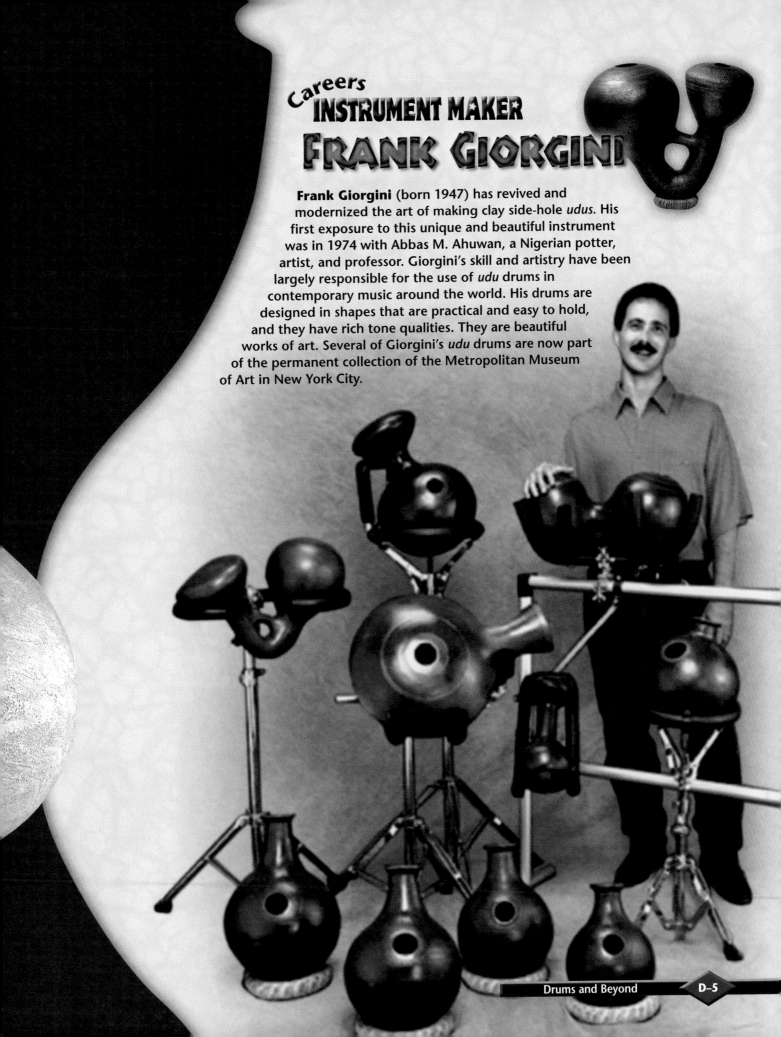

Careers
INSTRUMENT MAKER
FRANK GIORGINI

Frank Giorgini (born 1947) has revived and modernized the art of making clay side-hole *udus*. His first exposure to this unique and beautiful instrument was in 1974 with Abbas M. Ahuwan, a Nigerian potter, artist, and professor. Giorgini's skill and artistry have been largely responsible for the use of *udu* drums in contemporary music around the world. His drums are designed in shapes that are practical and easy to hold, and they have rich tone qualities. They are beautiful works of art. Several of Giorgini's *udu* drums are now part of the permanent collection of the Metropolitan Museum of Art in New York City.

Evolving African Music

Much of the world's popular music today is a mix of West African and European music. One type of popular African music is highlife, a **fusion** of African, European, and Caribbean musical styles.

Listen to *Mensu*, a contemporary highlife piece. You will hear instruments from West African, Caribbean, and North American cultures.

A Song from Ghana

Listen to *Samanfo, begye nsa nom*, a traditional Ghanian song arranged by W. Komla Amoaku.

Mensu

by Kwame Twusasi-Fofie

8-14   Other forms of popular West African music include *juju*, *fuji*, palm-wine, *kwassa kwassa*, *benga,* afrobeat, and *axe*.

Samanfo, begye nsa nom

Traditional from Ghana
arranged and performed by W. Komla Amoaku and group

8-15   The song begins with a two-toned bell, followed by shaker. Then the other percussion instruments join in one at a time.

Samanfo, begye nsa nom

Twi Song from Ghana
Arranged by W. Komla Amoaku

Sa - man - fo e, be-gye nsa nom. Sa - man - fo e, be-gye nsa nom.

Sa - man - fo e be-gye, A - o Sa - man - fo e, be-gye nsa nom.

Ya - da Nya - me a - se o. ___ Ya - da Nya - me a - se o. ___

Sa - man - fo e be-gye, A - o Sa - man - fo e be-gye nsa nom. Ya - da nom.

fusion A combination of two or more distinct musical styles.

Kwame Twusasi-Fofie ▶

Highlife Ensemble

Arranged by W. Komla Amoaku
Based on the Ghanaian Highlife "Osibi"

Play a Little Highlife

Practice "Highlife Ensemble" by learning to **play** the bell part first. Then add the *clave* and rattle parts, followed by the drums. **Play** the ensemble to accompany *Samanfo, begye nsa nom.*

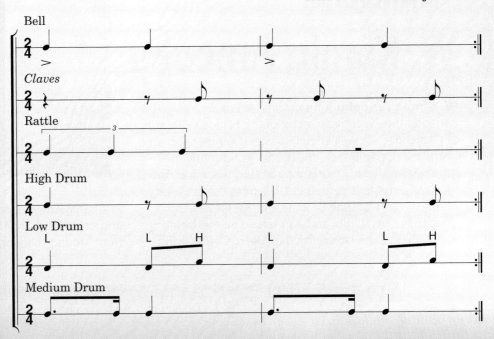

Take It to the Net For more information on West African drumming and vocal styles, go to *www.sfsuccessnet.com.*

Music MAKERS

W. Komla Amoaku

W. Komla Amoaku [uh-MOH-uh-koo] (born 1940) is currently the executive director of the National Theatre of Ghana. He is a well-known master drummer and an instructor of traditional African and world music. He has presented many workshops around the world. He received a master's degree in 1971 from the University of Indiana and later he became a professor at Central State University, Ohio, and also served on the faculty at California State University, San Marcos. Now living in Ghana, Amoaku continues to teach traditional and contemporary African drumming. Musicians from around the world come to study with him.

◀ *adinkra* cloth designer

African Art

Adinkra is a traditional West African cloth that is hand-printed with special stamps. The motif, or pattern, of each stamp is a symbol that represents a traditional proverb, attitude, behavior, or historical event. Originally used by royalty and spiritual leaders, *adinkra* cloths are now used by many people for various events, such as weddings, naming ceremonies, and festivals. Today, some companies even have their own *adinkra* stamps.

Adwo—symbol of peace, calmness, spiritual coolness, and continuity ▼

Nkyinkyim—symbol of toughness, adaptability, devotion to service, and resoluteness ▼

Juju Music

Africa has many types of popular music. *Juju* originated in Nigeria and was originally based on the traditional drum-based music of the region. As with many forms of popular music throughout the world, *juju* is the result of different influences and continues to change. *Juju*, which sounds similar to highlife, is now heard in various parts of Africa and around the world.

Listen to this example of *juju* music by Chief Commander Ebenezer Obey. **Compare** this example to the highlife recording *Mensu*.

▲ Chief Commander Ebenezer Obey

Awa ewe iwoyi

8-16

by **Chief Commander Ebenezer Obey** as performed by **Chief Commander Ebenezer Obey and His Inter-Reformers Band**

International recording artist Chief Commander Ebenezer Obey modernized *juju* music by adding multiple talking drums, guitars, and often a Hawaiian steel guitar soloist. Before his retirement from entertainment in 1992, he had recorded about 100 records.

"It's like cooking a soup. If you put in many different ingredients, it tastes richer and better."

—Chief Commander Ebenezer Obey,
talking about adding many different musical instruments and styles into juju music.

DRUMMING FROM GHANA

rums in Ghana, West Africa, are played during many occasions, from parties and social gatherings to official government functions and religious observances. Drumming is accompanied by singing and dancing. Often, drum ensembles feature a master drummer who leads the ensemble and plays solos. Most drum ensembles include a time line, often played by a bell, which serves as the rhythmic anchor for all other parts.

The Ewe [EH-vay] people who live in Ghana, Benin, and Togo once used the following drum ensemble during wartime. Today, it is used for funerals. This piece is just a small part of the Ewe's longstanding drumming tradition. Many Ewe drum ensembles include a master drum or *atsimevu* part. The master drummer's role is to lead the other drummers in call-and-response "conversations."

Prepare for "*Agbekor* Ensemble"

Play this *axatse* [ahks-AHT-see] (rattle) 2 part. Hold one hand about twelve inches above your thigh. Hold the rattle in the other hand and bounce it between your thigh and your hand. Say *yah* as the rattle goes down and say *boo* as it goes up.

Once you can play the *axatse* (rattle) 2 pattern with ease, lift your hand so that the rattle hits your thigh only on the *yah* syllables. This is the rhythm for the double bell called the *gankogui* [gahn-KO-gwee]. **Play** both the *axatse* (rattle) 2 and the *gankogui* parts together.

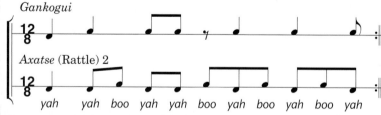

Now practice the *axatse* (rattle) 1 part with the *kaganu* [KAH-gahn] or high drum. **Play** both parts at the same time by holding a rattle in the non-dominant hand while playing open tones on the drum with the dominant hand. To put the parts together, **play** the rattle part instead of hitting the side of the drum on the "x."

Axatse (Rattle) 1

yah   yah   yah   yah

Kaganu (High Drum)

* hit side of drum

Play the remaining two drum parts, the *kidi* [KEE-dee] and *kroboto* [KROH-boh-toh], along with *axatse* (rattle) 1. Notice that each part comes in right after the rattle. The *kroboto* answers the *kidi*.

Axatse (Rattle) 1

yah   yah   yah   yah

Kidi (Medium Drum)

Kroboto (Low Drum)

* press fingertips in drum center

Ewe drum set ▶

Ewe-Style Ensemble

Play the *"Agbekor* [AH-boh-koh] Ensemble" by adding one part at a time. *Axatse* rattle parts 2, 3, and 4 are optional.

Agbekor Ensemble

Traditional Music of Ghana

Feel the Time Line

Tap the rhythms below while singing the *gankogui* part for the *"Agbekor* Ensemble."* Notice how each pattern brings out different features of the *gankogui* time line. Then with your classmates try all parts at once, using rattles on the "x" notes.

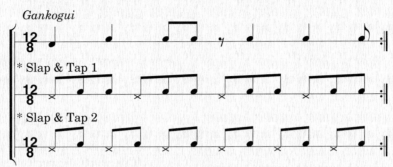

Gankogui

* Slap & Tap 1

* Slap & Tap 2

* *Slap the side of your thigh with one hand on the "x" notes or play a rattle; then tap the other thigh on the regular notes.*

Tap these rhythms on your thighs and you will feel the 3-against-2 rhythms that underlie the *gankogui* time line. The 3-against-2 feeling is common in West African rhythms and has found its way into Latin American, Caribbean, and African-American music. Play the top notes with the dominant hand and the bottom notes with the non-dominant hand.

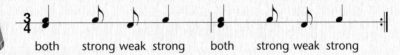

both   strong weak strong   both   strong weak strong

More Music for Ewe

Listen to this recording of another Ewe piece called *Adzogbo-Ovitse.* It uses a faster version of the same time line as the *"Agbekor* Ensemble."

Adzogbo-Ovitse

Ewe drumming ensemble
8-17   as performed by the Africa West Trio (Josh Ryan, Jamie Ryan, and Ryan Korb)

The Ewe proverb *Ovitse, Ovitse,* which is spoken at the beginning of the recording, introduces rhythmic elements that are later echoed in the drums and percussion.

The Cuban Connection

The *gankogui* time line you learned for the *"Agbekor* Ensemble" is also found in music from Cuba. **Listen** to this piece from Cuba and tap the time line along with the recording.

Eleggua

Yoruban-style song from Cuba
8-18   as performed by Los Munequitos de Matanzas

The time line is played on a single (rather than double) bell that interacts with rattles and drums.

◀ Noblemen in Kumasi

Xylophones and Marimbas

The marimba, a member of the xylophone family, is played worldwide. The word *xylophone* comes from the Greek words *xylon,* which means "wood," and *phone,* which means "voice." Marimbas and xylophones can play both melodies and harmonies. Some are designed with whole-step or pentatonic scales, while others have complete diatonic or even chromatic scales. Marimbas can have a range of up to five octaves and can be almost nine feet long!

Listen to *Crunchy, Crunchy, Crunchy.* **Read** the notation on page D-15 as you listen. **Identify** the repeated rhythmic **motives** in each part. How are the four parts related?

Crunchy, Crunchy, Crunchy

by Walt Hampton
8-19   as performed by students from Marcus Whitman Elementary School, Richland, Washington
This ensemble is based on a familiar Caribbean melody.

Play Crunchy

Play the melody of the Ⓐ section of "Crunchy, Crunchy, Crunchy" on the soprano xylophone. When you can play Ⓐ, learn the Ⓑ section melody.

Identify the three pitches of the contrabass bars part. These pitches are the roots of the chords that create the harmonies of "Crunchy, Crunchy, Crunchy." **Play** the contrabass bars part.

Listen to the alto xylophone part. Notice that it has the same rhythm as the melody. Echo each phrase, and then **play** the entire part.

Compare the bass xylophone part to the other parts, and then play this part by ear.

Play a steady beat with a pair of *hosho* or gourd rattles.

African xylophone ▶

motives Rhythmic or melodic fragments that serve as the basic elements from which a more complex musical structure can be created.

D-14

Crunchy, Crunchy, Crunchy

Music by Walt Hampton

Guatemalan Marimbas

The marimba has been around for centuries in Guatemala. Images of marimbas are seen in ancient Mayan manuscripts. Resonators for Guatemalan marimbas are made from gourds or rectangular-shaped wooden boxes. These marimbas have a distinctive buzzing sound called the *charleo* or *tela*. This sound is produced by a thin animal membrane that covers a small opening near the bottom of each resonator.

Listen to this marimba music from Guatemala. **Analyze** what you hear. **Describe** the **timbre** of the marimba and the layering of the parts. **Identify** similarities and differences between the various parts in the texture.

San Miguel Jolonicapan

8-20 Folk music for marimba from Guatemala as performed by *Marimba Guatémaltéque*
The characteristic buzzing sound of Guatemalan marimbas is clearly present in this recording.

The Imbarimba

Listen to *Flight of the Ibis*, played on the Imbarimba, an instrument invented by Richard Cooke. **Describe** the timbres you hear at the beginning of the piece. **Compare** this sound to the xylophones of Guatemala.

Flight of the Ibis

by Richard Cooke

8-21 The design of the Imbarimba combines aspects of two African instruments: the marimba and the *kalimba (mbira)*.

▲ Imbarimba

◀ Musician playing a marimba with wood resonators in Chichicastengo, Guatemala.

Note This

In 1999 the Congress of Guatemala declared the marimba a national symbol.

timbre The unique sound of a musical instrument or voice.

INSTRUMENT INVENTOR
Richard Cooke

Richard Cooke (born 1955) is an American instrument inventor and musician. Born in Louisville, Kentucky, he studied piano, voice, and trumpet in his youth. Later, he traveled the world and studied the music of many cultures. Cooke models his creations after Javanese and Balinese gamelan instruments. He makes artful mallet percussion instruments of wood and metal that can easily be played and enjoyed by all people, regardless of their musical training or age. With his instruments there are no "wrong notes" because they are built on harmony-based scales. Cooke wants everyone to feel the joy of creating music effortlessly, so he designs instruments with shapes that allow almost anyone to reach the bars easily. Cooke connects music with visual arts. His pieces are both musical instruments and unique sculptures that entice the observer to explore their beauty.

More Xylophones

Listen to *Hornpipe and Jig* and *Wilder Reiter*. **Analyze** and **describe** the similarities and differences in timbre, meter, melody, and harmony between the two performances.

 ### Hornpipe and Jig

8-22
from *Two Dances for Three Xylophones*
by Margaret Murray
These pieces are written for soprano, alto, and bass xylophones. They are pentatonic melodies and rhythms based on the traditional hornpipe and jig.

 ### Wilder Reiter

8-23
by Robert Schumann
arranged by Leigh Howard Stevens
Leigh Howard Stevens is regarded as one of the world's foremost classical marimba players. This performance sounds as if more than one person is playing but Stevens is actually the only player!

Richard Cooke's musical creations are also used as art. ▶

ON YOUR OWN
Design an instrument that could also be used as a sculpture in an outdoor setting. Describe in detail what it would look and sound like. What materials would you use?

5

Puerto Rican Style

Bomba and *plena* are two musical styles native to Puerto Rico. *Bomba* is a style of music and dance that originated with African slaves who were brought to Puerto Rico in the 1600s. The only instruments used are two drums, a pair of hardwood sticks, and a maraca. *Plena* is an African-influenced Puerto Rican folk music style with elements of *bomba*. In addition to percussion instruments, a variety of melodic and harmonic instruments are also used.

Listen to *Zoila* and *Bembe de Plena*. **Analyze** the differences between the two styles.

Zoila
8-24
Bomba song from Puerto Rico as performed by *Paracumbé*

As is typical in southern *bomba* style, a female soloist performs with female backup singers.

Bembe de Plena
8-25
Plena Song from Puerto Rico as performed by *Plena Libre*

In this *plena* song the drums are joined by a brass section and guitars.

Island Ensemble

Music by Jeff Bush

Play *Bomba*

Practice "Island Ensemble." **Play** the maracas and *guiro* parts. Then add the cowbell and drum parts. Finally, **perform** all parts together.

Maracas/Cabasa

Guiro

Cowbell

Bongos

Congas

¡Viva Puerto Rico!

Listen to "La borinqueña," the official anthem of the Commonwealth of Puerto Rico. **Perform** the "Island Ensemble" with the recording. Start playing when the voices begin.

Puerto Rican Folkloric Dance ▶

La borinqueña

(Beloved Island Home)

Words by Manuel Fernández Juncos
English Words by Kathleen Bernath

Music by Félix Astol Artés

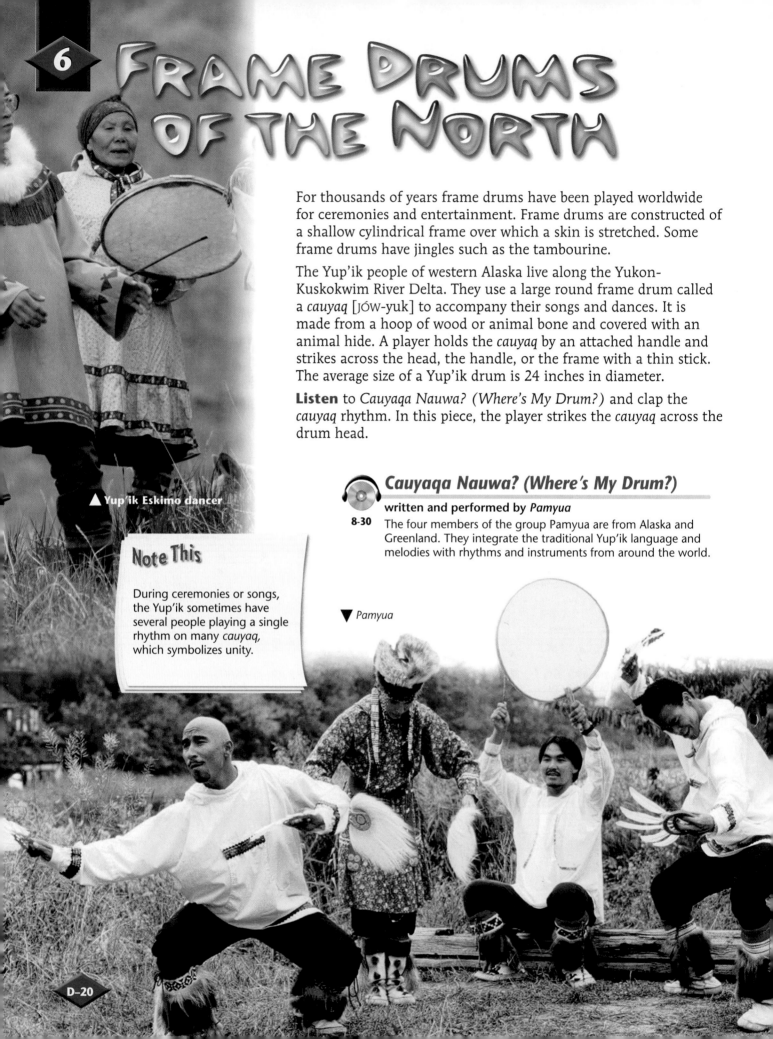

6

FRAME DRUMS OF THE NORTH

For thousands of years frame drums have been played worldwide for ceremonies and entertainment. Frame drums are constructed of a shallow cylindrical frame over which a skin is stretched. Some frame drums have jingles such as the tambourine.

The Yup'ik people of western Alaska live along the Yukon-Kuskokwim River Delta. They use a large round frame drum called a *cauyaq* [JÓW-yuk] to accompany their songs and dances. It is made from a hoop of wood or animal bone and covered with an animal hide. A player holds the *cauyaq* by an attached handle and strikes across the head, the handle, or the frame with a thin stick. The average size of a Yup'ik drum is 24 inches in diameter.

Listen to *Cauyaqa Nauwa? (Where's My Drum?)* and clap the *cauyaq* rhythm. In this piece, the player strikes the *cauyaq* across the drum head.

▲ Yup'ik Eskimo dancer

Note This

During ceremonies or songs, the Yup'ik sometimes have several people playing a single rhythm on many *cauyaq*, which symbolizes unity.

Cauyaqa Nauwa? (Where's My Drum?)

written and performed by *Pamyua*

8-30   The four members of the group Pamyua are from Alaska and Greenland. They integrate the traditional Yup'ik language and melodies with rhythms and instruments from around the world.

▼ *Pamyua*

Where's Your Drum?

Play the "Where's your Drum? Ensemble" on frame drums. **Play** the low frame drum 1 part first, then layer the others. Strike a dowel flat across the head of the drum, as in the Yup'ik tradition. Traditional Yup'ik drummers play a single rhythm, repeated throughout an entire piece of music. This ensemble has four layers of contrasting rhythms. Increase the tempo to play along with the recording of *Cauyaqa Nauwa?*

Where's Your Drum? Ensemble

Music by Anne Fennell

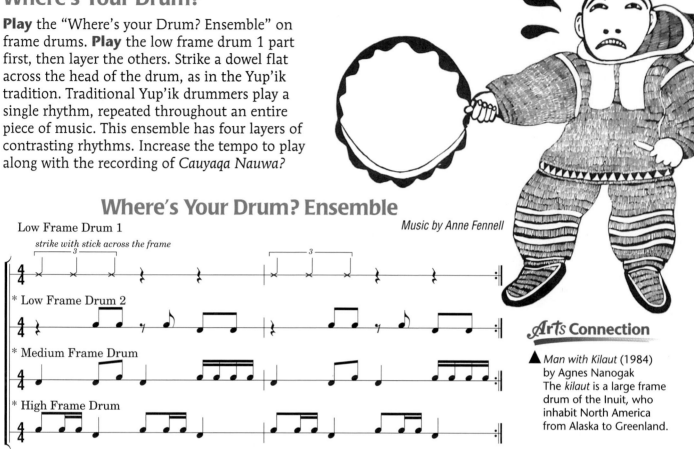

Low Frame Drum 1

strike with stick across the frame

* Low Frame Drum 2

* Medium Frame Drum

* High Frame Drum

* Play notes below the line on the drum center. Play notes above the line on the drum rim.

Arts Connection

▲ *Man with Kilaut* (1984) by Agnes Nanogak
The *kilaut* is a large frame drum of the Inuit, who inhabit North America from Alaska to Greenland.

Outside the Frame

Listen to *Apu Min'Tan* performed by Kashtin, a Canadian folk-rock duo. They sing in the *Innu* language of the Algonquin people of Eastern Québec. **Describe** aspects of the music that show how this group supports their traditional heritage through contemporary music.

Apu Min'Tan

8-31 by Florent Vollant and Claude McKenzie
as performed by Kashtin
Apu Min'Tan means "leave me alone."

▲ Kashtin performing at the Inuvik-Inuit Circumpolar Conference

7

Batucada to Capoeira

Carnaval is a festival celebrated throughout the Caribbean and in many other parts of the world just prior to Lent. It is a time for music, parades, costumes, and fun! One of the best-known *Carnaval* celebrations is held in Rio de Janeiro, Brazil. One type of music heard at *Carnaval* in Rio is the percussion street music known as **batucada**. The percussion groups at *Carnaval,* called *bateria,* can have hundreds of members. They work for many months to perfect their *batucada.* Because this is street music, all of their percussion instruments must be easy to play and carry. Typical instruments include Brazilian-style bass drums, snare drums, shakers, hand drums, and two-tone bells.

Play "*Batucada* Parade Ensemble." Begin by learning each part. Practice the ensemble by starting with the bass drum, then adding each instrument group one at a time. On cue from a leader, play either the unison bridge 1 or unison bridge 2 before going back to your assigned rhythm. On a different cue from the leader, play the unison ending. **Perform** the ensemble in class and as part of a parade.

---

batucada A samba composition utilizing only percussion instruments.

▲ Man playing the *cuíca* in a *Samba* school parade in Brazil

Batucada Parade Ensemble

Music by Jeff Bush

CD-ROM Find samples of *samba*-style accompaniments in *Band-in-a-Box*. Modify the tempo so that you can use one of them to accompany the ensemble "*Batucada* Parade Ensemble."

Brazilian Percussion

Brazil has instruments which are both similar to and different from instruments one might find in the United States. Look at the photos and read the description of the instruments.

◀ *surdo* [SUR-doh]—Similar to a bass drum, it is usually played with a single padded stick in one hand while the other hand muffles and changes the pitch of the drum.

◀ *caixa* [CAY-sha]—A type of snare drum, it comes in many sizes and is made of either wood or metal.

◀ *cuica* [KWEE-kah]—A small drum with a stick inserted into the middle of the drumhead. The stick is dampened so that it produces a squeaking sound when rubbed, causing the drum to vibrate. Pressing on the drum head will change the pitch. The *cuica* works like the squeaky straw in the plastic top of a fast food drink.

◀ *caxixis* [kah-SHEE-shees]—Small shakers similar to maracas. The outside is usually made from heavy straw, and it is filled with seeds or rice.

◀ *berimbau* [BEH-rihm-bow]—A bow strung with wire that has a gourd resonator attached to the bow with cotton string. The *berimbau* is played by striking the wire with a small stick, or baton. To produce one of three tones, the wire is touched with a rock, coin, or similar object held in one hand. The *berimbau* is played together with a *caxixi*, which is shaken while striking the string.

Listen to the *batucada* performance of *Sai da frente* by *Bateria Nota 10*. **Identify** and **classify** the instruments you hear.

Sai da frente

9-1

Batucada from Brazil
as performed by *Bateria Nota 10*
This is a recording of a small *bateria*. It includes various percussion solos.

Let's Samba!

Many events take place during *Carnaval* in Rio. One very popular event is the *samba* parade. In this event, community groups, known as *samba* schools—often numbering 3,000 to 5,000 people—march on the streets or ride on floats. The members of each *samba* school wear the same colorful costume, designed to represent the theme of the group. Each school also has its own special theme song, known as a *samba enredo*. The song is sung by one or two soloists and accompanied by a chorus and a *bateria*.

Listen to this *samba enredo* from Rio de Janeiro.

Talaque talaque o romance da María

9-2

by Pestana/Jorginho do Pandeiro
as performed by G.R.E.S. Arrastão de Cascadura

All *samba* school names in Brazil, and many around the world, start with the G.R.E.S. abbreviation to show that they are official *samba* schools.

Video Library Watch the video episode *Batucada: samba–Brazil* to see and hear percussion instruments of Brazil.

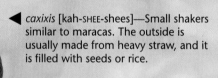

The World of *Capoeira*

Capoeira is an ancient combination of martial arts, dance, and music. Although originally from Africa, *capoeira* has become an art form associated with Brazil. The music is used to excite the participants. When the action becomes too intense, it is used to calm them. The most prominent musical instrument in most *capoeira* music is the *berimbau*, which is often accompanied by *caxixis*, two-tone bells, and drums.

Listen to this contemporary example of *capoeira*.

Capoeira na vila

9-3 by the *Ensemble Amaro de Souza* directed by Coaty de Oliveira

Two pitches produced on the *berimbau* are accompanied by the *caxixis*. As the music progresses, the other instruments of the *capoeira* orchestra are added.

Capoeira practice ▶

Checkpoint

Form a group of four or more players. Choose one of the ensembles listed below and practice it in your group. Have individual group members take turns **listening** to the others play to make sure that they are playing their parts accurately. Group members should also prepare short talks about the instruments they will play. Prepare the presentation and the ensemble, and **perform** it for the class. **Evaluate** your group's performance in a music journal.

1. "Bora Bora Boom Ensemble"   page D-3
2. "Highlife Ensemble"   page D-7
3. "*Agbekor* Ensemble"   page D-12
4. "Crunchy, Crunchy, Crunchy"   page D-15
5. "Island Ensemble"   page D-18
6. "*Batucada* Parade Ensemble"   page D-23

Take It to the Net Go to *www.sfsuccessnet.com* to learn more about music and dance in Brazil.

Gongs-Cymbals-Drums

8

Many types of metal, wood, and skin percussion instruments can be heard in the classical and folk music in China. One of the numerous types of traditional Chinese musical groups is the percussion *luogu* ensemble. The *luogu* ensemble has many functions. They perform for rituals and parades, and they accompany shows and dances. The *luogu* can be heard alone or in combination with melody instruments. The music is so bright and exciting that whenever the *luogu* are playing, many people stop what they are doing to watch and listen to the gongs and drums!

Prepare to play the "*Hsù chu* [SOO choo] (Prelude) Ensemble. **Play** the drum part, using two fingers on your desk then on the instrument. Add the two gong parts, followed by the woodblock. Then play the cymbal part. Play the muted notes by clapping the cymbals and holding them together. Finally, play the drum part and **perform** the entire ensemble.

Luogu ensemble ▼

Hsù chu (Prelude) Ensemble

Music by Jeff Bush

* mute by holding cymbals together

---

luogu [LOH-gooh] The name of a Chinese percussion ensemble; "*luo*" means "gongs" and "*gu*" means drums.

Flower Drum Song

Listen to *Huagu ge* [hoo-AH-goo guh], a popular Chinese folk song also known as the "Flower Drum Song." The melody is played on *yunluo* [yoon-loh], or cloud gong, which is a set of ten or more small, flat-tuned gongs suspended on a frame.

Huagu ge

9-4

Folk song from China arranged for *luogu* ensemble by Han Kuo-Huang

The *luogu* ensemble begins the piece. The melody is then accompanied by two woodblocks, small bells, and cymbals. The gongs and drums return quietly part way through and then loudly end the song.

Arts Connection

Detail of a funeral procession by Guo Zihong (Qing Dynasty) ▼

▲ *Yunluo* (cloud gong)

Dragon Dance

The dragon is one of the most famous symbols in Chinese culture and is associated with strength, wisdom, and good luck. The Chinese celebrate the dragon by performing a dragon dance at New Years' events. It is believed that the longer the dragon, the more luck it brings. The actual dragon may be so long that it takes 20 or 30 people to hold it up! *Luogu* ensembles are an important part of the dragon dance; the lead drummer often controls both the dancer's and musician's actions.

Chinese Dragon Dance ▼

Note This

Percussion instruments have been found in China dating back to the Shang Dynasty, which lasted from the sixteenth to the eleventh centuries B.C.E.

Take It to the Net Go to *www.sfsuccessnet.com* to find out more about the music of China and Taiwan.

WOOD WORKS!

Tap your pencil on a wooden cabinet or knock your knuckles on a wooden table. Imagine everyone in your class using the wooden objects in the room to create a piece of music. Your classroom would become a percussion studio! Imagine the sound each wood object will make. The sound depends on its thickness, the type of tree from which it is cut, and the type of mallet or stick used to play it.

Play each part of the "Wood Works Ensemble" separately. The first part should be played on an instrument or object that has two distinct pitches. Strike the wood with wooden sticks or with hard rubber mallets. Play parts 2 through 5 on a variety of small wooden percussion instruments or objects that vary in timbre and pitch.

Wood Works Ensemble

Music by Anne Fennell

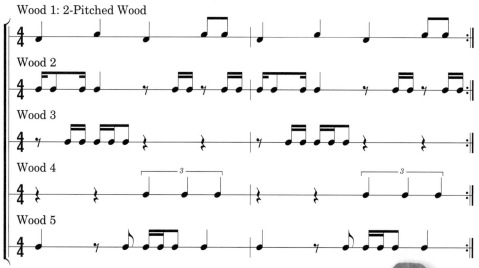

Arts Connection

▲ *Tapestry* by David C. Roy is a wooden kinetic sculpture—it moves, driven by the energy of a spring and wheels that rotate in opposite directions. Visualize the opposing curved lines moving toward one another and overlapping as they circle around and around. The symmetry in the design creates continuous symmetrical overlapping patterns.

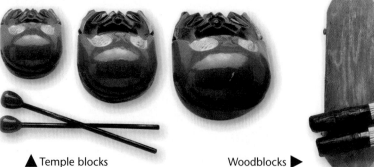

▲ Temple blocks

Woodblocks ▶

More than Wood

Listen to *Daphne of the Dunes* by Harry Partch.
Describe the timbres you hear and determine what
material is producing the sounds. Read about Partch
below and then **describe** how his talent as an
inventor influenced and supported his music.

Daphne of the Dunes
by Harry Partch

Daphne of the Dunes is played by
eight musicians accompanied by a
prerecorded tape. The tape is a
recording of five segments played
back at double speed.

Music MAKERS

HARRY PARTCH

Harry Partch (1901–1974) was an innovative American
inventor, theorist, and composer. He created his own
tuning system and invented instruments to play these
new sounds. His musical compositions often had
spoken, rhythmic text. Partch's works were performed
primarily on his unique instruments, including the
bass marimba, the diamond marimba, and
cloud-chamber bowls—12-gallon bowls or jars
cut in half and suspended from a
wooden frame.

▼ **Cloud-chamber bowls**

▲ **Diamond marimba**

◄ **Bass marimba**

ON YOUR OWN
Invent a
wooden percussion
instrument. Explore ways to
produce various timbres and
pitches. If your instrument
is melodic, create a new scale.
Name your instrument and
compose a piece
of music for it.

Find It— Play It

Make music with whatever is available! You do not have to buy expensive instruments. Have fun by finding things wherever you are that sound good. Now you are ready to play music in the *go-go* street music tradition that originated in Washington D.C.

Get into the *go-go* groove by beginning with the large frame drum (plastic trash can) part. **Play** this part in the manner of a basic drum part you might hear on hip-hop or rock music recordings. Once the basic beat is solid, play the rattle parts until you feel the subdivision of the beat in three as shown.

Play "Go-Go Street Ensemble" using regular drums and rattles. Then play it with sticks on trash cans and buckets made of plastic and metal. Do you prefer one sound over the other? Why?

Play *Go-Go*

Play the entire "Go-Go Street Ensemble" by adding one part at a time. When you feel comfortable with the basic ensemble, add a soloist who will improvise on an instrument that stands out from the rest.

Go-Go Street Ensemble

Music by Will Schmid

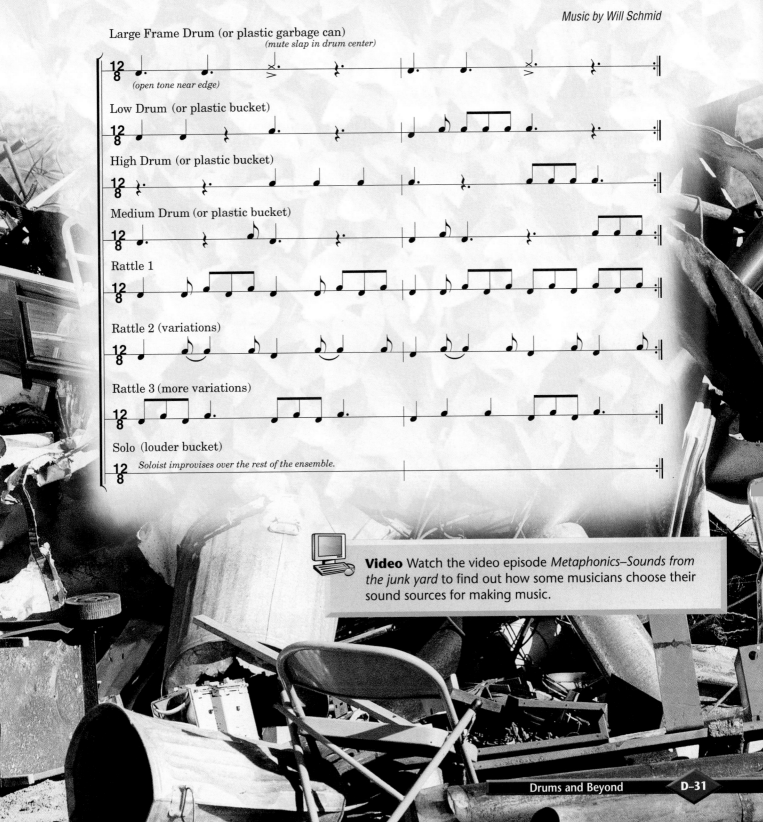

Video Watch the video episode *Metaphonics–Sounds from the junk yard* to find out how some musicians choose their sound sources for making music.

Starting a Street Band

Listen to the Junk Yard Band perform *The Rippa Medley*.
Analyze the meter and compare it with the meter of
"Go-Go Street Ensemble."

The Rippa Medley

written and performed by Junk Yard Band

9-6   Members of the Junk Yard Band were only eight-to-eleven years old when they started performing together.

Junk Yard Band started in 1980 when a group of Washington D.C. youth were inspired by the *go-go* bands in their neighborhood. The band members lived in housing projects and had little money, so they decided to find junk (hubcaps, crates, buckets, cans, and old pots) from their neighborhood to use as instruments. Performing on the streets of Washington D.C., the Junk Yard Band became a tourist attraction and gradually caught the attention of concert promoters and record companies. They appeared in two movies, *D.C. Cab* with Mr. T. and *Tougher Than Leather* with Run DMC. They also had a hit single *Sardines* on the hip-hop Def Jam label. As the kids grew into adults, they stayed together as their music matured. Over the years they have performed with such national acts as Salt-N-Pepa, Tupac, the Roots, and the Beastie Boys.

ON YOUR OWN
Look around your area for objects to use as instruments and start your own group. You might want to add vocal melodies to the group, or rap over your percussion sounds.

D–32

Get the B.E.A.T.

In many areas of the United States, students use "found sounds" for creating music. **Listen** to the group B.E.A.T. in this live performance of *Cow Barn Cha Cha*, an original composition by Kim Bejot.

Cow Barn Cha Cha

9-7

by Kim Bejot
as performed by B.E.A.T.

The "instruments" in this piece are cowbell, cow skull, cow spine, cob fork, cream can, milk jugs, corn shakers, and a "cattle crossing" sign.

B.E.A.T (Bejot's Ensemble of Acoustic Troubadoures) started when music teacher Kim Bejot, from Ainsworth, Nebraska, had her creative problem-solving students look for interesting musical sound makers in their rural area of Nebraska. They discovered a cow skeleton, farm implement disks, buckets, and lots of other interesting materials. Students created their own highly imaginative ensembles using these found sounds. They also used the instruments to play other existing percussion ensemble music.

Review and Assess

Throughout Drums and Beyond, you have

- Listened to drumming ensembles from all over the world.
- Learned to play some representative examples of several important drumming traditions.

Your performance during this module has focused on ensemble playing—making music with other musicians. Ensemble playing is an important part of making music. It requires you not only to play your own part well, but also to listen and play together with other members of the ensemble to produce an effective performance.

Review What You Learned

Review what you have studied and practiced. Consult with your teacher and select drumming pieces that allow you to demonstrate excellent musicianship. This will take some careful thinking on your part, but selecting the right music to perform is an important part of becoming a successful musician.

Not everyone will be able to play all of the parts in every ensemble piece. Some require different skills than others. What is most important is that you perform accurately, musically, and beautifully.

For this assessment you will form percussion ensembles to rehearse and perform for your class and for other audiences. Select an ensemble piece to perform from the following list.

Ensemble	Number of parts	Instrumentation/Origin/Style
"Bora Bora Boom Ensemble"	5	slit drum
"Highlife Ensemble"	6	highlife
"Agbekor Ensemble"	8 (5 required)	Ghanaian
"Crunchy, Crunchy, Crunchy"	4	keyboard percussion
"Island Ensemble"	5	Puerto Rican
"Where's Your Drum? Ensemble"	4	frame drums of the north
"Batucada Parade Ensemble"	9	Brazilian
"Hsù chu (Prelude) Ensemble"	5	gongs and cymbals
"Wood Works Ensemble"	5	found instruments
"Go-Go Street Ensemble"	8	found instruments

Show What You Know

With the help of your teacher, select several pieces to perform in which you can do at least two of the following well.

- Conduct the ensemble, providing clear starting and stopping cues, a clear, steady pulse throughout, and cues for changing dynamics.
- Play a single-instrument part that defines the pulse of the music.
- Play a part with multiple sounds that remains steady throughout the piece.

- Play a percussion part with rhythms that change from measure to measure.
- Play a keyboard part.

In choosing the pieces to perform, your goal is to show all of the qualities of good musicianship. You want performances of which you can be proud; do not choose a piece to perform simply because it is difficult. The goal for this assessment is quality, not difficulty.

Share What You Know

Select one of the recorded pieces from the module that is your personal favorite. Prepare a presentation for a class of younger children or your peers that will help them understand the music and why you like it. You may use poster board, overhead transparencies, or slides made with presentation software. Your presentation should include basic facts about the piece—title, composer or arranger (if known), the approximate time of its composition, the instruments used— and explanations of how the music plays a part in the culture of the society from which it comes. Also, be sure to include four aspects of music description that you will use this year: the actual sounds that make up the music (timbre); the organization of the sounds (rhythm, structure, dynamics); the emotional effects that the sounds elicit from the listener; the cultural function of the music. In your presentation, you should play excerpts from the piece to illustrate your points. Some of these may be from recordings while others may be live performances.

What to Look and Listen For

Excellent musicians often record themselves so they can evaluate their own work and refine their performances. You may wish to record your performances using digital audio, cassette tape, or video tape.

Ask yourself whether all these things are true about your performance. Use this checklist to see how you're doing and to identify aspects of your playing and singing that are in need of further refinement.

Drumming

- Posture is upright and relaxed.
- Sticks (when used) are held loosely and comfortably.

- Arms, hands, and fingers move easily (no tension evident).
- Strokes, whether with hands, fingers, or sticks are even and relaxed.
- Playing motion is efficient and smooth.
- Instrument tone is open and resonant.
- Notes are accurate (keyboard).
- Tempo is steady and even.
- Rhythm is accurate.
- Volume level is balanced with other members of the ensemble.
- Dynamic and rhythmic changes are used to create expressive effects.

KEYS and CHORDS

Playing Keyboard Chords and Progressions

▲ Recording workstation

"The piano is able to communicate the subtlest universal truths by means of wood, metal, and vibrating air."

—Kenneth Miller

▲ Italian-made accordion

MAKING IT EASY

The piano is a very versatile musical instrument. It is the instrument of choice for accompanying most songs. You will learn to play songs by reading chord symbols and playing those chords as you accompany songs.

Listen to "Goodbye, Julie," an African American call-and-response song. Notice how the soloist changes the melody beginning on verse 3. The singer is **improvising.** Observe how the singer's improvisation changes on each succeeding verse.

CD 9-8

GOODBYE, JULIE

African American Folk Song

VERSE

Call F(I)   *Response*   C₇(V₇)

1. Miss   Ju - lie Ann John - son,   Oh,   oh!
2. Oh,   where's __ my   Ju - lie?   Oh,   oh!

Call C₇(V₇)   *Response*   F(I)

Miss   Ju - lie Ann John - son,   Oh,   oh!
Oh,   where's __ my   Ju - lie?   Oh,   oh!

REFRAIN

Call F(I)   *Response*   C₇(V₇)

Good - bye, ____ Ju - lie,   Oh,   oh!

Call C₇(V₇)   *Response*   F(I)

Good - bye, ____ Ju - lie,   Oh,   oh!

3. She's gone to Dallas, . . .

4. Going to catch that train, yes, . . .

5. Going to find my Julie, . . .

TRO–© 1936 (Renewed) 1959 (Renewed) 1964 (Renewed) Folkways Music Publishers, Inc., New York, NY. Used by permission.

improvise To make up music as you perform.

Make Your Own Music

Comping is a type of accompanying. To comp at the keyboard, you follow the melody and **play** the given **chords** in your own style.

Getting Started

Look at the photograph of hands on page E-2. Notice that the numbers written above the fingers are the same for the left and right hand. When playing piano, the thumb is finger 1, the index finger is number 2, and so on. Now look at the chords below and find the numbers next to the notes on the page. Match the finger number to the key to play the chord.

At the keyboard, put your thumb (finger 1) on middle C. Now move your thumb up three white keys to find F. Build the F **root position** chord as shown. Your thumb is on the root of the chord. Now move to a **first inversion** C₇ chord as shown below.

Study page H–25 of Sounds and Symbols to learn more about building chords.

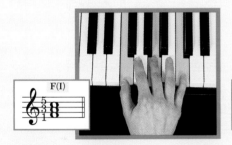

Practice the chord change from F to C₇ and back to F. Make the change as smoothly as possible.

Find the F and C₇ chord markings above the melody of "Goodbye, Julie." F is called the I chord and C₇ is called the V₇ chord. **Play** the appropriate chord on each beat of the measure as you sing the song.

Improvise a different rhythm pattern for the chords as you **listen** to the song again.

For another song using F and C₇ chords, play "I Shall Sing" on page I-38 in Performance Anthology.

---

comping To improvise and provide a chord accompaniment for a song. An abbreviation of *accompany*.

chord Three or more pitches played or sung simultaneously.

root position The arrangement of a chord in which the root of the chord is the lowest pitch.

first inversion A chord in which the pitch called the third is the lowest note of the chord.

PRO TIPS

Be sure to keep the fifth finger of your right hand (the top note of the chord) on C when changing from the F chord to the C₇ chord.

A Bunch of Pros

Most professional musicians read music notation. However, those who perform in jazz and rock bands tend to use a **lead sheet,** also called a chart, when they play. Lead sheets provide the melody and chords for a song. Musicians improvise on the melodic and harmonic structure.

Follow the lead sheet as you **listen** to the Jeff Hellmer Trio perform *Peak Moments.* Observe the introduction (**vamp**) and the ending (*coda*). Determine how many different times the trio performs the melody.

Peak Moments

Music by Jeff Hellmer

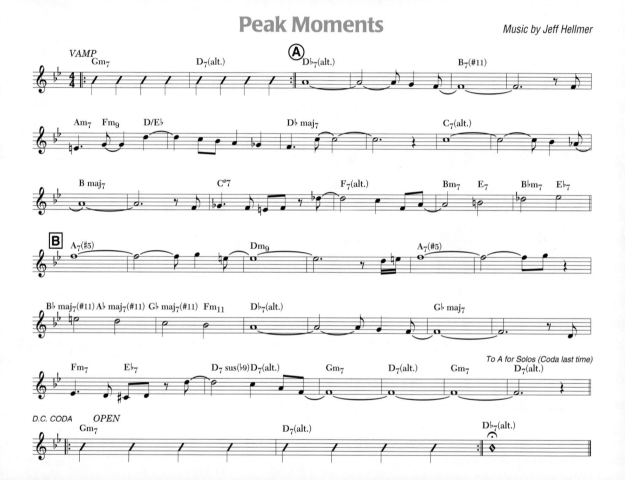

Peak Moments

by Jeff Hellmer

9-10   as performed by the Jeff Hellmer Trio

The Jeff Hellmer Trio consists of a pianist, a bassist, and a drummer. A saxophonist joins the trio to play the melody of the song.

---

lead sheet A shorthand score or part, which can provide melody, chord symbols, accompaniment figures, or lyrics.

vamp A simple passage that repeats until the soloist enters.

Music MAKERS JEFF HELLMER

As a young child in Iowa, **Jeff Hellmer** (born 1959) dreamed of playing the piano. As a matter of fact, his favorite childhood toy was a toy piano. Hellmer's mother, a pianist, began teaching him when he was five years old.

In the fourth grade, Hellmer started trumpet lessons so he could play in the band. In eighth grade, he joined the school jazz band. There Hellmer learned to improvise on the trumpet and soon began to improvise on the piano.

In college he studied both classical and jazz piano.

Hellmer now lives in Austin, Texas, where he is Director of Jazz Studies at the University of Texas. He performs as a soloist and with his trio at jazz clubs and jazz festivals throughout the country. He also conducts workshops and clinics for high school and college students. Although best known as a jazz musician, Hellmer still enjoys playing classical music. He frequently performs as a soloist and an accompanist for other classical musicians.

Comping in a New Key

Musicians who comp can play music in other keys. You can **transpose** "Goodbye, Julie" to the key of C. You will need to play C(I) and $G_7(V_7)$ chords. Practice the F root and C_7 chords again. Then move your hand down until the thumb rests on middle C and play the first chord in the same position there. That is your C root chord. Move your hand to the V_7 position and play the G_7 chord. Remember that the top note of the chord is shared. Practice playing the I and V_7 chords in C major, then **play** in the new key while the other students **sing** the song.

For more information on key signatures, see page H–19 in Sounds and Symbols.

ON YOUR OWN
Find another song in the book that is harmonized by I and V_7 chords and comp an accompaniment for that song. Ask someone to sing the melody as you play the accompaniment.

transpose To write or perform music in a new key.

On Board with Three Chords

The Orange Blossom Special was a passenger train that operated on the East Coast of the United States from 1925 to 1953. It traveled between New York and Florida, bringing winter tourists to the "Sunshine State." The train was well known for its food and attentive service.

As you **listen** to the recording of "Orange Blossom Special," **analyze** what in the music might suggest a train. Listen for the variations in the **interludes** between the verses.

▼ Orange Blossom Special circa 1950

CD 9-11
MIDI 2

Orange Blossom Special

Words and Music by Ervin T. Rouse

C(I)

do

1. Look-a yon-der com-in', com-in' down that rail-road track!
2. I'm go-in' down to Flori-da and get some sand in my shoes.
3. Talk a-bout a-trav-'lin', she's the fast-est train on the line.

C(I)   F(IV)   C(I)

Hey, look-a yon-der com-in', com-in' down that rail-road track!
Or may-be Cal-i-for-nia and get some sand in my shoes.
Talk a-bout a-trav-'lin', she's the fast-est train on the line.

C(I)   G₇(V₇)   C(I)

It's the Or-ange Blos-som Spe-cial bring-in' my ba-by back.
I'll ride that Or-ange Blos-som Spe-cial and lose these New York blues.
It's that Or-ange Blos-som Spe-cial roll-in' down the Sea-board line.

interlude Any kind of instrumental music inserted between the sections of a song.

Chord Training

Practice each of these chords separately.

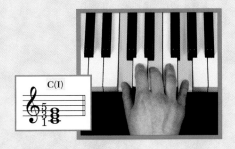
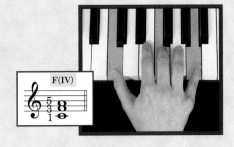
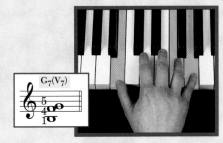

Note that one of the chords is in root position, and two are in **inversion.** Keyboard players often choose inversions so that their hands stay in the easiest **playing position.**

Make Playing Easy

Clap these rhythms. Then **play** them with the indicated chords in inversion.

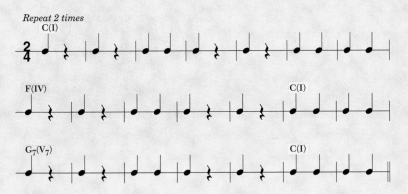

▼ Postcard showing The Orange Blossom Special

By "Streamliner" Thru Tropical Florida

A Chord Challenge

Use the rhythm you just learned to accompany the song. Practice the chord progression with the rhythm slowly, and gradually increase the tempo. When you are comfortable, **play** and **sing** with the recording.

inversion A chord in which the pitch called the third or fifth is played as the lowest note.

playing position In keyboard, where fingers are placed so that the same fingers play tones shared by different chords.

A Lion's Share of CHORDS

"The Lion Sleeps Tonight" is based on a South African folk song. The Tokens, a singing group from the 1950s and 1960s, made it a hit.

"The Lion Sleeps Tonight" is printed on page I-56 in Performance Anthology. Look at the notation. The harmony for the song includes three chords: F(I), B♭(IV), and C_7(V_7). **Move** as you **listen** to the recording. Pat your knees when you hear the F(I) chord, clap your hands when you hear the B♭(IV) chord, and snap your fingers when you hear the C_7(V_7) chord.

Review the F and C_7 chords. Then learn the B♭ chord. You will want to perform the B♭ chord in **second inversion**.

Practice each chord separately, and then **play** this progression.

When ready, **sing** the song while you **play** an accompaniment following the chords in the music.

Listen to this recording of *The Lion Sleeps Tonight*. How is this performance different from the one you just heard?

The Lion Sleeps Tonight

9-13 music by Solomon Linda
lyrics by Hugo Peretti, Luigi Creatore, and George Weiss
as performed by the Tokens

The Lion Sleeps Tonight was originally titled *Mbube*, which means "lion" in the Zulu language.

---

second inversion A chord in which the pitch called the fifth is the lowest note of the chord.

▼ The Tokens

PRO TIPS

Remember to use the same finger when playing tones common to different chords.

Two Hands Together

Create a bass part to play with "The Lion Sleeps Tonight." Place your left-hand thumb on middle C. Now find the B♭ under your index finger, and F under your pinky finger. Following the chord progression, play the chord roots with your left hand.

Review the chord progression on page E-8, playing the chords with your right hand. When you can play both the left and right hand patterns, **play** this progression as you follow the song notation.

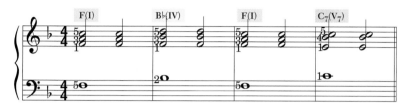

A Challenge on the Refrain

Clap the rhythm of the melody as you sing the refrain of "The Lion Sleeps Tonight." Then play the chords with the right hand, using that rhythm. **Play** the chord roots on the first beat of the measure. This is how the rhythm is notated.

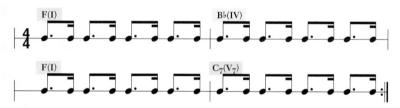

Be sure you play with a bright and energetic style. **Play** "The Lion Sleeps Tonight," performing the above accompaniment pattern during the refrain and the first accompaniment pattern during the verses.

For another song using I, IV, and V_7 chords, see page I-22 in Performance Anthology, "*El rancho grande.*"

MIDI Using the MIDI file, transpose "The Lion Sleeps Tonight" to the keys of C, D, and G. Each time you play the song, select a different instrument timbre to play the melody.

ON YOUR OWN

"The Lion Sleeps Tonight" has been recorded many times. Research the performers who have recorded "The Lion Sleeps Tonight" and compare the singing style of the various groups.

A Night on the Town

One of the best things about playing the piano is its versatility in performing different styles. It can be dressed up, as in a classical symphony performance, or dressed down for a rock or jazz concert.

Look at the photograph on this page. What are the audience members wearing? What type of performance is this?

Listen to this famous song by a rock 'n' roll legend. How would you describe his piano playing?

Good Golly, Miss Molly

9-14 **by Robert Blackwell and John Marascalco**
as performed by Little Richard
Little Richard continues to be one of the most recognized performers of rock 'n' roll.

The Jazz Scene

At a jazz club, the audience is often seated at tables. They usually applaud at the conclusion of a solo passage in addition to applauding at the end of a piece of music. You might hear this tune at a jazz club.

Listen to the piece and **describe** the role of the piano.

The Queen's Suite: Sunset and the Mockingbird

9-15 from *The Ellington Suites*
by Duke Ellington
as performed by Duke Ellington and his Orchestra
The Queen's Suite was composed in 1958 as a gift to the Queen of England.

◀ **MTV Europe Music Awards, 2001**

Classical Style

inset ▶

In a symphony orchestra concert, the audience sits and listens quietly as the music is played. In a piece with more than one movement or section, the audience usually does not applaud until the entire piece has ended. When the conductor's hands drop, and the performers put their instruments in their laps, it is time to applaud. At that time, the audience shows appreciation for the music with applause. If the performance has been exceptionally enjoyable, the audience might give a standing ovation. Sometimes, people also shout, *"Bravo!"* or *"Brava!"* or even *"Bravi!"*

Piano concertos feature a piano soloist with orchestral accompaniment. **Listen** to this performance of Edvard Grieg's *Piano Concerto in A Minor.* How does the piano and orchestra remind you of a conversation?

Piano Concerto in A Minor, Op. 16

Movement 1
9-16 **by Edvard Grieg**
as performed by Leif Ove Andsnes, with the Bergen Philharmonic Orchestra
This is Grieg's only piano concerto.

▼ A chamber orchestra concert

Time for Good Behavior

There are several "golden rules" of audience behavior. Here is a breakdown of what would be appropriate etiquette in any type of performance.

- Be on time. Some theaters will not let you in until there is a break.
- Stay in the theater once the performance has begun. Use the restroom, open cough drops, and make yourself comfortable before the lights go down.
- If it is a classical concert, refrain from talking during the performance, including the overture.
- Make sure any cell phones and pagers are turned off.
- Applaud at the appropriate times. In a classical performance, that would be at the end of an entire piece. In a jazz or pop concert, it could be at the end of a solo as well.
- Check the theater's policy before photographing or recording a concert.
- Most theaters do not allow the audience to consume food or beverages.
- Don't leave before the performance ends.

ON YOUR OWN

Find out what concerts are playing in your area. Attend two different types of concerts and compare them. What are people wearing? How do they respond to the music? How is the playing style of the musicians different? Report your findings to your class.

◀ inset

Arts Connection

◀ *Woman in Black at the Opera* American-born artist Mary Cassatt (1845–1926) was fascinated with the vivid colors and the unfocused excitement of the concert hall.

The Pampered Piano

Like any musical instrument, pianos need to be tuned and cared for.

Here are rules for good piano care.

- Keep it clean.
- Avoid putting drinks or flowers on top, which could cause water damage.
- Keep it away from direct sunlight and wide swings in temperature.
- Keep the piano tuned.

Tuning a piano is an important job, since the strings attached to each of its 88 keys must be tuned separately. Each key can have one, two, or three strings. Sometimes pianos require more work than tuning, such as reconstructing or replacing parts of a piano.

Behind every great piano player, there is a piano that has been kept in great condition.

Careers
PIANO TECHNICIAN
JIM WOOTEN

By the time he was in elementary school, besides playing the piano and violin, **Jim Wooten** (born 1951) was helping his father tune and restore pianos. In fourth grade, he began tuning pianos entirely on his own. After high school, Wooten moved from Greenwood, Mississippi to Greenville, South Carolina, where he received a degree in music from Furman College. In 1973, he moved to New York City, to study violin at The Juilliard School. There, he realized he would rather be a piano technician than a performer. He got a job tuning pianos for the Metropolitan Opera and was soon responsible for maintaining all the pianos in the opera house.

Wooten has served as Director of Artists' Services for the Yamaha Corporation, where he has worked with many well-known performers, including Elton John and Chick Corea.

Wooten believes that to do an outstanding job maintaining and repairing pianos, a piano technician must create a sort of dialogue with each instrument. The technician listens to the piano and makes adjustments accordingly, so the instrument will both sound its best to the listener and play its best for the performer. Wooten believes that being a piano technician is a rewarding career for someone who enjoys music, is analytical, a good listener, and a perfectionist.

COLORS AND CHORDS

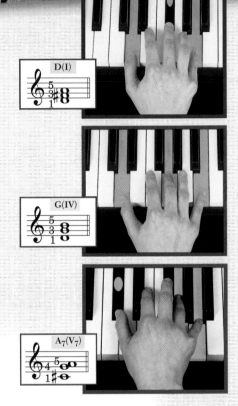

"De colores" is a Mexican American folk song. It became the theme for struggling Mexican American workers who were seeking better working conditions. Today, the song is popular with *mariachi* performers.

"De colores" is written in the key of D. Its harmony contains three chords: D(I), G(IV), and $A_7(V_7)$. Here are the chords in playing position. Which one is in root position?

Playing Colors and Chords

"De colores" is printed in Performance Anthology on page I-14. As you **listen** to "De colores," follow the lead sheet below and note the chord changes.

Play the song using this lead sheet. Add a left-hand part by playing the root of the chord on the first beat of each measure.

De colores

English Words by Alice Firgau

Folk Song from Mexico

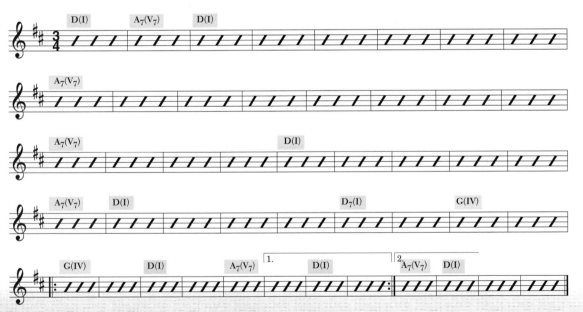

Break the Chord

Create a broken-chord accompaniment pattern for *"De colores"* by playing each pitch of the chords separately. Practice these patterns.

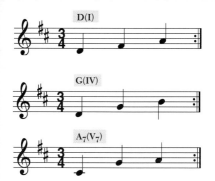

D(I)

G(IV)

A₇(V₇)

Practice the chord progression on page E–14 using the broken-chord pattern, and then use it to accompany the song. Add the root with your left hand when you can.

PRO TIPS

You can make your accompaniment more interesting. With your left hand, alternate the root of the chord on beat 1 and the rest of the chord on beat 2.

Checkpoint

Select one of the songs you have already learned to play. **Play** an accompaniment for your classmates, using one of the accompaniment patterns you have learned so far. **Describe** how your choice of a pattern matches the song style.

ON YOUR OWN

Research other Mexican American songs and listen for accompaniment styles, chord patterns, meter, and so on. How are they similar to *"De colores"*? How are they different?

6 Moving to Minor

"Keep Your Eyes on the Prize" is an African American song based on a spiritual. Its lyrics were changed in the 1960s, and it became a popular Civil Rights Movement song. Follow the song notation as you **listen** to the recording. Watch for the chord changes.

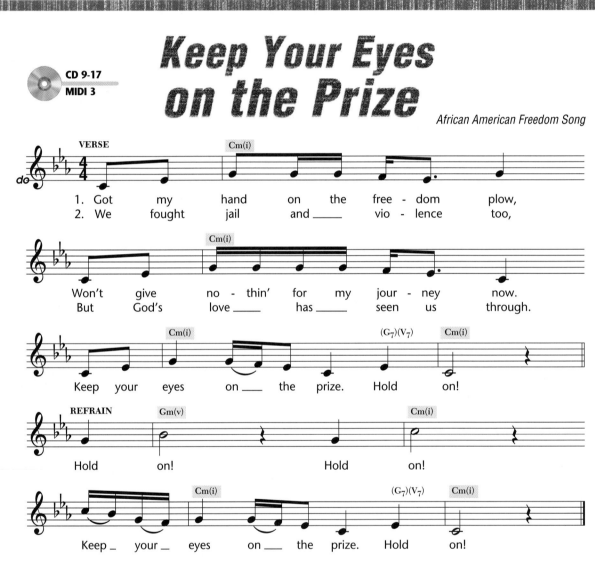

Keep Your Eyes on the Prize

CD 9-17
MIDI 3

African American Freedom Song

VERSE

Cm(i)

1. Got my hand on the free - dom plow,
2. We fought jail and _____ vio - lence too,

Cm(i)

Won't give no - thin' for my jour - ney now.
But God's love _____ has _____ seen us through.

Cm(i)   (G₇)(V₇)   Cm(i)

Keep your eyes on _____ the prize. Hold on!

REFRAIN Gm(v)   Cm(i)

Hold on!   Hold on!

Cm(i)   (G₇)(V₇)   Cm(i)

Keep _ your _ eyes on _____ the prize. Hold on!

3. Work all day and work all night,
   Tryin' to gain our civil rights.
   Keep your eyes on the prize.
   Hold on! *Refrain*

4. The only chain that a man can stand
   Is the chain of a hand in hand.
   Keep your eyes on the prize.
   Hold on! *Refrain*

Major to Minor

"Keep Your Eyes on the Prize" is in minor mode. Play a C major chord. Then lower the third of the chord one half step and make it a C minor chord. Notice the difference between the sound of the major chord and the sound of the minor chord. Then play the G major chord in closest playing position. Make it minor by lowering the third.

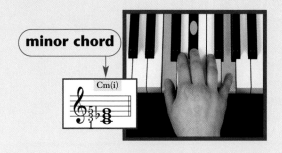

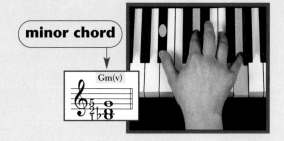

Play the chords separately. Then practice moving smoothly from Cm to Gm. **Play** your chord accompaniment as you **listen** to "Keep Your Eyes on the Prize." Play the chords on beats 1 and 3 of each measure.

Add a Rhythm

Practice tapping this rhythm.

Play the chords with the song as you play the root of the chord with your thumb and the top two pitches of the chord with your other fingers as marked.

For another song in minor, see page I-36 in Performance Anthology, *"Hanuka, Hanuka."*

A Song of Tribute

The 1960s Civil Rights Movement in the United States was led in part by the Reverend Martin Luther King, Jr. His nonviolent pursuit of justice made him an American hero. **Listen** to *Shed a Little Light* by James Taylor. How does it capture King's philosophy?

▼ James Taylor

Shed a Little Light

9-19

written and performed by James Taylor

Taylor uses the word *light* to remind us to look for truth and fairness.

A Spiritual in Minor

"Joshua Fought the Battle of Jericho" is an African American spiritual written here in E minor. Learn more about minor keys on page H-22 of Sounds and Symbols. As you **listen** to the song, observe the **syncopation** in the melody in measures 2–4. The syncopation, combined with the dotted rhythms, gives the spiritual a lively feeling. Find other measures that include syncopated rhythms.

CD 9-20

JOSHUA FOUGHT THE BATTLE OF JERICHO

African American Spiritual

REFRAIN

Em(i)   Am(iv)   Em(i)

Josh - ua fought the bat - tle of ___ Jer - i - cho, _ Jer - i - cho, _ Jer - i - cho, _____

Em(i)   B7(V7)   Em(i)   Fine

Josh - ua fought the bat - tle of ___ Jer - i - cho, _ And the walls came tum - blin' down.

VERSE

Em(i)

You can talk a-bout your king of Gid - e - on, _ You can talk a-bout your man of Saul, _

Em(i)   B7(V7)   Em(i)   D.C. al Fine

But there's none like good old Josh - u - a ___ At the bat - tle of Jer - i - cho.

___

syncopation A rhythm where the note that is stressed comes between two beats.

◀ Tell Al-sultan, among the ancient excavations of Jericho, circa 1966

Following Form

As you **sing** and **play** the song, observe the *D.C. al Fine* in the last measure. This means to go back to the beginning and play until you see the *Fine*.

New Chords to Play

Practice the three chords needed to perform "Joshua Fought the Battle of Jericho." Notice that the B_7 chord is not a minor chord.

Note This

Excavations begun early in the twentieth century show that Jericho is the oldest known settlement in the world. This city may date from as early as 8,000 B.C.

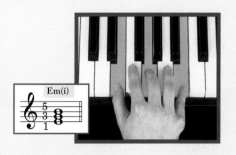

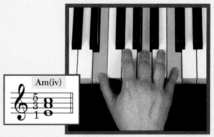

Practice the chord progression until you can maintain a steady beat. Then **play** the progression with chord roots on the first and third beats of each measure and chords on the second and fourth beats.

When ready, **play** an accompaniment for the song with the recording, following the chords in the notation. Which chord appears in the refrain but not in the verse?

A Walking Bass Variation

Make your accompaniment more interesting by playing two accompaniment patterns. During the refrain, **play** the rhythm pattern above. Then for the verse, comp a new rhythm pattern, playing the chords and chord roots together.

Play this **walking bass** line in the last measure of each verse. The letter following the slash (/) indicates the note to play in the bass.

PRO TIPS

The chords Am and B_7 have the pitch A in common. Use finger 3 to play A in the minor chord. Then switch and play A with finger 4 to play B_7.

---

walking bass A repeating bass line that moves stepwise using one note value.

KEYS YOU CAN SQUEEZE

The accordion, a relatively new keyboard instrument, is found in different types of ensembles in cultures all over the world. It sounds great as a solo instrument, as well. Its versatility and portability have made it a popular musical instrument.

Many accordions have a keyboard that plays melodies, a bellows that pumps air across reeds attached to keys, and buttons that play chords to accompany the melody.

Blowin' in the Reeds

The accordion belongs to a family of instruments known as free-reed instruments. These instruments make sound when air blows over reeds that vibrate and produce sound. All free-reed instruments

have a separate reed for each pitch. Some of the instruments, such as the harmonica, make sounds when the player blows directly into the instrument. Others, like the accordion, have a bellows that must be pumped to make the air blow across the reeds. Ancestors of the accordion in the free-reed family tree include the *sheng*, from ancient China, which does not have a keyboard. Other free-reed instruments that do have a keyboard are the regal, the reed organ, and the harmonium.

A Harmonica with Keys

In 1821, Christian Buschmann of Germany created the first harmonica. He then added a keyboard and a leather bellows, which a player could pump. He called his instrument the "Handaeoline." An Austrian named Cyril Demian improved Buschmann's design. He called his 1829 instrument an accordion, because it could play chords as well as a melody line.

The accordion was an overnight success in Europe. It was portable and could play melodies and accompaniments. It became popular in North and South America, China, and parts of Africa.

◀ Regal, circa 1580
A free reed is attached on one end, while the other end is left "free," so it can vibrate.

Planet Accordion

Accordions are used across the world, from the *Tejano* music of Texas and the *zydeco* music of Louisiana, to the tangos of Brazil and the polkas of central Europe. They are also used in the pop music of artists such as Paul Simon, Los Lobos, Ry Cooder, and Tom Waits. In the twentieth century, a classical tradition of accordion music sprang up. There are now many works for solo accordion and accordion performing with orchestras and chamber groups.

Listen to the sound of the accordion in this *zydeco* piece.

▲ Twentieth century Italian accordion

My Girl Josephine

9-21

by Fats Domino and Dave Bartholomew as performed by Queen Ida
This song was originally a rock 'n' roll hit in the 1960s.

Music MAKERS Guy Klucevsek

Guy Klucevsek [KLOOH-suh-vek] (born 1947) saw his first accordion on television when he was five years old and begged his father to buy one for him. His father bought an accordion, and Klusevcek took lessons all the way through college, studying classical and popular music, as well as polkas and waltzes from his Slovenian heritage. His college, Indiana University of Pennsylvania, didn't allow students to major in accordion, so he majored in music theory and composition. By the time he finished college, he had decided to be a composer as well as a performer. Today, Klucevsek tours the world as a soloist and as part of a number of ensembles.

Listen to this composition for solo accordion.

Altered Landscapes: Part One

9-22

by Guy Klucevsek
Notice the multiple layers of sound created by the solo accordion.

Take It to the Net For more information on accordions and other free-reed instruments, go to *www.sfsuccessnet.com*.

A Texas Tune

"Deep in the Heart of Texas" is a well-known Texas song. It has been arranged for many groups, including orchestra, marching band, and chorus. As you **listen**, **analyze** how many different chords you will play. The song is printed on page I-18 in Performance Anthology.

Play with Old Friends

You already know the F chord in root position and the C_7 in first inversion. **Play** the chords on this lead sheet as you listen to the recording of "Deep in the Heart of Texas."

Deep in the Heart of Texas

Words by June Hershey

Music by Don Swander

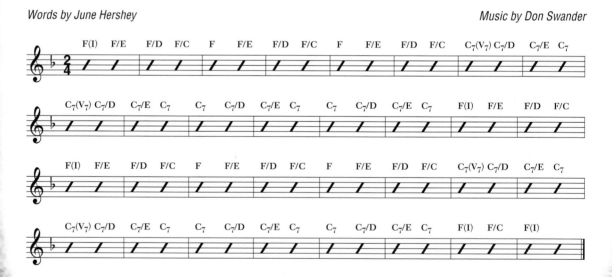

Bass a-Walkin'

"Deep in the Heart of Texas" can be played using two walking bass patterns. Review walking bass on page E-19. Practice the left hand pitches in this pattern and **play** the fingering as notated.

When you are comfortable with this left-hand pattern, comp an accompaniment for "Deep in the Heart of Texas." Use the walking bass pattern as notated in the slash chords on the lead sheet, and **create** an interesting rhythm pattern for the chords in the right hand. Here are two examples.

▲ Left-hand position for walking bass

Note This

Texas bluebonnets (*lupinus texensis*) grow naturally only in Texas. The flowers have been loved since people first traveled across the vast prairies of Texas. They bloom only in spring.

Checkpoint

Below are several chord progressions. Find the most efficient hand positions for these chord progressions on your keyboard. Then play the chords and add the root of the chord with your left hand.

1. C G_7 C G_7 C
2. D   G   D A_7 D
3. Cm   Gm   Cm   Gm   Cm

10

Notes in Common

Jerry Leiber and Mike Stoller wrote many famous songs, such as *Yakety Yak, Charlie Brown, Kansas City, Hound Dog, Jailhouse Rock, Little Egypt, On Broadway,* and *Spanish Harlem.* Perhaps their best-known song is "Stand By Me," which was co-written and performed by Ben E. King.

This song contains four chords: F, Dm, B♭, and C₇. You already know F and C₇. Learn the new chords you will play with "Stand By Me" on the next page.

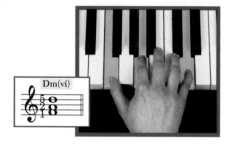

Play the chords in order until you can make the moves easily.

As an added challenge, add a left hand pattern. Put your left thumb on F below middle C and your ring finger on C. Play the F root on the first beat of the measure for the F, Dm, and B♭ chords. Play the C root for the C₇ chord.

A Matter of Style

Listen to the original pop version of *Stand By Me,* from 1961. **Describe** how the opening bass pattern provides unity throughout the song.

Stand By Me

9-23   by Ben E. King, Jerry Leiber, and Mike Stoller
as performed by Ben E. King
This song was derived from an old gospel song.

PRO TIPS

Note that F, Dm, and B♭ all share the F root as a common tone. Hold the common tone as you change the other pitches in the chords.

Ben E. King ▶

Time to Play

Play your new chord progression with "Stand By Me." A classmate can play one hand while you play the other, or you can play both parts yourself.

11

Electrifying Keyboard

In the twentieth century, new technology allowed people to experiment even further with keyboard instruments. Pianos could now be plugged in and hooked up to amplifiers. Many portable electric pianos have the ability to produce almost the same sound quality as a large **acoustic** grand piano. An electronic keyboard is a piano that musicians can combine, or interface, into the international electronic music standard called Musical Instrument Digital Interfacing, or MIDI for short. There are also many other types of interfaces, or controllers, including drum, saxophone, guitar, bass, and vocal MIDI interfaces. Today's performers have a spectrum of sound at their fingertips that musicians in the past would have never dreamed possible.

Synthesizers produce sounds electronically. The first synthesizers created sound using **oscillators** and voltage control. The sound that a synthesizer makes can be changed, allowing the instrument to imitate the sound made by other acoustic instruments, such as flutes, trumpets, and drums. Synthesizers can create completely new sounds as well. Some digital synthesizers create sound by making a virtual reality model of instruments that could not physically exist, such as a bowed flute or a plucked tuba.

The effort to imitate acoustic instruments has slowed with the advent of samplers. Samplers play digital versions of acoustic sound. Certain synthesized sounds are preferred by many pop musicians. Many of the instruments we hear on the radio, on recordings and live at a concert are produced by a sampler or synthesizer.

◀ Recording workstation

acoustic Term for an instrument that is not electronically modified; for example, an acoustic guitar.

oscillator A device that converts currents of a particular frequency.

The First Synthesizers

Early synthesizers, which were developed in the late 1920s and early 1930s, had no keyboards. They were massive machines on which electrical impulses traveled through **patch cords** to create sound. Because of their expense, most synthesizers were only found in laboratories or on university campuses. A few musicians saw the potential of these machines as musical instruments and began writing music for them.

A Taste of Moog

Listen to an example of music created using only Moog [mohg] synthesizers. What do you notice about its timbre?

Popcorn

10-1 **written by Gershon Kingsley**
realized by Hot Butter
This selection was a huge radio hit in 1972.

▲ Physicist and inventor Robert Moog with a 1974 model of his synthesizer

patch cord A cord with a plug on either end used to make electrical connections. They are used to connect phone calls and to transfer electrical signals among units and controllers.

Sounds of the 1960s

In 1964, Robert Moog, a physicist who was interested in the electronic reproduction of sound, developed a synthesizer that he manufactured and sold to the public. Several music groups, including The Beatles, George Clinton, and the German group Tangerine Dream, purchased and used them. The sound of the Mini Moog is so distinctive that it is still used by musicians today such as Lenny Kravitz and Jamiraquoi.

Listen to the sound of the Mini Moog in this popular Beach Boys song.

Good Vibrations

by Brian Wilson

10-2 **as performed by the Beach Boys**

Good Vibrations, written in 1967, not only uses a synthesizer, but also an early electronic instrument called the *electro-theremin*.

▼ Mini Moog

Keyboards Today

By the end of the 1960s, larger companies developed more sophisticated and cost-effective instruments based on the Moog synthesizer. Not only were these new instruments more portable, they became more reliable because of digital technology which sounded more like the instruments they were imitating. During the late 1980s, a process called sampling emerged. Sampling uses a short recording of an acoustic sound and changes it to match the pitch of the controller. These sounds are very realistic. It can be difficult to tell when samples are being used instead of acoustic instruments.

Listen to this selection and determine which sounds are performed on an electronic keyboard and which are performed by acoustic instruments.

Quiet City

by Jim Beard

10-3 **as performed by Michael Brecker**

Brecker is a well-known saxophonist known for his jazz fusion style. He blends non-traditional jazz percussion and synthesized sound in this recording.

Electronica vs. Electronic Music

Electronica is a popular style of music that uses synthesizers and samplers. The sounds that are used are not intended to sound like acoustic instruments. The composer uses different techniques of synthesis to create music with new and interesting timbres. Often a computer will be the only performer on stage, and sometimes the computer interacts with a musician who is using a controller.

Listen to this piece created entirely from electronic instrumentation.

A Miniature Odyssey

written and generated by Timothy Polashek

10-4 *A Miniature Odyssey* was generated using a computer and a software sampler.

Many musicians now blend electronic instruments with live vocals. Occasionally, they use electronic alterations on the vocals as well. **Listen** to this pop group's use of electronica.

Solsbury Hill

by Peter Gabriel

10-5 **as performed by Erasure**

This selection is an electronic version of Gabriel's 1977 hit.

◀ Pet Shop Boys, a popular group known for its use of Electronica

12

Rockin' Out

"Those Magic Changes" is from *Grease*, a musical about teenagers of the 1950s. You already know the chords in this song. **Play** them as you **sing** the song. Then play the progression again using the highlighted rhythm pattern.

PRO TIPS

When moving from C(I) to Am(vi), change from playing E with finger 3 to playing it with finger 2.

CD 10-6

THOSE MAGIC CHANGES

(from *Grease*)

Words and Music by Warren Casey and Jim Jacobs

E-30

13

The Color BLUE

"Blues with a Feeling" is a classic blues song with lyrics all about heartache and loss. The best part about playing and singing the blues is that you almost always feel better when you finish!

Listen to "Blues with a Feeling." It is in 12-bar blues form. The song notation is found on page I-6 in the Performance Anthology. Follow along with the notation to observe the form. Look for repetition of the lyrics.

Shape and Style

Practice the following new chords with your right hand, and then add the root of the chord with your left hand.

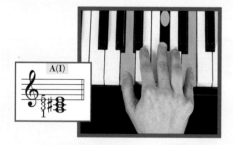

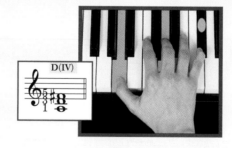

Which chord is in root position? Which chord is in first inversion? Which chord is in second inversion?

Perform one chord each beat. Try some of the rhythm patterns you have learned so far to reflect the mood of the song.

Great Blues Players

Pianist **Sunnyland Slim** (1907–1995) was born Albert Luandrew in Vance, Mississippi. He taught himself to play on a pump organ. He played at social clubs and silent-movie houses in Mississippi. In 1928, Slim wrote a classic blues song entitled *Sunnyland Train* and earned his nickname.

In the 1940s, Slim moved to Chicago and began recording as a soloist and back-up artist for the founders of the Chess Record label. He introduced blues star Muddy Waters to Chess in 1947. Having performed in the Chicago area into his 80s, Sunnyland Slim is a blues legend.

Eurreal Wilford **"Little Brother" Montgomery** (1906–1985) grew up in a house whose visitors included Jelly Roll Morton and Cooney Vaughan. At five, he was playing piano. At the age of 11, he ran away to work as a musician. In 1928, Montgomery headed for Chicago where he performed live and worked as a recording pianist and accompanist. On a single day in 1935 he recorded 18 songs and five accompaniments, including his instrumental masterpiece, *Farish Street Jive*. The sound is a daring blend of boogie and stride piano. His career took him to Carnegie Hall in 1949 and on a European tour in 1960.

▲ Little Brother Montgomery with Barrelhouse Chuck

One of the few Chicago blues pianists to have studied with Sunnyland Slim, Little Brother Montgomery, and other greats, Charles **"Barrelhouse Chuck"** Goering (born 1958) has a blues, boogie-woogie and barrelhouse piano style all his own. Goering learned to play piano at an early age. Soon he had formed his own band and began opening shows for Willie Dixon, B.B. King, and Bo Diddley, among others. Goering often played with Sunnyland Slim's fellow musicians. Goering also became friends and worked with Little Brother Montgomery. Goering has played all over North and South America and tours Europe regularly. He has also appeared often at the Chicago Blues Festival.

Listen to this recording of a song dedicated to pianist Sunnyland Slim.

Salute to Sunnyland Slim

10-8 written and performed by Charles Goering
Goering's piano style in this recording echoes Slim's teaching.

Sunnyland Slim ▶

KEYS and CHORDS

Review and Assess

Throughout Keys and Chords, you have

- learned to play and sing at the keyboard.
- learned chords in root position and inversions.
- practiced different accompaniment patterns with several songs.
- learned about several types of keyboards and how they produce sound.

Playing and singing the notes and rhythms and remembering the words to the songs are just the first steps of excellent music making. Real musicianship involves playing and singing beautifully, using all of the good habits that you've been practicing. It's not so important what you play; it's how well you play and sing that matters.

Review What You Learned

Review what you have studied and practiced. With your teacher, choose performance activities that permit you to demonstrate excellent musicianship. This will take some careful thinking on your part, but selecting the right music to perform is an important part of becoming a successful musician.

Not everyone will be able to play with both hands and sing at the same time. What is most important is that you perform accurately, musically, and beautifully. Think about the songs that you enjoy and that you can play and sing well.

Song	Key	Chords	Progression
"Goodbye, Julie"	F major	F, C_7	I-V_7-I
"Orange Blossom Special"	C major	C, F, G_7	I-IV-I-V_7-I
"The Lion Sleeps Tonight"	F major	F, B♭, C_7	I-IV-I-V_7-I
"De colores"	D major	D, G, A_7	I-V_7-I-IV-I
"Keep Your Eyes on the Prize"	C minor	Cm, G_7, Gm	i-V_7-i-v-i
"Joshua Fought the Battle of Jericho"	E minor	Em, Am, B_7	i-iv-i-V_7-i
"Deep in the Heart of Texas"	F major	F, C_7	I-V_7-I (walking bass)
"Stand By Me"	F major	F, Dm, B♭, C_7	I-vi-IV-V_7-I
"Those Magic Changes"	C major	C, Am, F, G_7	I-vi-IV-V_7-I

Show What You Know

1. With the help of your teacher, select several songs to perform in which you can do at least two of the following well.

- Play one hand of the keyboard accompaniment while a partner plays the other hand. The rest of the class sings.

- Play both hands of the keyboard accompaniment while the rest of the class sings.

- Play one hand of the accompaniment and sing with your classmates.

- Play both hands of the accompaniment and sing with your classmates.

In choosing the songs to perform, your goal is to show all of the qualities of good musicianship. You want performances for which you can be proud, and not just to perform something that is hard to do. The goal for this assessment is quality, not quantity or difficulty.

2. Compare and contrast three listening selections from Keys and Chords in a two-paragraph essay. Consider the following.

- Types of keyboards used in the selections

- How the sounds are produced

- Style of each selection

What to Look and Listen For

Excellent musicians often record themselves so they can evaluate their own work and refine their performances. Record your performance using digital audio, cassette tape, or video tape.

Use this checklist to see how you're doing and to identify aspects of your playing and singing that are in need of further refinement.

Keyboard

- Seat is positioned so that shoulders are relaxed and forearms are parallel to the floor.
- Posture is upright and relaxed.
- Wrists are comfortably straight.
- Fingers are curved.
- Tone is resonant and even.
- Notes and rhythms are played accurately.
- Dynamic levels of the chord pitches are balanced.

- Accompaniment is softer than the melody.
- Accompaniment reflects the character of the music.
- Dynamic and rhythmic changes are used to create expression.

Singing

- Posture is upright and relaxed.
- Jaw and mouth are relaxed and open.
- Breath is inhaled with natural, relaxed expansion of the body.
- Tone is free, open, and even throughout range.
- Singing is accurate and in tune.
- Diction is clear (all words are understood).
- Dynamic and rhythmic changes are used to create an expressive effect.

POWER STRUMMING

Playing Guitar Chords, Progressions, and Strums

◀ Stevie Ray Vaughan

"My first guitar was one of the most beautiful sights I'd ever seen in my life. It was a magic scene. There it is. The guitar. It was real and it stood for something . . . I had found a way to do everything I wanted to do."

—Bruce Springsteen
(born 1949)

◀ Sheryl Crow

Know Your Guitar

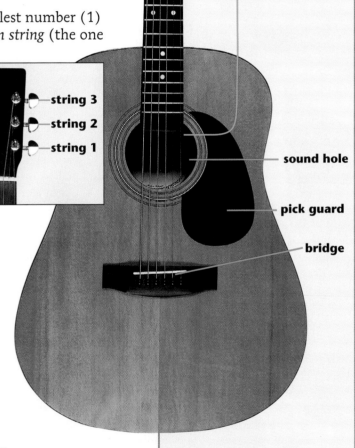

Parts of the Guitar

- tuners
- head
- nut
- frets
- neck and fingerboard
- sound hole
- pick guard
- bridge

The history of the guitar can be traced back to Spain, earlier than the sixteenth century! Guitars come in many sizes and shapes, and almost anyone can learn the basics of playing them. Because of the guitar's ability to produce a wide variety of sounds, it has remained current and popular for a very long time. You can hear guitar-playing in many styles of music around the world.

If you have played guitar before, review the information below. If you are just starting, learn the names of the parts of the guitar.

String Numbers

The strings are numbered 1 through 6 with the smallest number (1) assigned to the thinnest string. Remember, *one = thin string* (the one closest to the floor).

Locate the strings and find the tuners attached to them.

Strings: 6   5   4   3   2   1

E   A   D   G   B   E

string 4 — string 3
string 5 — string 2
string 6 — string 1

Tuning the Guitar

Now tune your own guitar by following these steps for each string.

- Locate the correct tuner for the string you are tuning.

- **Listen** to the pitch on the recording.

- Pluck the string that you are tuning.

- Match the pitch on the recording by tightening or loosening the tuner. Keep plucking the string as you turn the tuner.

- If the pitch of your string is getting closer to the pitch on the recording, keep turning the tuner in the same direction.

- If the pitch of your string is getter farther away, turn the tuner in the other direction.

- Your string is in tune when the pitch of your string matches the sound on the recording.

 Guitar Tuning

Guitar pitches E, A, D, G, B, E

10-9   The recording starts with bass string 6 and each string has its own track.

Playing Position

Experiment with different ways of holding your guitar. Depending on your body size, type of guitar, and style of playing, you may prefer one of the positions shown. See which works best for you.

When you choose your playing position make sure that

- The guitar neck tilts upward (never downward)
- Your body and arms are relaxed.

Standing position with guitar strap ◄

Seated position ◄

PRO TIPS

Many professional guitarists play standing up. If you want to play this way, you will need a guitar strap.

Take It to the Net Explore the world of guitars by reading "Guitars and Guitar Music" at *www.sfsuccessnet.com*.

Hand Positions

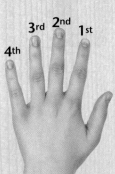

3rd 2nd 1st
4th

The fingers of the left hand (or chording hand) are numbered, starting with 1 for the index finger.

Fingers should arch over the strings. Press the tips straight down onto the strings. The thumb is placed at the back of the neck.

You will begin strumming with the thumb of the right hand (or strumming hand) by brushing down across the strings over the sound hole.

When you use a pick, hold it like this.

Chords & Strums

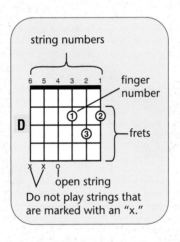

string numbers

6 5 4 3 2 1

D

finger number

frets

x x o

open string

Do not play strings that are marked with an "x."

As with the piano, the guitar allows one musician to play many notes simultaneously, producing chords and harmonies. Chords are the main vocabulary for guitar music. Because the guitar is frequently used to accompany songs, knowing how to play chords is the most important thing to master. The ability to change quickly from one chord to another can be challenging, but once you have that skill, you will be able to play many songs.

Reading Chord Frames

Look at the chord frame for D to learn what the symbols mean. Compare the chord frame to your guitar's fingerboard. Form the chord with your fingers. Then review the finger positions for the G (full and partial) and A₇ chords.

Practice forming the chords as you look at the photos. Check your finger positions and then strum each chord.

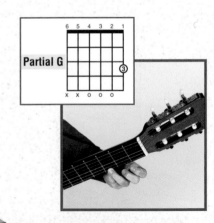

Partial G

6 5 4 3 2 1

x x o o o

G

6 5 4 3 2 1

o o o

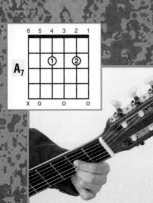

A₇

6 5 4 3 2 1

x o o o

Grab and Strum

"Grabbing" the chords is like doing pushups with your fingers and helps to build finger strength and chord memory. To grab a chord, press down on the strings but do not strum. Remember to always keep the beat steady as you grab the chords. Anticipate where your fingers need to go to play the next chord.

PRO TIPS

If you hear buzzing as you play a chord, press a little harder on the string closer to the fret.

- Grab the chords eight times each in this order D, A_7, G, and then back to D.

- Grab the chords four times each in the progression D-A_7-D-G-D-A_7-D.

- Play the same chord progression. Strum each chord eight times. Use a basic thumb strum.

- Play a new chord progression, D-G-D-A_7-D, strumming four times on each chord.

- Super challenge! Strum each chord in the progression two times.

A Song to Strum

Play "The Lion Sleeps Tonight," which is printed on page I-56 in Performance Anthology. Place a **capo** at fret 3 as shown, and play the chord progression D-G-D-A_7 (the chords will sound F-B♭-F-C_7). Play this strum, using a thumb strum or flat pick. The symbol above the first four notes shows that you should strum downward.

capo ▲

down

Once you can play the strum and chords throughout the song, try this strum, which gives the music a little swing.

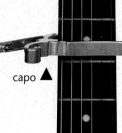

---

capo A small clamp-like device that is used to raise the pitch of the guitar strings.

Rockin' Reggae

Reggae style characteristics are heard in much of the dance, rap, and rock music of today. The music of Eric Clapton, Paul Simon, and the band No Doubt, among others, has clearly been influenced by this music native to Jamaica. One of the greatest pioneers of reggae music was Bob Marley.

Music MAKERS

Bob Marley

Bob Marley (1945–1981) had an extraordinary influence on popular music. He was regarded as a folk hero and prophet in Jamaica and in the rest of the Caribbean. He also spoke to the needs of the politically oppressed worldwide. Early in his career, Marley was influenced by American rhythm and blues, and later by British punk rock music. He wrote many songs, and his fans believe that Marley wrote a song for each important issue in life.

Reggae Family

Bob Marley's son, Ziggy Marley, branches out from his father's musical roots. His music retains some elements of reggae while implementing a mix of other popular music genres. **Listen** for a rhythm pattern in the accompaniment of *I Get Out*, which emphasizes beats 2 and 4.

I Get Out

10-15

written and performed by Ziggy Marley
Ziggy Marley writes song lyrics that touch on spiritual and social topics much the same as his father's lyrics do.

Reggae Strum

Review the chord progression D-G-A$_7$ that you learned in the previous lesson. **Play** the song "Three Little Birds" by Bob Marley, using a pick and a new strumming pattern called the *reggae strum*. Notice that the down strum occurs on beats two and four. This gives the song its characteristic reggae sound.

CD 10-16

Three Little Birds

Words and Music by Bob Marley

REFRAIN

D

Don't wor-ry   a-bout   a   thing

G   D

'cause ev-'ry lit-tle thing   gon-na be all-right.

D

Sing-in' don't wor-ry   a-bout   a   thing

D   G   D   *Fine*

'cause ev-'ry   lit-tle thing   gon-na be all-right.

VERSE D

Rise up this morn-ing,   smile _ with the ris-ing sun.

A$_7$ D   G

Three _ lit-tle birds   sit by my door-step,

G   D   A$_7$

Sing-in' sweet _ songs   of mel-o-dies pure and true,

A$_7$ G   D   *D. C. al Fine*

Sing-in':   "This is my mes-sage to you-hoo-hoo."   Sing-in'

 Take It to the Net For more information on reggae read "Jamaican Music and Instruments" at *www.sfsuccessnet.com*.

POPULAR Changes

The singing duo, the Everly Brothers, Don (born 1937) and Phil (born 1939) were just teenagers in 1955 when they were hired to write songs for publisher Roy Acuff. By 1957 they had recorded several popular tunes, including "Bye Bye, Love," which became an international hit.

"Bye Bye, Love" uses three chords that are often used together in progression: G, C, and D_7. Examine the chord frames for the full and partial C chord. The bass note for the full C chord is string 5. If you play the partial chord, strum only strings 3, 2, and 1.

Now examine the D_7 chord frame. Practice changing between the partial C chord and the D_7 chords. Then practice changing between the full C and D_7 chords.

Now **play** along with the song recording. Choose whether you will play a basic down strum or another strum such as the reggae strum.

▼ Everly Brothers

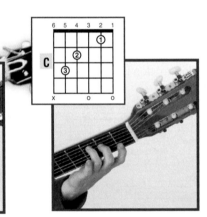

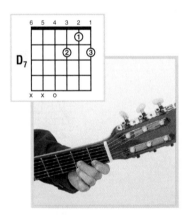

Beyond Strumming

Eric Johnson is a well known guitarist from Austin, Texas. **Listen** to him as he demonstrates a way of playing with the strumming hand, called fingerpicking. He also plays **harmonics** to add interesting tone colors or timbres to the music. **Identify** the places in the recording where you hear the harmonics.

 Song for George

by Eric Johnson

10-18 In this solo guitar piece, Johnson allows the strings to buzz and squeak, adding to its raw, emotional quality.

▲ Eric Johnson

---

harmonics High-pitched, bell-like sounds produced by lightly touching a string directly over the fret and then plucking the string.

Bye Bye, Love

CD 10-19

Words and Music by Felice Bryant and Boudleaux Bryant

REFRAIN

Bye __ bye __ love; _ Bye __ bye, __ hap - pi - ness. __

Hel - lo lone - li - ness. __ I think-a I'm-a gon - na cr - y. __

Bye __ bye, __ love; _ Bye __ bye, __ sweet _ ca - ress. __

Hel - lo emp - ti - ness. __ I feel like-a I could _ d - ie. __ Bye

Fine

bye, my love, good - b - ye. __

VERSE

1. There goes my ba - by _____ with some - one new. She sure looks hap - py. __
2. I'm through with ro - mance. ____ I'm through with love. I'm through with count - ing __

I sure am blue. She was my ba - by __ till he stepped
the stars a - bove. And here's the rea - son __ that I'm so

D.C. al Fine

in. Good-bye to ro - mance _ that might have been. _____
free. My lov - in' ba - by __ is through with me. _____

Guitar Art

Guitar manufacturers produce standard or "stock" instruments to meet public demand, but they also make special or "custom" instruments for famous guitarists. Custom instruments help performers develop their own sound and allow other players to get the look, feel, and sound of some of their favorite stars. Here are some examples.

One of the most important developments in rock 'n' roll music is the growing visibility of women guitarists. Gibson makes a Sheryl Crow signature acoustic guitar that is modeled after the 1962 Gibson Country Western. The guitar is a square shoulder dreadnought with a rosewood fingerboard and a pick guard in the shape of a hummingbird.

Carlos Santana has a sustained, lyrical style that is unlike many other famous guitarists who are often known for playing "lightning fast." This guitar has 24 frets (two octaves), an extrawide neck, and specially designed pick-ups.

Sheryl Crow plays a Sheryl Crow Signature Gibson guitar ▼

◀ Carlos Santana plays a Paul Reed Smith Santana III guitar

The Sand Sound

Listen to Doyle Dykes, a guitarist from Nashville who plays a Kirk Sand guitar on this recording. How does he use harmonics?

Jazz in the Box

by Doyle Dykes

10-21

Jazz in the Box is a mixture of various fingerstyle techniques and is considered to be one of Doyle Dykes's signature compositions.

▲ Doyle Dykes in Kirk Sand's Shop

▲ Detail of mother-of-pearl inlay on a Kirk Sand guitar made for Doyle Dykes

Careers LUTHIER
Kirk Sand

Kirk Sand (born 1953) is a **luthier** from Springfield, Illinois. He moved to the West Coast when he was nineteen years old to study classical guitar. He opened a guitar shop and learned how to repair guitars and in 1979 he began designing his own. His original love for the classical guitar and the modern demand for high-tech features can be seen in his designs. He makes guitars for many well-known performers, who visit him in his shop in Laguna Beach, California.

luthier A person who makes and repairs string instruments.

URBAN ARTS

Music and art can bring renewal and inspiration to urban areas that are dominated by the presence of brick and concrete. In her song "God Bless the Grass" Malvina Reynolds finds beauty in the grass growing through a concrete sidewalk in a city.

The artist Alexander Calder (1898–1976) is well known for his giant mobiles and stabiles (mobile-like forms that do not move). His works bring vibrant color into urban environments all over the world.

New Chords

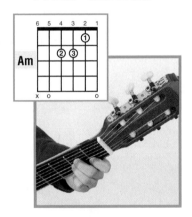

Examine the chord frames for the A minor (Am) and E₇ chords. Determine where your fingers need to be placed and on which strings and frets. **Play** this short Am–E₇ chord progression.

Arts Connection

This stabile, *Flamingo* (1974) by Alexander Calder is located in Chicago. It weighs 30 tons and stands six stories high. ▶

A New Strum

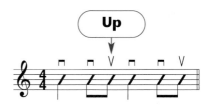

Once you are getting a clear sound changing from the Am to E_7 chords, experiment with a different strum. Instead of playing all down strums, create rhythmic interest by making the second beat a down-up strum. Notice the symbol that shows you when to strum upward.

Play the song "God Bless the Grass." Use the down-down-up strum to play the chord changes. **Swing** the eighth notes.

---

swing A practice of performing eighth notes with the first note slightly longer than the second note.

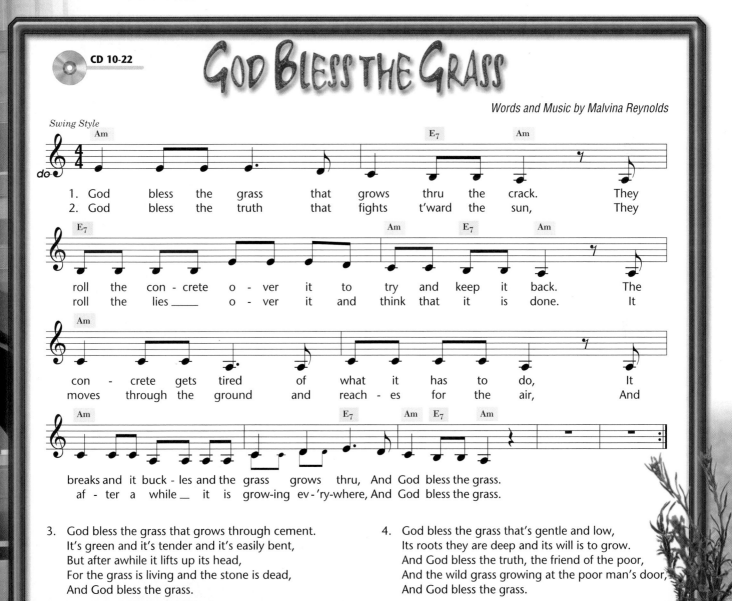

CD 10-22

GOD BLESS THE GRASS

Words and Music by Malvina Reynolds

Swing Style

1. God bless the grass that grows thru the crack. They roll the con - crete o - ver it to try and keep it back. The con - crete gets tired of what it has to do, It breaks and it buck - les and the grass grows thru, And God bless the grass.

2. God bless the truth that fights t'ward the sun, They roll the lies ___ o - ver it and think that it is done. It moves through the ground and reach - es for the air, And af - ter a while __ it is grow-ing ev-'ry-where, And God bless the grass.

3. God bless the grass that grows through cement.
   It's green and it's tender and it's easily bent,
   But after awhile it lifts up its head,
   For the grass is living and the stone is dead,
   And God bless the grass.

4. God bless the grass that's gentle and low,
   Its roots they are deep and its will is to grow.
   And God bless the truth, the friend of the poor,
   And the wild grass growing at the poor man's door,
   And God bless the grass.

7

Bass Strum Basics

A great way to accompany a melody on the guitar is to use a variety of strumming patterns. When you learn more complex strums you will be on your way to learning new techniques such as fingerpicking.

Listen to Etta Baker's fingerpicking on *Railroad Bill.* The most common keys to play the blues are E or A, but Baker plays this old-time blues song in the key of C.

Railroad Bill

10-24 **Piedmont-style blues**
as performed by Etta Baker

Etta Baker tunes her guitar a bit lower than standard tuning, so this song, though played in C, actually sounds in the key of B.

Minor Workout

Examine the chord frame for E minor (Em). Then, strum the Em chord four times. Practice changing from Em to Am by grabbing the chords four times each. Move fingers 2 and 3 together as you move between the two chords.

Now use a basic down strum to play the Em and Am chords.

Music MAKERS Etta Baker

Etta Baker (born 1913) is a virtuoso performer of the Piedmont blues style of fingerpicking. She uses a two- and three-fingered technique. Baker grew up in the foothills of the Blue Ridge Mountains in North Carolina. Her father was an early bluesman and her grandfather played banjo. She learned to play guitar, fiddle, banjo, and piano.

Em and Am Bass Strums

The bass strum is an early step toward fingerpicking. The bass note for Em is string 6 and the bass note for Am is string 5. Use your thumb or flat pick to play the bass. Use your thumb, fingers, or flat pick to play the other strings. Notice that the strings you strum on the Am chord are different from the ones you use for the Em chord. Now **play** the bass strum on each chord several times until you can perform it easily.

Strum Along

Play the bass strum patterns above with the recording of the song "Chicka Hanka," an African American work song.

CD 10-25

Chicka Hanka

African American Work Song

Cap-tain, go side - track your train! ___
Chick-a hank-a, chick-a hank-a, chick-a hank-a, chick-a

Cap - tain, go side - track your train! ___
hank - a.
Chick - a hank - a, chick - a

Num - ber three in line a - com-in' in on time.
hank-a, chick-a hank-a, chick-a hank - a.

8

Tricks of the Trade

There are as many guitar-playing techniques as there are musical styles and cultures. Some styles use very percussive techniques on the guitar, for example the *lift-off* and the *slap*.

A Four-Finger Chord

The B₇ chord requires you to use all four fingers of your chording hand. Examine the chord frame and place your fingers in position to play.

Notice that the bass note for the B₇ chord is on string 5 and your 2nd finger is at fret 2. Do not strum string 6. Practice this strum on the B₇ chord.

Now **play** the strum again, this time adding a lift-off on the up strums on beats 2 and 4. The lift-off is done by lifting your 4th finger off of string 1, then replacing the finger in time for the next down strum.

Play the song "Ain't Gonna Let Nobody Turn Me 'Round," using the strum with a lift-off.

CD 10-27
MIDI 04

Ain't Gonna Let Nobody Turn Me 'Round

African American Civil Rights Song

1. Ain't gon-na let no-bod-y turn me 'round, — turn me 'round, —
2. Ain't gon-na let no jail ___ turn me 'round, — turn me 'round, —
3. Ain't gon-na let no doubt-ers turn me 'round, — turn me 'round, —

turn me 'round. _ Ain't gon-na let no-bod-y turn me 'round, —
turn me 'round. _ Ain't gon-na let no jail ___ turn me 'round. _
turn me 'round. _ Ain't gon-na let no doubt-ers turn me 'round. _

I'm gon-na keep on a-walk-in', keep on a-talk-in', March-in' to the free-dom land. _

More Strums and Effects

Play the chord progression, Em-Am-B₇, using a variation of the *huapango* strum that is very popular in Mexico and throughout Latin America. For all of the down strums, brush the strings with your thumb. This is important because it puts your hand in position to **perform** a slap, which is done by gently laying your palm on the strings over the sound hole.

Now use the *huapango* strum as you **play** the song *"Canto del agua,"* which is printed on page I-10 in Performance Anthology.

Next, place a capo at fret 3 and practice this bass strum. Now **play** it to accompany the song "Deep in the Heart of Texas," which is printed on page I-18 in Performance Anthology. Note that the D and A₇ chords will sound as F and C₇.

Play the song again with more of a country music sound. On the D chord, alternate bass strings 4 and 5, and on the A₇ chord, alternate bass strings 5 and 6, like this.

Strum and Sing

With the capo still set at fret 3, **play** the song "I Shall Sing," which is printed on page I-38 in Performance Anthology. Use a bass strum throughout.

9

Strummin' on the Bayou

When you are learning to play a new song, you may find different combinations of chords than you played before. Many times you will need to review all of the chords and strumming patterns that you already know in order to perform the new song. The song, "Jambalaya," by Hank Williams, uses the chords A and E_7. You already know the E_7 chord (see Lesson 6), and A is a new chord. The A chord is very similar to A_7, but has one added finger. Examine the chord frame. Which finger is added, and where do you place it? Now **play** the A chord.

Notice that the bass note for this chord is string 5. Practice this strum.

Now **play** the strum to accompany the song "Jambalaya," which is printed on page I-46 in Performance Anthology. Use your thumb for the bass notes and the rest of your fingers or a flat pick for the down strums.

PRO TIPS

Solo guitarists sometimes mute their strings to give them a more percussive sound. Lightly rest the outside palm of your strumming hand on the strings at the bridge. Then strum. You can adjust this muting effect as you become more comfortable with the technique.

Checkpoint

Review the fingerings for all of the chords you have learned so far—D, G, A_7, C, D_7, E_7, Am, A, and B_7. Draw chord frames for each one to show where the fingers are placed on the fingerboard. Next, **play** each chord with a basic down strum and check for clear-sounding strings. Then play a bass strum pattern on each chord.

MAKERS
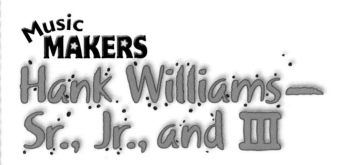
Hank Williams— Sr., Jr., and III

Hank Williams (1923–1953), the composer of "Jambalaya," was the first superstar of country music. He was born in Alabama. As a young child his mother, a church organist, encouraged him to sing in church. By the age of eight he was playing guitar and at thirteen he organized his first band. Williams slowly gained a reputation for writing catchy, irresistible songs and eventually became the best-known country and western singer in the country. He died at age 29 while on a road trip.

His son, **Hank Williams, Jr.** (born 1949), had a remarkably similar childhood. He was encouraged to take the stage early on and at age 11 he made his debut at the Grand Ole Opry. He became a country music star in his own right, and he was the first country music performer to win an Emmy Award. During the 1980s Hank, Jr. won the Entertainer of the Year Award

multiple times. He currently has twenty-four gold and ten platinum albums, as well as one double and one quadruple platinum album. He has become an international star for his opening segment on Monday Night Football.

Hank Williams III (born 1976) is carrying on the family's musical tradition in his own way. Although he is not yet as famous as his father and grandfather, he is quickly developing a following. His musical style departs from the traditional country sound and has been described by his recording company as "hard-twang, punkabilly, ...alternacountry, ...or honky punk." To keep the older country music fans happy, Hank III presents concerts where the first half is country, including covers by his grandfather, Hank, Sr., and the second half is punk rock.

ON YOUR OWN

Find other examples of musical families. Some well-known family members are John and Bonnie Raitt, Frank and Dweezil Zappa, Woody and Arlo Guthrie, and Bob and Jakob Dylan. Identify shared musical talents and the unique qualities of each musician. Share your findings with the class.

Hank Williams, Jr. ▶

Hank Williams ▶

Hank Williams III ▶

fingerstyle Guitar

Fingerstyle is one of the most popular types of guitar playing. In fingerstyle, the guitarist uses the strumming fingers to pluck each string individually. Classical fingerstyle players use nylon-string guitars, while blues, country, jazz, folk, and new age fingerstyle players usually use steel-string guitars. Listen to examples of classical (nylon) and steel-string guitar playing to hear how those two types of guitars sound distinctly different.

Classical Fingerstyle

Listen to the Los Angeles Guitar Quartet play *"Danza ritual del fuego"* from *El amor brujo* by Manuel de Falla, one of Spain's best-known composers. This piece was originally written for orchestra.

Danza ritual del fuego

10-29
from *El amor brujo*
by Manuel de Falla
as performed by the Los Angeles Guitar Quartet
This piece illustrates the fiery quality of Spanish dance.

Steel-String Fingerstyle

Now **listen** to American guitarist Michael Hedges play one of his signature pieces *Aerial Boundaries*. Hedges's career as one of the world's best fingerstyle guitarists was cut short by a tragic car accident near his home in California.

Aerial Boundaries

10-30
by Michael Hedges
Hedges achieved his distinctive sound by playing with both hands on the fingerboard.

▲ Nylon-string classical guitar

◄ Steel-string acoustic guitar

Music MAKERS
Los Angeles Guitar Quartet

The **Los Angeles Guitar Quartet (L.A.G.Q.)** is a world-acclaimed group of virtuoso classical guitar players, John Dearman, William Kanengiser, Scott Tennant, and Andrew York. The group has greatly expanded the classical guitar quartet repertoire to include transcriptions of orchestral and keyboard works, as well as new works based on popular music, such as variations on a song by Led Zeppelin. The L.A.G.Q. has appeared in concerts throughout the world, from Lincoln Center and Carnegie Hall in New York to Munich, Paris, Singapore, and Beijing.

Playing Fingerstyle

When you play fingerstyle guitar, your thumb and fingers are assigned to pluck specific strings. The diagram shows the names of the fingers of the picking hand.

Play this finger exercise, using a chord you already know.

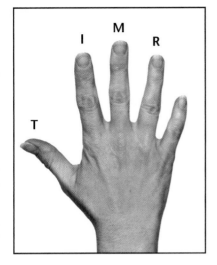

- Thumb (T) plucks bass string 4, 5, or 6. Choose the string that is the bass note of the chord you have chosen to play.
- Index (I) plucks string 3.
- Middle (M) plucks string 2.
- Ring (R) plucks string 1.

Guitar Tablature

Guitar music is sometimes written on a six-line staff called tablature, also known as TAB. In tablature, each line represents a string on the guitar. The bottom line is bass string 6 and the top line is treble string 1.

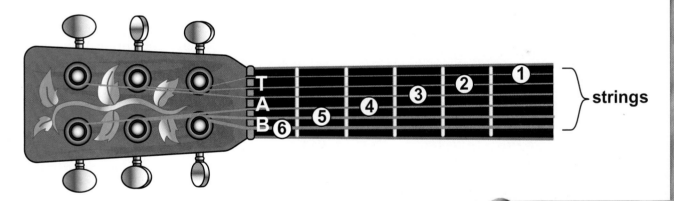

Read the following tablature, or TAB, and **play** the basic fingerstyle patterns on the chords indicated. Notice that the only change occurs in the bass-string thumb (T) positions.

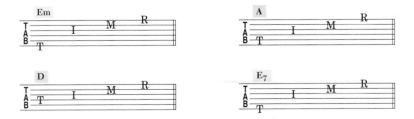

PRO TIPS

Many guitar method books show fingerstyle patterns, using *p-i-m-a.* This labelling system is based on the Spanish names for the fingers–*pulgar*=thumb, *indice*=index, *medio*=middle, *anular*=ring.

11

Picking with Style

What makes one guitarist sound different from another? How can you tell whether you are hearing Bonnie Raitt or Manuel Barrueco? Strumming and picking styles, pitch bending, and slurring techniques such as **hammer-on** and lift-off, all contribute to the expressiveness of the guitar. The way guitarists combine these techniques contributes to their signature sound. What techniques will you use to play the guitar expressively?

Hammer-on Lift-off

Listen to the fingerstyle technique of Richard Thompson in his *Roll Over Vaughan Williams*. Thompson is known as one of "modern music's best-kept secrets." He has been playing guitar and writing songs for nearly fifty years. He is not only considered a formidable guitarist, but a songwriting genius as well, writing on all manner of topics. Listen for the techniques of hammer-on lift-off, and **pitch-bending**.

Roll Over Vaughan Williams
by Richard Thompson
11-1 Richard Thompson's deep roots in British traditional music can be heard in this live performance.

Classical Picks

Listen to the fingerpicking style of classical guitarist Manuel Barrueco as he plays *Sevilla* by Isaac Albéniz. Barrueco has been a leading figure in the classical guitar scene since his acclaimed 1974 debut at Carnegie Hall in New York City. **Compare** his playing style with Richard Thompson's style.

Sevilla
by Isaac Albéniz
11-2 **as performed by Manuel Barrueco**
Barrueco's virtuosic technique and passionate style is clearly demonstrated on this recording.

hammer-on A technique of plucking the string before placing a finger at a fret on the fingerboard.

pitch-bending A technique of pushing a string on the fingerboard to make the pitch change.

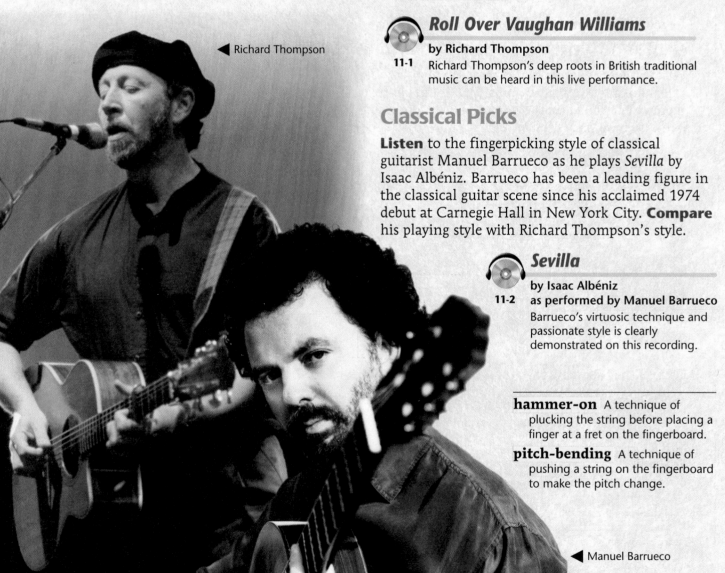

◄ Richard Thompson

◄ Manuel Barrueco

Pick a Song

Review fingerstyle technique that was introduced in Lesson 10. Remember that your thumb will typically play strings 6, 5, or 4, and your fingers will play strings 3, 2, and 1.

Practice fingerstyle technique on the A, D, and E₇ chords.

Arts Connection

The *Koru* is a symbol for the harmonic life wheel. It depicts waves in a circle. ▶

Play along with the recording of *"Karangatia ra,"* a *Maori* [MOW-ree] song from New Zealand. Use the picking patterns above for each chord.

CD 11-3

Karangatia ra

Maori Song from New Zealand

Ka - ran - ga - ti - a ra ___ Ka - ran - ga - ti - a ra ___

Po - whi - ri - ti - a ra nga i - wi o te mo - tu

Ki te - nei ma - rae ha - e - re mai ___

He hui a ro - ha mo kou - tou e te - i - wi

Na - u nei te a - ro - ha me te ma - mae. ___

12

POWER CHORDS

One of the essential types of chords to learn in order to play rock 'n' roll guitar is the **power chord.** Beginning in the 1960s, guitarists played these simple, yet powerful, chords to bring innovation to their performances of rock, blues, punk, and heavy metal music. Power chords have an open sound and can be used to accompany almost any song because they are neither major nor minor.

Power chords are labeled with a letter, which indicates the bass note of a chord, or the root, followed by the number 5, which indicates the fifth scale degree up from the root.

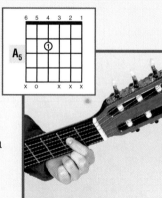

A_5

Play the A_5 chord, using an open string 5 and the 1st finger on string 4 at fret 2. Strum only strings 5 and 4.

Now place a capo at fret 3 and strum the A_5 chord on the beat to accompany "The Earth Is Our Mother."

Hammer-on for Power

Guitarists use the term *hammer-on* as a way of describing a musical **slur**. **Play** a hammer-on with the A_5 chord as follows.

- Strum open strings 5 and 4.

- While these strings are sounding, hammer your 1st fingertip down on string 4 at fret 2. Do not strum again for this step.

- Strum strings 5 and 4 again with the 1st finger down.

Play this hammer-on with "The Earth Is Our Mother."

---

power chord Two-note chords where the middle note of the triad is omitted.

slur A style of playing where the transition between notes is smooth and connected.

The Earth Is Our Mother

Cherokee Song
Arranged by Barbara Sletto

Guitar: capo 3

1.,3. The Earth __ is our Moth - er, we must take care of her. The
2. Her sa - cred ground we walk u - pon with ev - ery step we take. Her

Earth __ is our Moth - er, we must take care of her.
sa - cred ground we walk up - on with ev - ery step we take.

Hey ____ yan - na, ho ____ yan - na, hey ____ yan yan.

Hey ____ yan - na, ho ____ yan - na hey ____ yan yan.

D₅ and E₅ Power

You can use the fingering you just learned for A$_5$ on the D$_5$ and E$_5$ chords by moving to a different pair of strings. Study the chord frames, then play the power chord workout below.

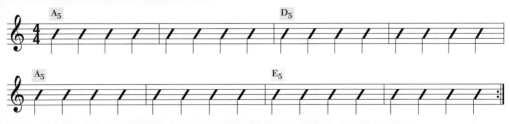

A₅   D₅

A₅   E₅

Blues Power

It is well known that rock 'n' roll has been heavily influenced by the blues. Sometimes, however, another style is influenced by rock 'n' roll and a new style is born. With blues rock it is hard to know which came first, the blues or rock 'n' roll. One of the most important performers of blues rock style was Stevie Ray Vaughan.

Listen to Stevie Ray Vaughan's *Scuttle Buttin'*. Imagine how much you would need to practice in order to play that many notes in such a short time.

Scuttle Buttin'

by Stevie Ray Vaughan

11-10 The last performance of Stevie Ray Vaughan's career was in East Troy, Wisconsin, where he played an encore with blues greats, Eric Clapton, Buddy Guy, Jimmie Vaughan, and Robert Cray.

A_5 Blues

The 12-bar blues progression can be played using standard chords or power chords. First, strum this chord progression with standard chords. Think about their function in the key of A. You can learn more about chord function in Sounds and Symbols on page H-25. Second, strum the progression using power chords.

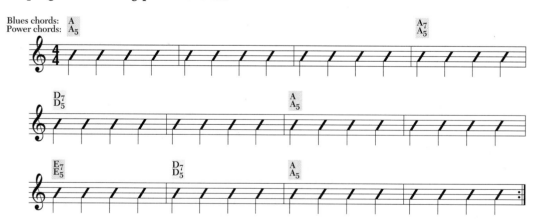

Next, **sing** and **play** "Blues With a Feeling," which is printed on page I-6 in Performance Anthology. This classic blues song is by "Little" Walter Jacobs, one of the best harmonica players of all time. Use the shuffle, or swing, rhythm to play along with the recording. Experiment with playing standard chords as well as power chords.

Stevie Ray Vaughan

Stevie Ray Vaughan (1954–1990) was one of the most important guitarists in the blues revival of the 1980s. Vaughan was influenced by blues players Muddy Waters and Albert King, rock guitarists such as Jimi Hendrix, and jazz players such as Kenny Burrell. Stevie Ray Vaughan developed an eclectic style that bridged the styles of blues and rock. A tragic helicopter accident in 1990 took Vaughan's life, and one of the best guitar players of the last fifty years was gone. Born and raised in Dallas, Texas, Vaughan played in garage bands while in school. In the mid-1970s he formed a band called the Cobras which played in the Austin area. Another band, Triple Threat, followed. When one of the members left, the band was renamed Double Trouble (after an Otis Rush song) with Vaughan featured as lead singer. After a 1982 appearance at the Montreux Festival, Vaughan caught the attention of both David Bowie and Jackson Browne. Bowie invited him to play lead guitar on his *Let's Dance* album, and Browne gave him free use of his Los Angeles recording studio. Shortly after, Vaughan and Double Trouble landed a contract with Epic Records.

Key to the BLUES

Blues is often credited with being the basis for rock 'n' roll, because many of its early performers modeled their playing and singing after blues artists such as Robert Johnson, B.B. King, and Big Bill Broonzy.

Listen to Buddy Guy perform *Key to the Highway*. As you listen, **analyze** the form of the song. Is it 12-bar blues?

Key to the Highway

by Big Bill Broonzy and Charles Segar
11-11   as performed by Buddy Guy and Junior Wells

Guy is well known as an electric blues guitar player but in this recording, made live in Chicago in 1989, he plays old-style blues on acoustic guitar.

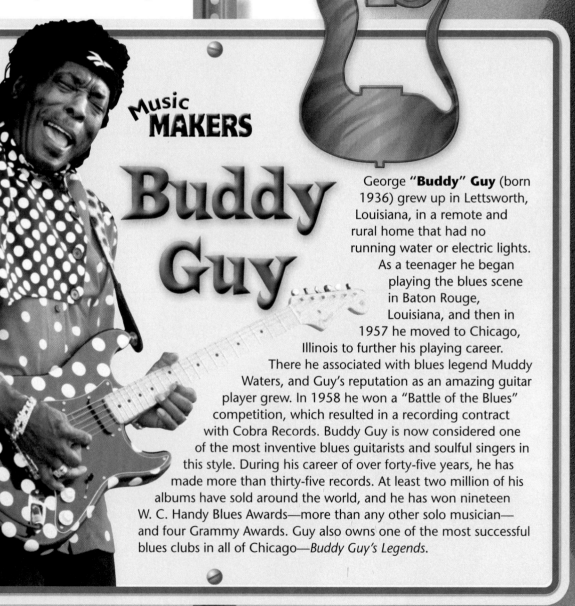

Music MAKERS

Buddy Guy

George **"Buddy" Guy** (born 1936) grew up in Lettsworth, Louisiana, in a remote and rural home that had no running water or electric lights. As a teenager he began playing the blues scene in Baton Rouge, Louisiana, and then in 1957 he moved to Chicago, Illinois to further his playing career. There he associated with blues legend Muddy Waters, and Guy's reputation as an amazing guitar player grew. In 1958 he won a "Battle of the Blues" competition, which resulted in a recording contract with Cobra Records. Buddy Guy is now considered one of the most inventive blues guitarists and soulful singers in this style. During his career of over forty-five years, he has made more than thirty-five records. At least two million of his albums have sold around the world, and he has won nineteen W. C. Handy Blues Awards—more than any other solo musician—and four Grammy Awards. Guy also owns one of the most successful blues clubs in all of Chicago—*Buddy Guy's Legends*.

Highway Blues

Play a blues progression using the chords E(I), $A_7(IV_7)$, $B_7(V_7)$. The E chord is new, so look at the chord frame to determine where to place your fingers.

Place a capo at fret 1 and **play** "Key to the Highway," using the chords E-A_7-B_7 which will sound as F-Bb_7-C_7. **Improvise** with various strumming techniques you have learned. Be inventive with the rhythm.

CD 11-12

Key to the Highway

Words and Music by Big Bill Broonzy and Charles Segar

Guitar: capo 1

1. I've got the key to the high - way, __ I'm packed and read - y to go. ___ I'm gon - na leave here __ run - nin', _ walk - in's just __ too slow. _
2. When __ the sun peaks over the moun - tain, __ I'll be on ____ my way. ___ I'm go - in' down this __ high - way _ at the break _ of day. _
3. So long and good - bye, _____ hate to say ____ good - bye. _ But I'm gon - na ride this __ high - way _ 'til the day __ I die. ___

ON YOUR OWN

Check your local newspaper for a calendar of musical events and look for a blues concert you can attend with your friends and family. If there are no blues performances listed, visit your local library and check out several blues recordings to share in class.

15

THE POWER OF E

No style of music has been so dominated by the power chord as heavy metal. The combination of heavy distortion added to pure power chords has become a trademark of metal bands for decades.

Listen to Alice in Chain's recording of *Would?* **Identify** sections of the recording where you hear power chords.

Would?

by Jerry Cantrell
11-14 **as performed by Alice in Chains**
This recording is a definitive example of the heavy metal sound of the early 1990s.

Express Your Power

Review the E_5 and A_5 power chords you learned in Lesson 12. In order to play in the key of E you will need to learn the B_5 power chord. Look at the B_5 chord frame. Then form the chord.

Strum the E_5 and B_5 chords below. Be sure to strum only the correct two strings for each chord.

Now **play** the 12-bar blues power chord progression in E.

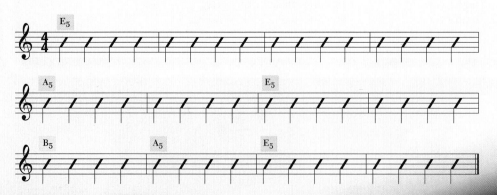

Play Lead

Many blues and rock guitar players start improvising on the five notes of the E minor pentatonic scale. Examine the notation and the diagram below to determine where you will place your fingers to play the pitches. Then **play** each note in the scale. To learn more about scales, see page H-23 in Sounds and Symbols.

On Your Own

ON YOUR OWN

Find a guitar partner and practice trading off solos. One person improvises a 4-beat solo and then the other echoes it back. Expand to 8-beat solos when you are ready.

Echo each of the following solos played by a leader. Remember that E is open string 1 and B is open string 2.

Ex. 1   Ex. 2   Ex. 3   Ex. 4

Ex. 5   Ex. 6   Ex. 7   Ex. 8

Ex. 9   Ex. 10

Solo Power

Play solos along with the recording of *12-Bar Blues Rock.* Choose two measures from the above exercises to play as your solo in measures 3–4, 7–8, or 11–12. Be sure to start and end your solo on E.

PRO TIPS

If you want to play a high B in your solos, slide your 3rd finger two frets up from the note A to B.

CD 11-15
MIDI 5

12-Bar Blues Rock

E_5 *Play your solo in these measures*

A_5 E_5 *Play your solo in these measures.*

B_5 A_5 E_5 *Play your solo in these measures.*

16

Songwriting

If you have a favorite performer, maybe it is because you can relate to the message or the feelings expressed in the music. Songwriters get their inspiration from a variety of sources. Some write their own lyrics based on personal experience. Others use words written by other people.

Listen to Ani DiFranco's *Angry Anymore*, a song she wrote about the challenges she faced while growing up.

Angry Anymore

by Ani DiFranco

11-16   This song is from DiFranco's album *Up Up Up Up Up Up* (1999).

Music MAKERS
Ani DiFranco

Ani [AHH-nee] DiFranco (born 1970) is a "punk folksinger" from Buffalo, New York, who began playing and singing professionally when she was nine years old. She is well known as a unique and gifted lyricist and guitarist. Her signature sound relies on alternative tunings of the guitar strings. She is perhaps best known for her efforts to professionalize the work of performing artists. She writes, publishes, produces, and distributes all of her own music on her own record label, Righteous Babe. She even creates original artwork for her recordings. Her infectious sense of humor, agile voice, and skill at weaving a heartfelt tale have earned her a following of loyal fans. As she says of herself, "Please let it [my grave stone] read: songwriter, musicmaker, storyteller, freak."

Jack Bruce wrote music to the poem, *Boston Ball Game*, by Pete Brown. It was recorded in 1969 on Bruce's album *Songs for a Tailor*. **Listen** to the recording and notice that the two stanzas are performed at the same time. This allows the words to take on a dual meaning.

Boston Ball Game 1967

by Jack Bruce and Pete Brown

11-17   Pete Brown wrote this poem specifically to be set to music.

Boston Ball Game

I. hey when

the time comes

will you

won't you

keep your head

in the games

of the

sunshine?

II. well, hello there, baby

if you hate it

hate it so much

why not leave it

maybe try like me too

we who were your fathers

have shared out all

tomorrow's sunshine

Write a Song

When you write a song, you can express yourself through the music. Before starting to write, it is helpful to have a plan, so here are some suggestions.

Ideas

Start with one idea, such as a tonal or rhythmic pattern, or lyrics. It is very difficult to create if you have too many ideas to express. An important part of the creative process is inspiration, so you may want to select a poem, a video clip, a painting, a dance, or some other piece of art to stir up your musical thinking.

Limits

Limits require creativity because you need to find ways to deal with them. If you do not have limits you could get lost in too many options. Decide, for example, that you will write a song that

1. Uses only two chords.
2. Is thirty seconds long.
3. Has three lines of lyrics.
4. Uses one type of strum.

Form and Balance

Many songs have a specific form or structure, such as ABA or 12-bar blues. Both of these forms use repetition, which provides unity. Both forms also use contrast, which provides variety. Include both repetition and contrast in your song. Too much repetition can be boring, and too much contrast can be chaotic, so it is important to balance the two when you are working with words, rhythms, melodies, chords, and other elements.

Writing Process

Start by establishing your limits. If you want lyrics in your song, write them first. Use the skills you have acquired on the guitar to help you develop the chord progression for the song. **Notate** your musical ideas on paper, such as the chord progression over the lyrics. **Play** your song ideas as you go along. **Evaluate** your work and **identify** the parts that you find acceptable and those that need revision. Keep working on it until you are satisfied, then **perform** your song for the class.

CD-ROM Use *Band-in-a-Box* to create an accompaniment for your song.

Review and Assess

Throughout Power Strumming, you have
- learned to play the guitar and sing.
- learned a number of different chords.
- practiced different accompaniment patterns with a variety of songs.

Playing and singing the notes and rhythms and remembering the words to the songs are just the first steps of excellent music making. Real musicianship involves playing and singing beautifully, using all of the good habits that you've been practicing. It's not so important what you play; it's how well you play and sing that matters.

Review What You Learned

Review what you have studied and practiced. With your teacher, review and choose performance activities that permit you to demonstrate excellent musicianship. This will take some careful thinking on your part, but selecting the right music to perform is an important part of becoming a successful musician.

Not everyone will be able to play a rhythmic accompaniment and sing at the same time. What is most important is that you perform accurately, musically, and beautifully. Think about the songs that you enjoy and that you can play and sing well.

Song	Key	Chords	Progression
"Three Little Birds"	D major	D, G, A_7	I-IV-V_7
"Bye Bye, Love"	G major	G, C, D_7	I-IV-V_7
"God Bless the Grass"	A minor	Am, E_7	i-V_7
"Chicka Hanka"	E minor	Em, Am	i-iv
"Ain't Gonna Let Nobody Turn Me 'Round"	E minor	Em, B_7	i-V_7
"Karangatia ra"	B♭ major (capo 1)	A, D, E_7	I-IV-V_7
"The Earth Is Our Mother"	C major (capo 3)	A_5	I (power chords)
"Key to the Highway"	F major (capo 1)	E, A, B_7	I-IV-V_7

Show What You Know

With the help of your teacher, select several songs to perform in which you can do at least two of the following well.

- **Play** the accompaniment chords and strum with your thumb on the beat while your classmates sing.

- **Play** a rhythmic guitar accompaniment while your classmates sing.

- **Play** the accompaniment chords by strumming on the beat with your thumb; while a partner plays a different accompaniment rhythm and you **sing** with your classmates.

- **Play** a rhythmic guitar accompaniment as you sing with your classmates.

In choosing the songs to perform, your goal is to show all of the qualities of good musicianship. You want performances of which you can be proud; do not choose a song to perform simply because it is difficult. The goal for this assessment is quality, not difficulty.

What to Look and Listen For

Excellent musicians often record themselves so they can evaluate their own work and refine their performances. Record your performance using digital audio, cassette tape, or video tape.

Ask yourself whether all these things are true about your performance. Use this checklist to see how you're doing and to identify aspects of your playing and singing that are in need of further refinement.

Guitar

- Posture is upright and relaxed.
- Face of the guitar is perpendicular to the floor.
- Guitar is positioned so that right and left hands remain relaxed.
- Wrists are comfortably straight.
- Fingers are curved.
- Left hand fingertips contact the fingerboard.
- All strings vibrate with a clear, resonant tone.
- Accompaniment chords and rhythms are played accurately.

- Chords change in tempo.
- Dynamic levels of the chord voices (individual strings) and bass notes are balanced.
- Accompaniment is softer than the melody.
- Lengths of individual notes and strums reflect the character of the music.
- Dynamic and rhythmic changes are used to create expressive effects.

Singing

- Posture is upright and relaxed.
- Jaw and mouth are relaxed and open.
- Breath is inhaled with natural, relaxed expansion of the body.
- Tone is free, open, and even throughout range.
- Rhythm is precise and sung with inflection.
- Singing is accurate and in tune.
- Diction is clear (all words are understood).
- Dynamic and rhythmic changes are used to create expressive effects.

Let Your Voice Be Heard

Singing in Unison and Parts

"The strongest and sweetest songs yet remain to be sung."
—Walt Whitman (1819–1892)

◀ Diana Ross and the Supremes

▲ The Mamas and the Papas

Metaphors and Music

Songwriters employ imagery and descriptive language to convey their message to the singer and audience. For example, the phrase *long road* is a metaphor that means a difficult learning experience in life. What might the words *fire* and *rain* mean?

As you listen to "Faith of the Heart," identify other metaphors that help create a mood and send messages to the listener. Then sing the song.

Singing Tips

Lower voices may find it more comfortable to sing parts of this unison song an octave lower than it is written. As you listen to the recording, determine which phrases are too high for your voice, and adjust your singing plan accordingly. Treble voices and unchanged male voices will be able to sing the song as written.

Sing a long *l* on the word *long* to help accentuate the meaning of the word. To create more resonance and a warmer sound, imagine that you have a gumball in your mouth and keep that space open as you sing.

Reading Music Tips

Read the rhythm patterns in the song with rhythm syllables before you sing. Identify phrases where repeating rhythm patterns occur so that you can sing them correctly.

Knowing the Score

"Faith of the Heart" has two time signatures. The quarter note always gets one beat. Watch for the two-beat measures so that there is no hesitation between the meter changes.

Faith of the Heart

Words and Music by Diane Warren

Music MAKERS

Diane Warren

Diane Warren (born 1956) is a phenomenally productive and successful songwriter. When Warren was ten, she received her first guitar from her father. She grew up listening to Top 40 hits on the radio, including songs by Buddy Holly and the Beatles. Other songwriters who inspired her include Carole King, Leiber and Stoller, and Burt Bacharach. Warren has written dozens of songs, which have been sung by such legends as Elton John, Tina Turner, Barbra Streisand, Aretha Franklin, and Patti LaBelle. Many other artists, including *NSync, Gloria Estefan, Enrique Iglesias, LeAnn Rimes, and Aerosmith have also performed her music. Warren's songs are featured in 80 motion pictures. She has won many awards, including a star on the Hollywood Walk of Fame, and induction into the Songwriters Hall of Fame. Warren also gives back to the community. The Diane Warren Foundation provides folios, sheet music, band arrangements, and methods books for a thousand middle schools.

Listen for Meaning

Songwriters often use metaphors to send a message in lyrics. Listen to *If You Asked Me To* as sung by Patti LaBelle. What metaphors does Warren use in the song?

If You Asked Me To

by Diane Warren

11-20 **as performed by Patti LaBelle**
Celine Dion and Johnny Mathis have also recorded this popular song.

What's Happening

In elementary school, boys and girls are able to sing the same pitches. The larynx, the part of the throat that holds the vocal cords, is about the same size. During adolescence the voice changes in many ways. The larynx grows, the vocal cords get longer, and the muscles that support singing strengthen and thicken. The singing and speaking voice often becomes lower in pitch. Good singing habits developed during adolescence lead to a lifetime of healthy singing.

Female Voices

Voice changes for females are sometimes subtle. Females may experience unsteadiness or breathiness. Singing range may also temporarily shift; the higher pitches may become harder to reach, and the lower pitches may become easier.

The biggest challenge to the changing female voice is the transition between head and chest. It sometimes sounds like two different people singing. Proper breath support helps smooth the transition between the parts of the range.

Male Voices

The voice change is more obvious for males. There may be a loss of control in both speaking and singing voices. The voice may crack or shift between pitches. It will also become lower, and may feel weak or not sound at all on certain transition notes. The speed of the change also varies. Some males will not experience a voice change until high school, while a few might experience the change in upper elementary school. One thing is certain: males will experience a voice change during adolescence.

How to Get There

Good breath support allows the vocal cords to vibrate freely. Here are a few good rules for singing as the voice matures.

- **Take a good breath just before you need to sing**. You can check your breathing by placing your hands on your lowest rib and inhaling through your mouth or nose. If your ribs expand against your hands, you're filling your lungs with air.

- **Start each pitch with breath**. You can check yourself by starting on an *h* the first few times to get the breath moving. Then eliminate the *h* as you gain confidence.

- When singing in parts, **experiment with singing different parts**. Challenge yourself to switch parts on a familiar or a new song. If you sing part 1 on one song, sing part 2 on another song. Use the full range of your voice whenever possible.

Start Your Sound

Performing vocal exercises before you sing a song is a great way to prepare for singing and extend your range. Here are some exercises to get the voice moving. Notice that the first two exercises take your voice through the transition. Use proper breath support and control to produce a more even sound.

Sing this exercise using the syllables provided. Sing each pattern four times—one for each vowel sound. Connect each note to the one before it. Repeat the exercise, moving down in half steps, five more times. Your bottom note will be middle C.

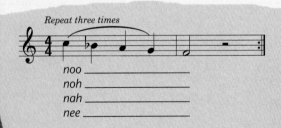

Repeat three times

noo _____
noh _____
nah _____
nee _____

Arts Connection

◄ *Oedipus' Riddle*, metal sculpture by Dick Kappel, 19

to My Voice?

Shape Your Sound

The next exercise helps start the sound. Notice that the *h* is in parentheses. Use it to help you feel the breath move as you begin. When you have done this exercise for several sessions, drop the *h* and start on the vowel.

(h)oo   (h)oo   (h)oo   (h)oo   (h)oo _____

Note This

The photograph and sculpture on this page represent the riddle of the Sphinx in the Greek myth of *Oedipus Rex*. The Sphinx asks Oedipus to name the creature that walks first on four legs, then two legs, then three legs. The answer? Man.

Singing Across the Range

This exercise opens up the bottom of the voice. Place your hand as if you were going to say the Pledge of Allegiance. Then **sing** this pattern. You should feel a "buzz" in your chest where your hand is resting.

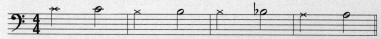

(breathe) eeyah (breathe) eeyah (breathe) eeyah (breathe) eeyah

Get the Words Out

Tongue twisters, like "Peter Piper picked a peck of pickled peppers" are often used for improving diction. **Sing** this tongue twister. Move up by half steps as you repeat. Concentrate on moving quickly through the *m* to the vowel. As you sing, focus on where the pitches resonate in your head and chest.

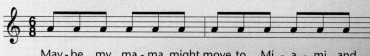

May - be   my   ma - ma   might move to   Mi - a - mi   and

may - be   my   ma - ma   might   not.

Singing Tips

Perform the syncopated rhythms in "Down by the Riverside" crisply to make your performance more interesting. **Sing** the consonants so that the words can be understood.

Reading Music Tips

Observe the rhythm in the highlighted measures. Tap, clap, and speak these rhythms, then speak the lyrics. **Describe** how measure 8 differs slightly from measures 2, 4, and 6.

Knowing the Score

Identify the 1st and 2nd endings and the repeat signs in "Down by the Riverside." Notice that the first ending indicates to repeat the refrain only.

"Down by the Riverside" is a popular African American spiritual. It is sung in schools, churches, and around the campfire. This version is arranged for treble and changed voices. **Analyze** the parts to determine which one matches your singing range best. **Listen** to the recording and determine which part has the melody. Then **sing** the arrangement, making sure the melody is slightly louder than the harmony part.

CD 11-21
MIDI 7

DOWN BY THE RIVERSIDE

African-American Spiritual
Arranged by Addie Brown

SING THROUGH THE WINTER

What comes to mind when you think of winter in your part of the country? Composer John Krumm wrote "Winter" to reflect the mood of the season in his home state of Pennsylvania.

Singing Tips

As you **sing** your part for "Winter," sing brightly and with energy so the combined parts sound clear and precise. When singing the word *gather*, make the first syllable slightly longer to give it more emphasis.

Reading Music Tips

Identify the different rhythm patterns in each of the voice parts and **compare** them.

Practice the rhythms in your part by singing with rhythm syllables.

Knowing the Score

"Winter" is best performed as three separate melodies sung at the same time. **Sing** the song straight through, and then choose the voice part that feels best in your range. Sing your part with other members of your group. Finally, beginning with part 1, add each part until all three parts are singing together.

Holiday Harmonies

Listen to another song often heard in the winter. How many vocal parts do you hear?

Carol of the Bells

by Mykola Leontovich

11-23　as performed by the Robert Shaw Chorale
This song was written to be performed *a cappella*.

CD 11-24
MIDI 8

WINTER

Words and Music by John Krumm

1
When the win - ter comes we gath - er to dance and sing to - geth - er.

When the win - ter comes we gath - er to dance our cares a - way. ___

2
Ev - 'ry - bo - dy clap hands. Ev - 'ry - bo - dy sing now.

Sing a song of glad - ness. Sing a song of joy. ___

3
Win - ter, cold win - ter blows hard a - gainst the win - dow pane.

Dance 'round the fire ___ 'til spring - time comes a - gain. ___

5

A Shona Song

"Wai bamba" is a wedding song of the Shona people who live in Zimbabwe and southern Mozambique. The harmony for "Wai bamba" is created by singing three melodies at the same time. **Listen** to the recording of the song, and describe how the three melodies are layered. Then choose the part that is most comfortable for you and **sing** with your classmates.

Singing Tips

To emphasize the rhythms of "Wai bamba," accent the b in the word bamba, and close your lips immediately on the m. Sing the i in Wai right after pronouncing the w to make the word sound like why rather than wahee.

Reading Music Tips

Notice that each melody in "Wai bamba" is written on a treble staff. Males with changed voices **sing** part 1 an octave lower than written, males with changing voices **sing** part 3 as written, and females and unchanged male voices **sing** part 2, or whichever part is most comfortable.

Zambezi River Gorge,
Victoria Falls, Zimbabwe ▶

▲ Shona students playing marimba, Zimbabwe

CD 11-26
MIDI 9

Wai bamba

Shona Wedding Song

Knowing the Score

Look at the song notation for "*Wai bamba.*"
Notice the repeat signs at the end of each
system. **Sing** your part as shown on system
1 and repeat it before going to system 2.

---

system Vocal or instrumental parts grouped by a bracket. The parts are
performed at the same time.

Arts Connection

◄ Serpentine Wedding Dancers by
anonymous Shona stone carver, 2003

6

Take a Chance

Swedish disco-pop vocal group ABBA was popular in the 1970s, and their songs are still heard today. This arrangement of their hit song "Take a Chance on Me" has two voice parts. **Analyze** the score to discover which part has the melody and which part has the harmony. Where do the two parts switch? Where are the parts sung in unison?

Singing Tips

Each time a word occurs after an eighth rest, put a slight vocal emphasis on the vowel or consonant. When singing words that are syncopated, be sure to accent the syncopated notes.

Practice part 2 at a slow tempo with the MIDI recording before performing it with the melody. Increase the tempo gradually, checking for accurate rhythms and clear diction.

Reading Music Tips

Practice the rhythm patterns in your part with rhythm syllables. Then practice singing your part with pitch syllables. Finally, add the lyrics.

Knowing the Score

Identify the *segno* 𝄋 in the music and *D.S.* for verses 1 and 2. When you see the *D.S.* instruction, skip back in the music to the *segno*. Go to the *Coda* when indicated.

Take a Chance on Me

Words and Music by Benny Andersson & Björn Ulvaeus

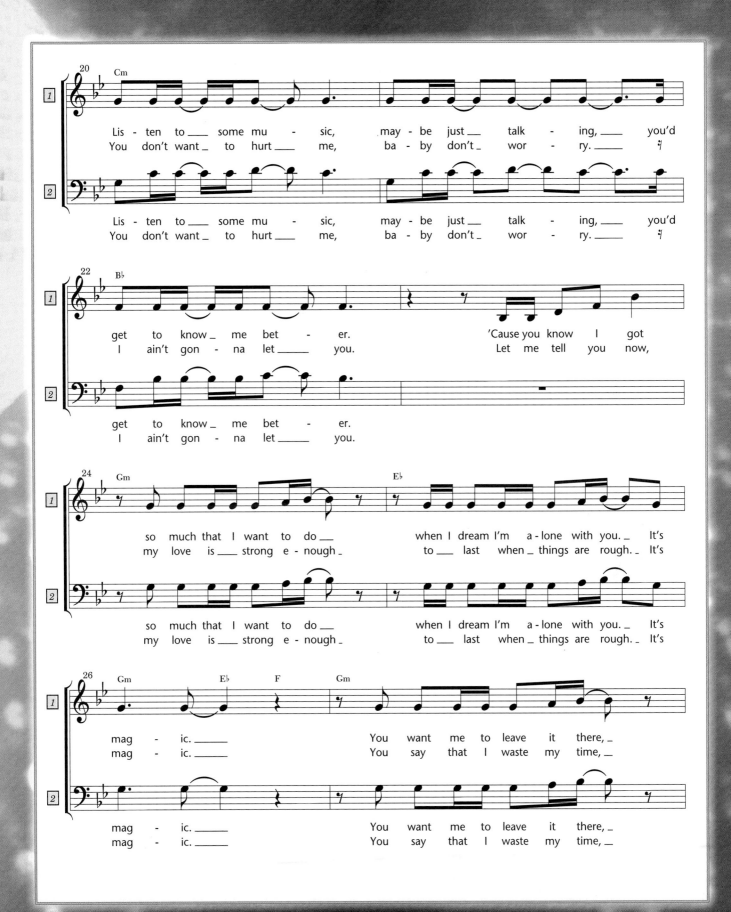

More ABBA-Inspired Sounds

Listen to *Dancing Queen*, another ABBA hit. **Compare** it to "Take a Chance on Me." What elements are the same? Which are different?

🎧 *Dancing Queen*
12-3
by Benny Andersson, Stig Anderson, and Björn Ulvaeus
as performed by the Real Group with Frida
The vocal harmonies in this version are typical of ABBA songs.

Music MAKERS ABBA

ABBA was a collaboration among four Swedish musicians—Agnetha Fältskog, Björn Ulvaeus, Benny Andersson, and Anni-Frid Lyngstad. The name ABBA is taken from the first letters of their first names. *Waterloo* was ABBA's first big hit in 1974. It was followed by a string of others including *Dancing Queen* and *Fernando*. In the late 1990s, Ulvaeus and Andersson took a number of ABBA's songs, wove a story around them, and created a hit musical, *Mamma Mia*. The musical has played in London, Toronto, New York, Melbourne, Sydney, Hamburg, and Tokyo.

At the Junction

"Tuxedo Junction" is a 1939 jazz tune written to celebrate the nightlife in Birmingham, Alabama. Glenn Miller and his orchestra made it famous with their 1940 instrumental recording. The song is considered a jazz standard today.

"Tuxedo Junction" is arranged in three parts. Part 1 is the melody and is sung by the highest treble voices. Part 2 is a harmony part arranged for a second group of treble voices. Part 3 is a countermelody arranged for changed voices.

Analyze the score to find the section that employs an echo effect. Are the parts in unison or harmony? **Sing** the arrangement with the recording, then determine the appropriate dynamics for each part.

Singing Tips

Find the half steps in your part and sing them in tune.

Notice that the bass line is a five-note pattern that repeats. Determine how many times the pattern appears in the song. Imitate the sound of a *pizzicato* string bass as you **sing** the bass line.

Reading Music Tips

There are two pitches in "Tuxedo Junction" that sound the same, but look different when written on the staff—A♭ and G♯. They are called enharmonic tones. Analyze why the two pitch spellings sound the same.

Knowing the Score

Read through your part to the 2nd ending. The music that occurs between measures 9 and 16 is called a *bridge*. *Crescendo* the ascending line at the end of the bridge to prepare the return of the main melody.

Note This

"Tuxedo Junction" has a walking bass line. This type of bass line is also found in Baroque music from the 1600s–1700s and in jazz tunes like the one in this lesson.

Tuxedo Junction

Words and Music by Buddy Feyne, William Johnson,
Erskine Hawkins, and Julian Dash
arranged by Susan Brumfield

8

Girls in Front

Girl groups have been popular for many years. How many of the groups here do you recognize?

"Light Up the World with a Song" is composed for women by Mark Patterson. Its theme of using art to create a better world is common to many songs. What movements could you add to make your performance more interesting?

Listen to the recording of the song. Then choose the part that is most comfortable for you and **sing** with your classmates.

Singing Tips

"Light Up the World with a Song" is intended to be bright and uplifting. Use crisp ending consonants and a bright tone.

Reading Music Tips

Read the song notation with pitch syllables. Notice where the harmony parts occur in the song so that you are ready to sing them.

Knowing the Score

The first eight measures of "Light Up the World with a Song" are sung three times. Follow the 1st and 2nd endings to determine when to return to the beginning.

Earth Mother Sound

Libana is a group of female musicians who research and perform women's traditional and contemporary music and dance from around the globe. **Listen** to this recording of *Yemaya*. Describe how its three melodies are layered.

Yemaya

12-6

by Marytha Paffrath
as performed by Libana

This contemporary song is written to honor the traditions of the Yoruba people of West Africa.

▲ The Spice Girls

▼The Bangles

▼The Supremes

▲ Libana

Light Up the World With a Song

Words and Music by Mark Patterson

CD 12-7
MIDI 12

f Light up the world with a song of glad-ness, shout for joy and sing all day long.

last time to Coda **1.**

Take a-way sor - row and end all sad - ness, light up the world with a song.

mp A friend may need a help - ing hand, their path may go a - stray.

2.

But e - ven in the dark-est night our song will guide the way. song.

We bring a song of hope for those who live in fear.

D.C. al Coda

mf We bring a song of peace for all the world to hear.

Coda

song. *ff* Light up the world with a song!

◀ The Indigo Girls

9

Boy Bands

The Monotones, a group of six men from New Jersey, had a hit record in 1958 with "Book of Love."

This arrangement of "Book of Love" is written in two parts for male singers. Higher voices sing part 1. Lower voices sing part 2. Be sure to observe the repeat signs as you **sing** this arrangement.

Singing Tips

To keep in tune, listen to the other singers on your voice part and keep your voice forward.

Reading Music Tips

Ledger lines are short lines going through pitches that are too high or low to fit on the regular five-line staff. As you read your part, **identify** what the ledger line pitches are. **Sing** them with pitch syllables to familiarize yourself before performing the song.

Knowing the Score

Identify the sections of the arrangement where the two voice parts sing in unison. Next, **analyze** the first six measures of the song, then find all the places where those measures repeat.

Book of Love

Words and Music by Warren Davis,
George Malone, and Charles Patrick

Oh, I won-der won-der who, who? Who wrote the book of love? ____

But who knew who?

1. Tell me, tell __ me, tell me. ___ Oh, who wrote the book of love?

I've got to know _ the an - swer. Was it some - one from a - bove?

Oh, I won-der won-der who, who? Who wrote the book of love? ____

But who knew who?

2. I _____ love __ you dar - ling, ba - by, you know I do.
3. Ba - by, ba - by, ba - by, I love you ___ yes I do.

But I've got to see this book of love, _ find out why it's true.
Well, it says so in this book of love _ ours is one that's true.

break up, but you give it just one more chance.

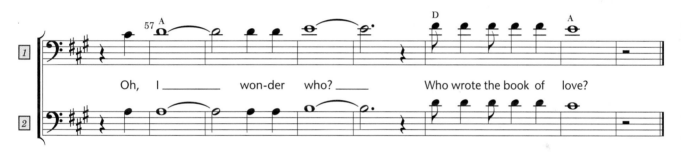

Oh, I won-der won-der who, who? Who wrote the book of love? _____

But who knew who?

Oh, I _____ won-der who? _____ Who wrote the book of love?

A cappella Boys

Listen to this *a cappella* rendition of a song in the Motown style. **Identify** the differences between this selection and "Book of Love."

Boogie Down

12-11 by Leroy Brown, Lawrence Smith
as performed by the Princeton Footnotes
This performance features a vocal soloist and quartet.

10

Song for the Season

John and Michelle Phillips, Denny Doherty, and Cass Elliot performed as the Mamas and the Papas in the 1960s. "California Dreamin'," recorded in 1966, was their first big hit.

Singing Tips

Notice that the melody is in part 3. Parts 1 and 2 echo the melody in harmony. As you sing the song, make sure the melody is more prominent than the harmony parts.

Reading Music Tips

Identify the whole and half notes in the music. Hold them for their full value when you perform. *Decrescendo* long notes during echo sections so that the echo is heard.

Knowing the Score

Identify the *segno*, the *to Coda*, the *D.S. al Coda*, and the *Coda* markings. Review the routine before you begin.

This arrangement of "California Dreamin'" is sometimes written in three parts, and sometimes in four. Identify the 4-part sections. What part will you sing? Find the instrumental section of the arrangement. Create movements to perform during the interlude.

A Beautiful Voice

Cass Elliot, or Mama Cass, as she was known to her fans, was the lead singer for many of the Mamas and Papas songs. Listen to Elliot sing another one of the group's popular songs.

Make Your Own Kind of Music

12-12 **by Barry Mann and Cynthia Weil as performed by Cass Elliot**
This song was a hit single for Cass Elliot in 1970.

ON YOUR OWN
Choose a song you have learned and create your own choreography to perform with your song.

◀ **Denny Doherty, Cass Elliot, Michelle Phillips, and John Phillips**

California Dreamin'

Words and Music by John Phillips and Michelle Phillips

The Legend Continues

The singing group Wilson Phillips was a women's trio comprised of the daughter of John and Michelle Phillips and the two daughters of Brian Wilson of the Beach Boys. Their first album contained three songs that ranked number one on the Billboard charts.

▼ Carnie Wilson, Wendy Wilson, Chynna Phillips

11

The Gift of Freedom

Freedom of speech, liberty, the right to vote, and the pursuit of happiness are a few of the most cherished rights of each citizen in the United States of America. Our constitution protects all of its citizens and guarantees multiple freedoms. Why is the singer in this song "proud to be an American?"

Singing Tips

"God Bless the U.S.A." can be performed as a two-part arrangement. Female voices sing part 1. Male voices sing part 2.

Before you begin, determine if anyone will sing the notes in parentheses in the last few measures.

Identify the phrases in this song. Take a deep breath prior to singing each phrase.

Reading Music Tips

Part 1 enters in the treble clef and part 2 enters two measures later in the bass clef. Notice that the pitches are different. **Identify** how many times in the song part 1 and part 2 sing the same rhythms.

Knowing the Score

Find the sections in "God Bless the U.S.A." that repeat, as well as the instructions that let you know when to go to the *coda*. Become familiar with these sections so you can move back and forth in the music easily.

The *coda* uses melodic and rhythmic material from the main part of the song. **Describe** how the rhythm in the last three measures of the song is different from the rhythm in measures 18–19.

Arts Connection

▼ Illustration of Flag art—Laura Stutzman, 1982

▲ Vietnam War Memorial, Washington, D.C.

God Bless the U.S.A.

Words and Music by Lee Greenwood
Arranged by Buryl Red

*Use an "h" to make the accent.

*Harmony notes are optional.

12

A Wonderful World

Composer André J. Thomas set Langston Hughes' poem *I Dream a World* to music as a tribute to the victims of September 11, 2001. It is arranged for three-part mixed chorus.

Singing Tips

The word *I*, when spoken or sung, contains two vowel sounds—*ah-ee*. This is called a diphthong. When singing the word *I*, be sure to sustain the *ah* sound as long as possible before adding the *ee* sound.

Reading Music Tips

Identify pitches in the melody for "I Dream a World" that use accidentals—sharps, flats, or naturals that do not appear in the key signature—so that you can sing them correctly.

Find the quarter-note triplet patterns in the song. These three notes are performed over two beats. Practice clapping and saying the rhythm with rhythm syllables.

Look for the measures in the song where group 1 will divide into two parts. Decide who will sing each part.

Knowing the Score

This arrangement looks a bit different from those in other lessons because it is written in octavo style. Octavos contain both the vocal and keyboard accompaniment parts on the same page. This enables singers, accompanists, and conductors to better understand how each part interacts.

CD 12-17
MIDI 16

I Dream a World

Words by Langston Hughes

Music by André J. Thomas

Of such I dream, ____ of such I dream,

Let Your Voice Be Heard

Review and Assess

Throughout Let Your Voice Be Heard, you have

- sung unison and two-, three-, and four-part music in a variety of styles.
- listened to vocal music in a variety of styles.
- learned how interesting and varied vocal music can be.

Singing notes and rhythms and remembering the words to the songs are just the first steps of excellent music making. Real musicianship involves singing with appropriate style, using all of the good habits of singing that you've been practicing. No matter what style of music you sing, *how well* you sing matters the most.

Review What You Learned

Review what you have studied and practiced. With your teacher, choose performance activities that demonstrate your excellent musicianship. Make careful choices that show your vocal skills and range. Selecting the right music to perform is an important part of becoming a successful musician.

Choose songs from this list that you like and sing well.

Song	Features
"Faith of the Heart"	unison
"Down by the Riverside"	two-part singing in gospel style
"Winter"	three-part singing in classical style
"Wai bamba"	three-part layered singing in African style
"Take a Chance on Me"	three-part singing in pop style
"Tuxedo Junction"	three-part singing in jazz style with bass ostinato
"Light Up the World with a Song"	two-part girls singing
"Book of Love"	two-part boys singing
"California Dreamin'"	three-part modified echo singing in pop style
"God Bless the U.S.A."	two-part singing in country style with extended range
"I Dream a World"	three-part singing in classical style

Show What You Know

1. Think about the songs that you enjoy and can sing well. With the help of your teacher, select several songs from the list to sing. Each one should demonstrate one of these skills.

   - Sing a unison melody with classmates and a live or taped accompaniment.

   - Sing the melody of a two- or three-part arrangement with classmates and a live or taped accompaniment.

   - Sing a harmony part in a two- or three-part arrangement with classmates and a live or taped accompaniment.

   - Sing a melody alone with a live or taped accompaniment.

   - Sing a harmony part in a two- or three-part arrangement with one person on each part.

2. Compare and contrast three song selections from the list of songs. You may also choose to review the listening selections in the module. In a two-paragraph essay, consider the following.

   - style of selection

   - number of vocal parts

   - difficulty of the melody

   - range

   - language or diction challenges

What to Look and Listen For

Excellent musicians often record themselves so they can evaluate their own work and refine their performances. Record your performance using digital audio, cassette tape, or video tape.

Use this checklist to see how you're doing and to identify aspects of your playing and singing that are in need of further refinement.

- Posture is upright and relaxed.
- Jaw and mouth are relaxed and open.
- Breath is inhaled with natural, relaxed expansion of the body.

- Tone is free, open, and even throughout range.
- Singing is accurate and in tune.
- Rhythm is precise and sung with inflection.
- Diction is clear (all words are understood).
- Dynamic and rhythmic changes are used to create expressive effects.

Sounds and Symbols

Music Theory and Fundamentals

"*Music needs to make sense, needs to have order. From what some people consider the lowest stuff— a cat in the middle of a cotton field shouting the blues, to what's considered the highest—a symphony or an opera—it has to be structured.*

—Ray Charles (born 1930)"

1 Rhythm Fundamentals

You've got your headphones on, listening to a favorite song. The steady pulse you hear is the **beat.** The combinations of sounds that are longer and shorter than the beat are **rhythms.** How do you show beats and rhythms in music? In the examples below, a **quarter note (♩)** shows a sound that lasts for one beat. A **quarter rest (𝄾)** represents silence for one beat. **Eighth notes (♫)** represent two even sounds per beat. Tap the beat while you **read** the rhythms. For more practice reading these rhythms, turn to pages F-25 and I-20.

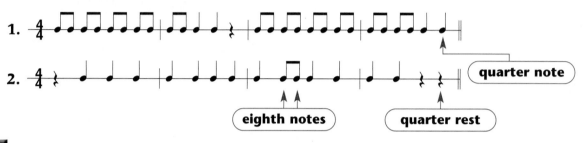

2 Meters, Measures, and More

Tap the beat as you **listen** to "The Marines' Hymn" on page C-39. Then tap the beat as you **read** this rhythm.

Read the rhythm again and emphasize the beats that have **accent marks (>).** How did the sound change?

In this music, beats are grouped in sets of two. The first beat in each set feels stronger than the second. The **time signature** shows the groupings of beats, or **meter,** of the music. The top number indicates that the beats in this example are grouped in sets of two. The bottom number indicates that a quarter note is the beat note. Each set of two beats is separated by a **bar line.** A **double bar line** indicates the end of a section. The space between bar lines is called a **measure.** Tap the beat as you **read** the rhythm.

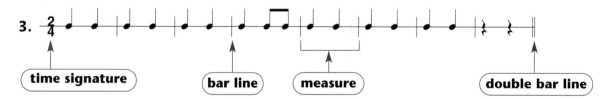

3 Conducting the Beat

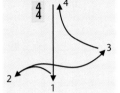

Another way to keep track of the beat is to **conduct** the music. When the time signature is ²₄, use this pattern to conduct the beat and meter. **Conduct** while you **read** the rhythm on page H-2.

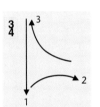

Identify the ⁴₄ time signature in the next example. What does it mean? Conduct the meter as you read the rhythm. For more practice, read similar rhythms on page F-25.

4 Meter in Three Plus Repeats

Listen to "*Gaudeamus igitur*" on page C-20, and **conduct** a three-beat pattern. **Analyze** the ³₄ time signature in the simplified rhythm below. What does it mean? **Conduct** as you **read** this rhythm.

1.

Identify measures that are the same or repeated in the music above. In notation, a **repeat sign** is used to indicate a repetition. **Identify** the repeat sign below. **Conduct** as you **read** this rhythm.

2.

repeat sign

5 Tie Two to Get a Half

Some musical rhythms are longer than a beat. For example, a sound that lasts for two beats can be notated with a **tie (⌒)** that connects two quarter notes (♩ ♩). Two tied quarter notes equal one sound that lasts for two beats. Tap the beat while you **read** the next rhythm.

1.

tie

Another way to notate one sound that lasts for two beats is to use a **half note (♩).** Tap the beat as you **read** this rhythm. Then find and **read** half notes in "Chicka Hanka" on page F-15.

half note

2.

6 And Now for the Rest

Like sounds, silences can also be longer than a beat. Two beats of silence can be written with a **half rest (-)** instead of two quarter rests. Tap the beat as you **read** the rhythm. Find more half rests in "California Dreamin'" on page G-31.

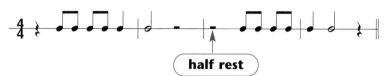

half rest

7 Dotted-Half Note and Whole Note

Observe the ties as you **read** the rhythm below. **Describe** the sound of the tied notes.

1.

One sound that lasts for three beats can also be notated as a **dotted-half note (♩.).** Tap the beat as you **read** this rhythm. Then **read** the rhythm of "I'll Fly Away" on page I-42.

2.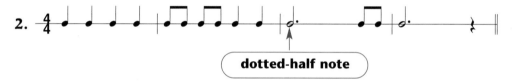

dotted-half note

Conduct as you **read** these rhythms in triple meter.

3.   4.

Solve this rhythm problem. How would you write a rhythm that lasts for four beats? You have two options—tie four quarter notes or write a single **whole note (♩ ♩ ♩ ♩ = o). Conduct** as you **read** these rhythms. Then **identify** and **read** whole notes on page F-15.

5.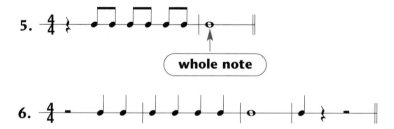

whole note

6.

H-4

 Dynamics

Listen to your favorite recording. Notice the changes in **dynamics**—the volume of the sound. In printed music, **dynamic markings** indicate that the music should be performed at different levels of loudness and softness.

pp	*pianissimo*	very soft
p	*piano*	soft
mp	*mezzo piano*	medium soft
mf	*mezzo forte*	medium loud
f	*forte*	loud
ff	*fortissimo*	very loud
————	*crescendo*	increase loudness
————	*diminuendo*	decrease loudness

Tap the beat as you **read** the rhythms. Observe and **perform** the dynamic markings in the **score,** or music notation. **Identify** and **read** the dynamics in the score on page G-40.

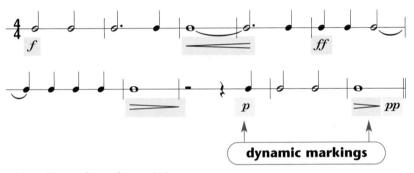

dynamic markings

Melody by Ear

Have you ever asked someone, "How does that song go?" If you have, you were probably asking them to help you remember the **melody.** The melody of a song is the arrangement of **pitches** and rhythms that makes the tune recognizable to you.

Sing the melody of "America, the Beautiful" or "The Star-Spangled Banner." On which words do the highest and lowest pitches occur? Sing again and listen for places where the melody ascends (gets higher), descends (gets lower), or stays on the same pitch.

Turn to page I-4 or I-62 to look at the notation for the song you chose. **Analyze** the melody to find the highest and lowest pitches. Look for ascending and descending parts of the melody. Find repeated pitches. Then **sing** your song again as you look at the notation.

Pitch Notation Fundamentals

Music can be notated on a group of five horizontal lines and spaces called a **staff.** Each line and space is assigned a number, starting at the bottom of the staff.

Pitches, the high and low sounds of music, appear as **notes** on the staff. The low pitches are notated at the bottom of the staff and the high pitches are notated at the top of the staff. **Ledger lines** can be added to write pitches that are higher or lower than the staff.

Line 5
Line 4 — Space 4
Line 3 — Space 3
Line 2 — Space 2
Line 1 — Space 1

Each note on the staff is assigned a letter name. Examine the letter names below to determine how many letters are used. How many As can you find? The names of the notes are determined by the **clef.** The circular line in the middle of the **treble clef** above surrounds line two and indicates that the note on line 2 is G.

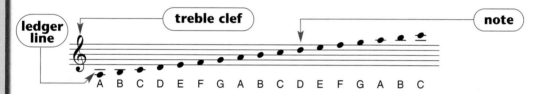

A B C D E F G A B C D E F G A B C

 mi-re-do

Sing the melody of "America" by ear. **Sing** the last three words of the song—*Let freedom ring.* Now **sing** the last three pitches—*freedom ring.* These three pitches move downward by step. Hum the pitches. Then **sing** them on the pitch syllables *mi-re-do.* Use hand signs as you **sing** this three-note melody.

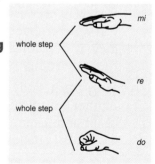

1.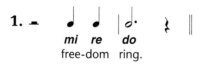

    mi   *re*   *do*
    free-dom ring.

In this melody, *do* is C. **Sing** the melody, first using hand signs and pitch syllables, and then using letter names. For a challenge, read a similar melody with *do* in a different place on page E-25.

2.

    do

12 Second or Third?

Sing *mi-re-do* using hand signs and pitch syllables. The distance, or **interval,** between *mi* and *re* is a **whole step,** or **major second.** The interval between *re* and *do* is also a major second. The interval between *mi* and *do* is a **major third. Identify** the major seconds and major thirds in this melody. Then sing the melody, first using hand signs and pitch syllables, and then using letter names.

1.

Do can be placed anywhere on the staff. In this melody, *do* is G. **Read** the melody, first using hand signs and syllables, and then using letter names. For an extra challenge, find the same melody with *do* in a different place on page I-28.

2. *do*

13 *fa* with 1st and 2nd Endings

Sing or **play** *do-re-mi* and add one more pitch. The syllable for the next highest pitch is *fa*. Use hand signs and pitch syllables to **sing** *do-re-mi-fa-mi-re-do*. The interval between *mi* and *fa* is a **half step.**

Identify the repeat signs, **1st ending,** and **2nd ending** below. When you perform the melody, sing the 1st ending, and then return to the beginning of the **phrase.** Repeat the first two measures, then skip to the 2nd ending.

Sing this melody, first using hand signs and pitch syllables, and then using letter names. For more reading practice, **sing** a similar melody with *do* in a different place on p. I-56.

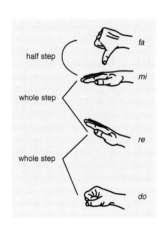

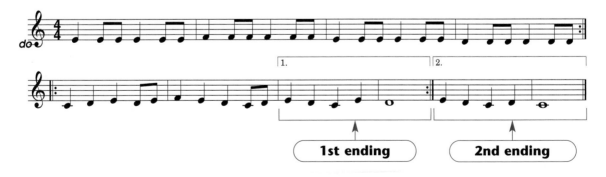

(1st ending)   (2nd ending)

14 Move up to *so*

Sing *do-re-mi-fa* using hand signs and pitch syllables. The syllable for the next highest pitch is **so.** **Sing** *do-re-mi-fa-so.* The interval between *fa* and *so* is a whole step. **Sing** the next melody, first using hand signs and pitch syllables, and then using letter names. Turn to "Rundadinella" on page I-60 for more reading practice.

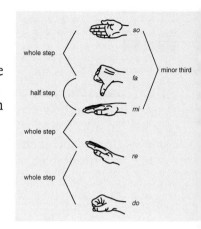

15 Intervals: 3rd, 4th, 5th

Listen as you **sing** *so-mi.* The interval from *so* to *mi* is a **minor third.** **Identify** the minor thirds in this melody. Find the major third (*do-mi*). Listen for the thirds as you **sing** this melody with hand signs and pitch syllables. For a challenge, **sing** a similar melody with *do* in a different place on page I-56.

1.

Look at the hand sign chart. **Sing** *do-so,* and then *do-fa.* These intervals are a **perfect fifth** and a **perfect fourth.** Listen for the fourth and fifth as you **sing** this melody using hand signs and pitch syllables. Then turn to page D-6 and find more fourths and fifths in a similar melody.

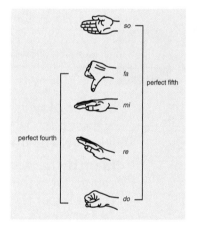

2.

16 Going Up: *la*

Sing all the pitches from *do* to *so,* and then go up one more step. The syllable for the next pitch is *la.* The interval *so-la* is a whole step. **Sing** all of the pitches from *do* to *la* and **identify** the half steps and whole steps. Then **sing** the next melody using hand signs and pitch syllables. **Read** a similar melody with *do* in a different place on page C-21.

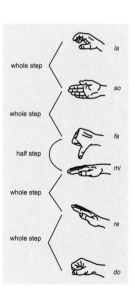

17 Transposing Practice

Do is G for the set of pitches below. **Sing** these pitches, first using hand signs and pitch syllables, and then using letter names. **Play** them on a keyboard. **Identify** the half step. How do you know where it is?

1.

Transpose the pitches to C-*do* on the staff and on the keyboard. Find C or *do*. **Sing** the pitches, first using hand signs and pitch syllables, and then using letter names. **Play** the pitches on a keyboard. **Identify** the half step.

2.

Analyze the next melody. **Identify** the half step. What other intervals can you find? **Sing** the melody, first using hand signs and pitch syllables, and then using letter names. **Play** it on a keyboard. Transpose it on your own to G-*do*. For more practice, find and **read** a similar melody in F-*do* on page I-2.

3.

18 Read the Signs

Identify the term **D.C. al Fine** in the music below. D.C. is an abbreviation for the Italian words **Da Capo.** *Da capo al fine* (dah KAH-poh ahl FEE-nay) tells the performer to go back to the beginning and end at the word **Fine.** Find the *Fine* in the music. A **final bar line** at the *Fine* also provides a clue that you have reached the end. Diagram the order of the phrases as you will perform them. Then **conduct** the beat as you **read** the rhythm.

final bar line

◆19◆ Syncopation

Two eighth notes can be written like this (♪♪) or like this (♪ ♪).
Read this rhythm.

1.

Now, listen to "Chicka Hanka" on page F-15 or *La borinqueña* on page
D-19. Both of these songs have syncopated rhythms. **Syncopation**
happens when an accented rhythm or long rhythm occurs off the beat or
on a weak beat. What does syncopation look like in written music? Tap
the beat as you **read** these rhythms. Find the syncopation. Then look for
syncopation in "Chicka Hanka" or *La borinqueña.*"

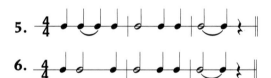

2.

3.

4.

Here is another way to write a syncopated rhythm. Tap the beat as you
read these rhythms. **Identify** the syncopation. **Compare** the sound of
these two examples. Look for syncopation in "I Dream a World" on
page G-40.

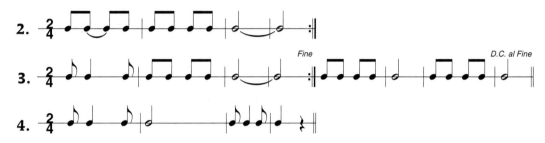

5.

6.

◆20◆ Eighth Rest

Music is sound and silence. Hum or **play** your favorite tune. Are there any
silences? You know the quarter rest and half rest—two symbols for silence.
An **eighth rest** (↱) indicates a half beat of silence in $\frac{2}{4}$, $\frac{3}{4}$, or $\frac{4}{4}$. **Conduct**
as you **read** this rhythm. Then **read** similar rhythms on page F-16.

eighth rest

21 Dotted-Quarter Notes and Anacrusis

Tap the beat as you **read** these rhythms. **Compare** the sound.

1.

2.

Another way to notate the sound of the tied rhythm is with a **dotted-quarter note (♩.).** **Conduct** the beat as you **read** the next rhythm. Determine the length or duration of a dotted-quarter note. Look for more dotted-quarter notes in "God Bless the Grass" on page F-13 and "Deep in the Heart of Texas" on page I-18.

3.

Analyze the next rhythm. What is the time signature? How many sounds occur before the first bar line? The first note is an **anacrusis,** or **upbeat,** that occurs before the first strong downbeat of the phrase. Tap the beat as you **read** the rhythm. Why is the last measure incomplete? **Read** this rhythm in "America, the Beautiful" on page I-4.

4.

22 Dotted-Quarter and Eighth Note—Backwards!

Perform one of the rhythms from the lesson above. What will happen to the sound if the rhythm is reversed and the eighth note comes before the dotted-quarter note? (♪♩.) **Identify** the new rhythm in the music below. Find the tie. **Conduct** as you **read** these rhythms. Then find and **read** similar rhythms in "Blues with a Feeling" on page I-6 and "*El rancho grande*" on page I-22.

1.

2.

23 Dotted Rhythm and Syncopation Practice

Identify the dotted-quarter and eighth note rhythms in the music below. Then **identify** the eighth and dotted-quarter note rhythms. **Conduct** as you **read** the music. Then **conduct** as you **read** these rhythms in "The Marines' Hymn" on page C-39 and "Deep in the Heart of Texas" on page I-18.

Analyze the music below to identify the dotted rhythms and the ties. **Conduct** the beat as you **read** the rhythms. Which rhythms are syncopated? For more practice, **read** similar rhythms in "Wade in the Water" on page I-64 and *"Wai bamba"* on page G-13.

24 Get Down to Low *la*

Sing this melody, first using hand signs and pitch syllables, and then using letter names. Play it on a keyboard. What is the pitch syllable for the last note of the melody? Melodies that end on *do* have a **major** tonality sound.

Analyze the next melody. It's exactly the same, except for the last note! The melody ends on **low la (la₁).** Low *la* is a minor third lower than *do*. Use the same hand sign as you did for *la* above *do*. **Sing** from low *la*, up to *mi*, and back down again. Then **sing** the melody using hand signs and pitch syllables. Melodies that end on low *la* have a **minor** tonality sound.

 la
 so
 fa
 mi
 re
 do
la₁

Show what you know by analyzing these minor melodies before you perform them. **Identify** syncopated rhythms and ties. How will you perform them? Which melody has an anacrusis? Where does the second melody end? What syllables will you sing for the starting and ending pitches of each melody? **Sing** the melodies, first using hand signs and pitch syllables, and then **play** them on a melody instrument of your choice. Turn to pages F-15 and F-16 for more minor melody reading practice.

Get Down to Low *so*

Sing *la₁-do-re-mi-so-la* and back down again. The next melody starts and ends on low *la*. **Identify** the pitch in the melody that is lower than low *la*. The syllable for this pitch is **low *so* (so₁).** Check the hand sign for low *so*. Then **sing** this melody using hand signs and pitch syllables. **Read** this melody in the song notation for "Wade in the Water" on page I-64.

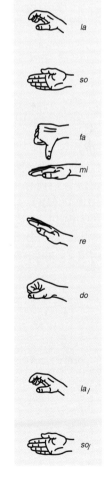

Sight Reading Practice

Practice your sight reading skills. Use this process for each example in this lesson.

First **analyze** the rhythm. What is the time signature? Are there any anacrusis notes? Practice measures with rhythms that look challenging. Then **conduct** the beat as you **read** the rhythm.

Next **analyze** the melody. Find *do*. On what pitch does the melody begin and end? Practice intervals or measures that look challenging. **Sing** the melody, first using hand signs and syllables, and then **play** it on a melody instrument of your choice.

For more practice, **read** similar melodies in the song notation on pages I-2, I-42, and G-3.

1.

2.

3.

ti̞ Time

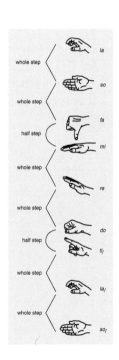

Look at the hand sign chart. **Listen** to the sound as you **sing** all of the pitches from *do* down to low *so* and back. The interval between *do* and **low ti (ti̞)** is a half step, or minor second. **Identify** low *ti* in each example, and then **sing** each melody using hand signs and pitch syllables. Find and **read** low *ti* in "God Bless the Grass" on page F-13 and "California Dreamin'" on page G-31.

1.

2.

More Minor Seconds

Listen for the half step between low *ti* and *do* as you **sing** from low *la* up to *mi* and back down. Then **listen** as you **sing** from *do* down to low *so* and back. The minor second between low *ti* and *do* has a different "feel" in each pattern. **Identify** the minor seconds in these melodies. **Sing** the melodies using hand signs and pitch syllables. What syllable did you sing on the last note of each example?

Melodies that end on *do* are usually major tonality melodies. Melodies that end on *la* are usually minor tonality melodies. **Analyze** the next two melodies. Which melody is major? Which is minor? How do you know? **Sing** the melodies. Then **play** them on a melody instrument of your choice. Find similar melodies on page F-9 and page E-18.

Practice Plus

Analyze these phrases from "The Star-Spangled Banner." What is the time signature? **Conduct** as you sing the text. What happens to your conducting and singing at the end of the first phrase?

In printed music, a **fermata** (⌒) means to prolong or lengthen a note. Another symbol in this example is a **slur** ♩ ♪ A slur indicates that pitches should be performed *legato,* or smoothly. **Identify** the slurs. Why do they occur in those places? Turn to page I-62 and **sing** "The Star-Spangled Banner," observing all slurs and the fermata.

ti on the Move

Sing the first phrase of "America, the Beautiful" from memory. Now look at the notation for this phrase. The syllable for the first pitch is *so*. **Identify** a **ti** that is higher than *so*. **Sing** the phrase using hand signs and pitch syllables. Then find the phrase on page I-4.

This phrase from "*De colores*" also includes *ti*. The phrase has a special challenge—it starts on *fa*. **Sing** the phrase using hand signs and pitch syllables. Turn to page I-14 and read the same phrase with *do* in a different place.

The Top *do*

Sing the pitches from *do* to **high *do* (*do*ˡ)** using hand signs and pitch syllables. The interval between *do* and *do*ˡ is an **octave.** **Sing** this melody using hand signs and pitch syllables. Turn to page F-23 and **sing** "*Karangatia ra,*" with *do* in a different place.

1.

Analyze the next two melodies. **Identify** *do* and *do*ˡ. Tap the beat as you **sing** the melodies using hand signs and pitch syllables. Find and **read** similar melodies with *do* in different places on pages E-25 and I-46.

2.

3.

32 The Major Scale

Find the pitch C on a keyboard. Starting on C, **sing** from *do* to *do¹* using hand signs and pitch syllables. You have just sung a **major scale.** In fact, you sang the **C major scale** because you started on the pitch C. **Analyze** the C major scale on the staff and the keyboard below. **Identify** the minor seconds. **Sing** the C major scale and then **play** it on the keyboard or a melody instrument of your choice. **Listen** for the minor seconds.

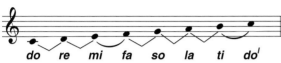 

33 Sixteenth Notes in the Rhythm

Tap a beat with your foot and **improvise** rhythms composed of quarter notes, eighth notes, and rests. If you wrote the rhythms in ⅔, ¾, or 4⁄4 the quarter note sounds for one beat. **Identify** the rhythms you know in the music below. What new rhythm symbol indicates four sounds on one beat? These are **sixteenth notes.** Tap the beat as you **read** the rhythm. Then find a similar rhythm in "Winter" on page G-11.

1.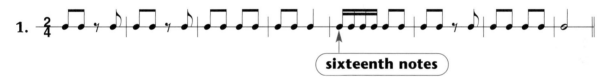

sixteenth notes

Identify the sixteenth notes in the music below. **Conduct** the beat as you **read** the rhythms. Look for more sixteenth notes on pages G-3 and I-41.

2.

3.

Now **improvise** 8-beat rhythms that include sixteenth notes.

34 One Eighth and Two Sixteenth Notes

Combine an eighth note with two sixteenth notes and you get two new rhythms:

Identify the new rhythms in the music below. Tap a steady beat as you **read** these examples. Then **read** the new rhythms on pages I-40, E-16, and G-15.

1.

2.

3.

35 Dot the Eighth Note

Analyze another pair of rhythm symbols that include eighth and sixteenth notes. These symbols include a **dotted-eighth note** and one sixteenth note. Will the sound of these rhythms be even or uneven? In which rhythm does the long sound occur first?

Identify the new rhythms in the music below. Tap the beat as you **read** the rhythms. Find and **read** these rhythms in the song notation on pages D-6 and E-16.

1.

2.

Analyze this melody before you read it. What is the time signature? Where is the new rhythm? **Conduct** as you **read** the rhythm only. **Identify** *do*. Find and practice any challenging intervals. **Sing** the melody using hand signs and pitch syllables. Then **read** a similar melody on page C-20.

3.

36 Major Review

Sing the major scale from *do* to *do'* and back again. **Listen** for the half steps, or minor seconds, from *mi* to *fa* and *ti* to *do'*. You can construct a major scale from any starting pitch if you know the formula of half steps and whole steps for a major scale. The formula is: whole-whole-half-whole-whole-whole-half. **Compare** the formula to the C major scale. **Sing** the C major scale using letter names, and then **play** it on a keyboard.

Analyze the next melody. What is the letter name of the last note? What syllable will you sing for that note? If *do* is C and the last pitch of the song is C, the song is usually in the key of **C major.** **Sing** the melody, first using hand signs and pitch syllables, and then using letter names. **Play** it on a melody instrument of your choice. **Read** a similar melody on page D-6.

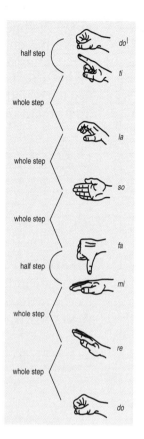

37 The Key of G Major

Find the pitch G on a keyboard and then **sing** a major scale using hand signs and pitch syllables. You are singing the **G major scale.** **Analyze** the notation for the G major scale. **Identify** the whole steps and half steps. Which pitch needs an accidental to maintain the pattern of the major scale formula? Find **F-sharp (F♯)** on a keyboard. **Play** the G major scale.

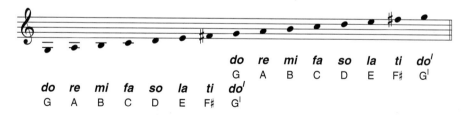

do	re	mi	fa	so	la	ti	do'
G	A	B	C	D	E	F♯	G'

do re mi fa so la ti do'
G A B C D E F♯ G'

Analyze the next melody. What is the letter name of the last note? What syllable will you sing? *Do* is G. The key of this melody is **G major.** Like the G major scale, a G major melody has an F♯ instead of F. The **key signature** at the beginning of the music indicates that the key is G and that performers should sing or play F♯. **Sing** or **play** this melody. Then **read** a similar melody on page C-20.

2.

(**key signature**)

38 Key of F Major

Apply the major scale formula of whole steps and half steps to a scale beginning on F. Use a keyboard to help you construct an **F major scale.** What adjustment must you make so that *mi-fa* is a half step? The F major scale includes a **B-flat (B♭).** On a keyboard, B♭ is the first black key to the left of B. **Sing** the F major scale. Then **play** it on a melody instrument of your choice.

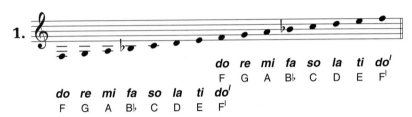

1.

do	re	mi	fa	so	la	ti	do'
F	G	A	B♭	C	D	E	F'

do	re	mi	fa	so	la	ti	do'
F	G	A	B♭	C	D	E	F'

Identify the key signature for the next melody. The B♭ in the key signature indicates that the melody is in the key of F major. Find the B♭ in the melody. **Sing** the melody using hand signs and pitch syllables, and then **play** it. **Read** this F major melody in the song notation on page I-2.

2.

39 Key of D Major

Find the pitch D on a keyboard. **Sing** a major scale, beginning on D, using hand signs and pitch syllables. The **D major scale** is written below in two different clefs. The scale in **bass clef** or **F clef** sounds one octave lower than the scale in treble clef. The two dots of the bass clef symbol show the location of the line F.

1.

(bass clef)

do	re	mi	fa	so	la	ti	do'	do	re	mi	fa	so	la	ti	do'
D	E	F♯	G	A	B	C♯	D'	D	E	F♯	G	A	B	C♯	D'

Analyze the D major scale. **Identify** the half steps. Why are there two sharps in this scale? What are the letter names of the two sharps? **Sing** or **play** the D major scale. Then **identify** the key signature for the next melody. What does the key signature tell you? **Sing** the melody and then **play** it on a melody instrument of your choice.

2.

40 Two More Keys with Sharps: A Major and E Major

Sing or **play** a major scale beginning on the pitch C, G, and then D. You can perform a major scale from any starting pitch, as long as you maintain the pattern of half and whole steps.

Solve a scale puzzle. **Notate** major scales beginning on A, and then on E. How many sharps will you need for each scale? **Sing** the scales using pitch syllables or letter names. **Play** the scales.

1.

|do|re|mi|fa|so|la|ti|do¹|
|A|B|C♯|D|E|F♯|G♯|A¹|

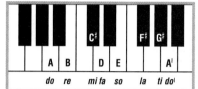

2.

|do|re|mi|fa|so|la|ti|do¹|
|E|F♯|G♯|A|B|C♯|D♯|E¹|

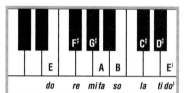

Analyze these melodies. Which is in the key of A major? The second melody is in **E major,** even though it ends on so. **Identify** the sharps in each key signature, reading left to right. Tap the beat as you **read** the rhythm. Then **sing** or **play** the melodies. **Read** similar melodies on page I-46 and I-32.

Compare the key signatures for C major and all of the keys that have sharps. What do you notice?

5.

Two More Keys with Flats: B♭ and E♭ Major

All of the scales you know so far have started on a white key of the keyboard. What happens when you begin a scale on a black key? Find the pitch B-flat on a keyboard. **Listen** as you **sing** a B♭ major scale using hand signs and pitch syllables. **Analyze** the B♭ and E♭ scales written below. **Identify** the half steps. **Sing** the scales using pitch syllables, and then letter names. **Play** the scales on an instrument of your choice.

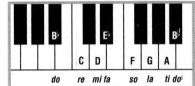

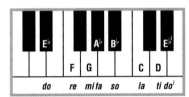

Identify the key signature of this melody, and name the flats from left to right. **Sing** or **play** the melody. Then **read** it on page C-21.

Minor Keys

When a song ends on *do*, it is usually in a major key. Songs or scales that end on *la* have a different sound. **Listen** as you **sing** from *la₁* to *la* and back. That sound is a minor tonality. The formula of half steps and whole steps for the **natural minor scale** is whole-half-whole-whole-half-whole-whole. **Listen** for the half steps as you **sing** from *la₁* to *la* again.

Every major scale has a minor scale related to it. The letter name of low *la* in a major scale is also the name of its **relative minor scale.** For example, if the major scale is G, its relative minor scale is E (low *la*). **Sing** the major and minor scales for each key signature, first using hand signs and pitch syllables, and then using letter names. Now **play** the scales. **Compare** the sound of major and minor.

C Major   A minor   G major   E minor   F major   D minor   D major   B minor   B♭ major   G minor

43 Scale Degrees

You have been singing scales and melodies using pitch syllables and letter names. Each note in a scale also has a number called a **scale degree.** In major keys, *do* is 1. **Sing** these scales, first using pitch syllables, and then using scale degrees.

1.

do	re	mi	fa	so	la	ti	do'
C	D	E	F	G	A	B	C'
1	2	3	4	5	6	7	8

2.

do	re	mi	fa	so	la	ti	do'
G	A	B	C	D	E	F♯	G'
1	2	3	4	5	6	7	8

3.

do	re	mi	fa	so	la	ti	do'
F	G	A	B♭	C	D	E	F'
1	2	3	4	5	6	7	8

Look at the minor scales below. What do you notice about the scale degrees for low *la, do, mi,* and *so?* **Sing** these natural minor scales, first using pitch syllables, and then using scale degrees.

4.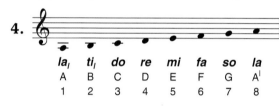

la,	ti,	do	re	mi	fa	so	la
A	B	C	D	E	F	G	A'
1	2	3	4	5	6	7	8

5.

la,	ti,	do	re	mi	fa	so	la
E	F♯	G	A	B	C	D	E'
1	2	3	4	5	6	7	8

6.

la,	ti,	do	re	mi	fa	so	la
D	E	F	G	A	B♭	C	D'
1	2	3	4	5	6	7	8

Identify the key signature of the next melody. Use hand signs and pitch syllables to **sing** the melody, and then use scale degrees. **Read** the melody in the song notation on page I-64.

7.

44 ▸ Harmonic Minor

Find the pitch A on a keyboard. **Sing** the A natural minor scale using hand signs and pitch syllables. Now **analyze** the A minor scale written below. The seventh scale degree (*so*) has been raised (sharped) one half step. This scale is called **harmonic minor. Sing** these harmonic minor scales using hand signs and pitch syllables. Use the syllable **si** for the seventh scale degree.

1.
la₁ ti₁ do re mi fa si la
A B C D E F G♯ Aᴵ
1 2 3 4 5 6 7 8

2.
la₁ ti₁ do re mi fa si la
D E F G A B C♯ Dᴵ
1 2 3 4 5 6 7 8

3.
la₁ ti₁ do re mi fa si la
E F♯ G A B C D♯ Eᴵ
1 2 3 4 5 6 7 8

Analyze these melodies. **Identify** the altered notes. What is the key of each melody? **Sing** the melodies. Then **play** them on a melody instrument. **Read** similar melodies in the song notation on pages G-11 and I-36.

4.

5.

45 ▸ Accidentals

Analyze the next melody before you perform it. **Identify** the time signature. Tap the beat as you **read** the rhythm. **Identify** the key signature and the starting and ending pitches. Find a note that has an **accidental**—a sharp or flat sign that is not in the key signature. In this melody, there is an added flat before the third scale degree near the end of the music. **Sing** *ma* for this pitch. **Sing** the melody using hand signs and pitch syllables. Then **read** a similar melody on page A-22.

1.

Identify the key signature of the next melody. What are the names of the sharps in this key? The accidental in this melody is a **natural sign.** The natural sign lowers C sharp a half step. Use the syllable **ta** for the lowered seventh scale degree. **Sing** the melody using hand signs and pitch syllables, and then **read** a similar melody on page I-28.

2.

Major Chords

Find a C, E, and G on a keyboard. **Play** these pitches simultaneously. You are playing a **chord.** The most common three-note chords are built on the first, fourth, and fifth scale degrees, which are the **roots,** or lowest pitches, of these chords.

Sing or **play** the C major scale. Now **sing** or **play** the first, third, and fifth scale degrees. This is the **I chord** or **tonic chord.** The first scale degree is the root. Scale degrees are identified with Arabic numerals (1-8) and chords are identified with Roman numerals (I, IV, V). Next, **identify** the intervals in the chord. There is a major third on the bottom and a minor third on the top of the chord. The sound of this combination of intervals is a **major chord.** **Sing** or **play** the C major chord.

1.

I chord in C major

Now build a chord starting on the fourth scale degree, or *fa.* Which pitches will you use? **Analyze** the intervals in the chord. This is the **F major chord.** Why is it also called the **IV chord** in C major?

2.

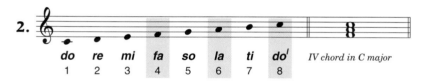

IV chord in C major

What pitches will you use to build the **V chord?** What is another name for the V chord in C major?

3.

V chord in C major

V or V₇

Analyze the chord below. It has four pitches instead of three, and it is also built using major and minor thirds. **Identify** the interval between the lowest and highest notes of the chord. This is the **V₇ chord. Sing** or **play** the V₇ chord in C major. **Compare** the sound to the V chord.

V₇ chord in C major

You can use your knowledge of chords to read chord symbols and play accompaniments for songs. **Sing** or **play** the roots of the I, IV, and V chords in C major. **Play** the chords on a keyboard. **Identify** the I and V_7 chord symbols in the music. **Play** the root of the chord indicated by the symbols on the down beat of each measure. **Play** the whole chord on each slash (/).

1.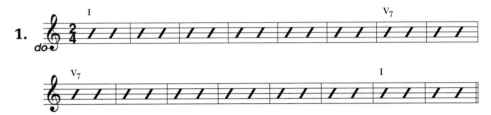

Patterns of chords are called **chord progressions.** Add a IV chord to the progression. **Sing** or **play** the root of the IV chord, low *fa*, in C major. **Play** the chord on a keyboard. **Sing** the chord roots as you **read** this progression. Then **play** the progression as an accompaniment to "The Marines' Hymn" on page C-39.

2.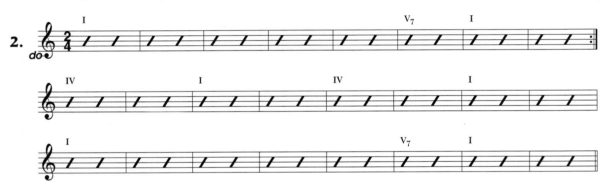

When you played the progressions above, you had to move your hand up and down the keyboard to play each chord. You can play the same chords without moving your hand as far. Stack the notes of the chords in different ways to make **inversions. Identify** and **play** the chord inversions in the chart below. **Play** the chord progressions in this lesson using these chord inversions.

3.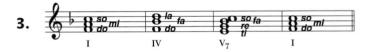

Minor Practice Plus

Review what you know about minor scales. **Sing** or **play** the D minor scales below. Which one is the natural minor scale? Which one is harmonic minor? **Identify** the scale degree that is raised in harmonic minor.

1.

la, ti, do re mi fa so la so fa mi re do ti, la,
1 2 3 4 5 6 7 1¹ 7 6 5 4 3 2 1

2.

la, ti, do re mi fa si la si fa mi re do ti, la,
1 2 3 4 5 6 7 1¹ 7 6 5 4 3 2 1

The next melody is in D minor. **Identify** the key signature and the last pitch of the melody. **Sing** or **play** measures 13–16 of the melody. Remember to use *si* for the raised 7th scale degree. **Sing** or **play** measures 1–8. Now **analyze** the melody in measures 9–12. What did you find?

3.

The melody above uses the **melodic minor scale. Sing** or **play** the entire melody. Use the syllable *fi* for the raised sixth scale degree. Notice that the sixth scale degree is raised in measure 9, but not in measure 11.

Now **analyze** the melodic minor scale. In this scale, the sixth and seventh scale degrees are raised when the scale ascends, and they are lowered when the scale descends. **Sing** or **play** the D melodic minor scale. Notice that when the scale descends, it is the same as the natural minor scale.

4.

la, ti, do re mi fi si la so fa mi re do ti, la,
1 2 3 4 5 6 7 1¹ 7 6 5 4 3 2 1

50 Tonic and Dominant Chords in Minor

You can build the **minor tonic** or **i chord** using the same technique you used to build the major tonic or I chord. Stack the first, third, and fifth scale degrees. **Analyze** the intervals of this chord. Notice that the minor third is on the bottom and the major third is on the top of the chord. **Play** the D minor chord.

1.

la₁	ti₁	do	re	mi	fa	si	la		i chord in D minor
1	2	3	4	5	6	7	8		

Remember, there are three different kinds of minor scales—natural minor, harmonic minor, and melodic minor. **Sing** or **play** these scales below to review their sounds. Because these scales are different, the **dominant** or V chord is also different. Sometimes it is major (V), and sometimes it is minor (v). Find the major and minor dominant chords for these scales. **Play** them on a keyboard.

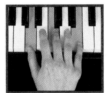

2.

| la₁ | ti₁ | do | re | mi | fa | so | la | ti | | v chord in D natural minor |

3.

| la₁ | ti₁ | do | re | mi | fa | si | la | ti | | V chord in D harmonic minor |

4.

la₁ ti₁ do re mi fi si la so fa mi re do ti₁ la₁   V Chord in D melodic minor   v Chord in D melodic minor

Identify the key of this example. **Sing** the roots of the tonic (i) and dominant (V) chords for this progression. Then **play** the chord progression as an accompaniment to *"Los reyes de Oriente"* on page I-58.

5.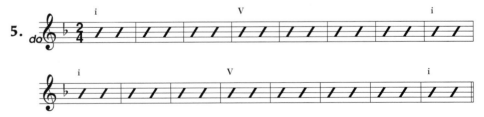

51 Subdominant in Minor

Play the tonic (i) and dominant (v or V) chords in the key of D minor. Now build the **subdominant** or IV chord. **Analyze** the scales and chords below. When is the subdominant a minor (iv) chord? When is it a major (IV) chord? **Play** both kinds of subdominant chords.

1.

la₁ ti₁ do re mi fa so la
1   2   3 4 5 6 7 8

iv chord in D natural minor

2.

la₁ ti₁ do re mi fa so la
1   2   3 4 5 6 7 8

iv chord in D harmonic minor

3.

la₁ ti₁ do re mi fi si la ti la so fa mi re do ti₁ la₁

IV chord in D melodic minor   *iv chord in D melodic minor*

Sing the roots of the tonic (i), subdominant (iv), and dominant (V₇) chords for this chord progression. Practice playing the chord inversions shown below the music. Then **play** the chord progression using the chord inversions.

4.

5.

i   iv   i

i   V₇   i

i

i   V₇   i

5.

i   mi do la₁   iv fa re la₁   V₇ mi re ti₁ si₁

Sounds and Symbols

Review and Assess

In this module you've been introduced to many music symbols and terms. Understanding these will require more than simply remembering their definitions; it requires practice using the terms to describe music in meaningful ways.

To practice using the terms you've learned, you will analyze and describe music that you already know and enjoy.

Review What You Learned

Review the elements of music you have learned in this module. These elements include:

- Rhythms from the eighth rest to whole notes.
- Pitch from so_1 to do^1
- Intervals from a half step to an octave.
- Dynamics from *pianissimo* to *fortissimo* including *crescendos* and *decrescendos.*

- Articulations including slurs and ties.
- Form including repeats and alternate endings.
- Musical notation including the staff, bar lines, clefs, and notes.
- Harmony from the I chord to minor iv chords.

Show What You Know

1. One of the best ways to develop understanding of music is to explain ideas verbally or in writing. Select two songs or listening selections referenced in this module. As you listen, write two sentences that describe the musical and expressive elements listed below.

- **timbre** What instruments and voices do you hear?

- **compositional elements** How fast is the tempo? How will you describe the rhythm? What does the harmony sound like?

- **dynamics** How are dynamics used?

- **form** How is the music organized? Are musical ideas repeated?

- **expression** What emotion does the music make you feel?

- **cultural function** When would you likely hear this music? Where would you expect this music to be performed? Does it have a public function, like a parade, or is it more personal?

In small groups, discuss each others' ideas and discover why different members of the same group came to different conclusions. The group need not agree, but the members should be able to explain their points of view.

2. Select a piece that uses dynamics to create expressive effects. Look at the music carefully. Conduct your classmates in a musical performance of the piece, using the conducting pattern that is appropriate for the meter of the piece. Make your conducting pattern larger and smaller to signal the performers to sing louder and softer. As you discuss the dynamics with the performers, be sure to use the appropriate terminology. For example, rather than asking the class to sing loudly, say "Sing *forte*." When you want the class to get louder in a phrase, make your conducting pattern larger. In rehearsal, say "*crescendo*."

Share What You Know

Select one piece from the module that is your personal favorite. Prepare a presentation for the class that will help students understand the music itself and why you like the music. Your presentation may be placed on poster board, on overhead transparencies, or on presentation software. You should start in your presentation with basic facts about the piece—title, composer, the approximate date of its composition—and explanations of how the sounds of the music convey the composer's intentions—the mood, the emotion, the picture, or idea. Be sure to include in your presentation the four aspects of music description that you've used before: the actual sounds that make up the music (timbre); the organization of the sounds (melody, rhythm, harmony, form, tempo, dynamics); the emotional effects that the sounds elicit from the listener; the cultural function of the music. In your presentation, you should play excerpts from the piece to illustrate your points.

Performance Anthology

"I have to create.
I have to dig in the earth;
I have to make something grow;
I have to bake something;
I have to write something;
I have to sing something;
I have to put something out.
It's not a need to prove anything.
It's just my way of life."

—Bette Midler (born 1945)

▲ Mariachi band

Ring and Sing
America

"America" and other patriotic songs celebrate pride in our nation and the freedoms we enjoy. **Sing** the verses of "America." Think about the freedoms that are most important to you.

CD 13-1
MIDI 17

America

Words by Samuel Francis Smith

Traditional Melody

1. My coun - try! 'tis of thee, Sweet land of lib - er - ty,
2. My na - tive coun - try, thee, Land of the no - ble free,
3. Let mu - sic swell the breeze, And ring from all the trees

Of thee I sing; Land where my fa - thers died,
Thy name I love; I love thy rocks and rills,
Sweet Free - dom's song; Let mor - tal tongues a - wake,

Land of the Pil - grims' pride, From ev - 'ry ___
Thy woods and tem - pled hills; My heart ___ with ___
Let all that breathe par - take. Let rocks ___ their ___

moun - tain - side Let _____ free - dom ring!
rap - ture thrills Like _____ that a - bove.
si - lence break, The _____ sound pro - long.

Bells or Chimes

Perform this accompaniment for "America" using bells or chimes. Find your assigned notes in the song notation. **Identify** the notes that will ring for an entire measure.

Inspiring Scene, Inspiring Song

The lyrics for "America, the Beautiful" were originally written as a poem in 1893 by Katharine Lee Bates. The poem was set to several melodies. The melody we know today was written by Samuel Ward for another song. What do the lyrics of the song mean to you?

Sing "America, the Beautiful."

ON YOUR OWN

Find a patriotic poem and create a melody for it. You can also write additional lyrics for Samuel Ward's melody.

CD 13-3

America, the Beautiful

Words by Katharine Lee Bates

Music by Samuel A. Ward

Bb   F   F7   Bb

1. O beau - ti - ful for spa - cious skies, For am - ber waves of grain,
2. O beau - ti - ful for Pil - grim feet, Whose stern im - pas - sioned stress
3. O beau - ti - ful for pa - triot dream That sees be - yond the years

Bb   F   C7   F7

For pur - ple moun - tain maj - es - ties A - bove the fruit - ed plain!
A thor - ough - fare for free - dom beat A - cross the wil - der - ness!
Thine al - a - bas - ter cit - ies gleam, Un - dimmed by hu - man tears!

Bb   F   Bb Bb7

A - mer - i - ca! A - mer - i - ca! God shed His grace on thee
A - mer - i - ca! A - mer - i - ca! God mend thine ev - 'ry flaw,
A - mer - i - ca! A - mer - i - ca! God shed His grace on thee

Eb   Bb   (N.C.)   F7   Bb

And crown thy good with broth - er - hood From sea to shin - ing sea!
Con - firm thy soul in self con - trol, Thy lib - er - ty in law!
And crown thy good with broth - er - hood From sea to shin - ing sea!

Chicago, Illinois, one example of an alabaster city. ▶

Voices

Analyze this harmony part for "America, the Beautiful." Look for patterns in the rhythm and in the melody. Find the accidentals. What do they mean? Practice the harmony part, then **sing** it while others sing the melody.

Harmony

do

1. O beau - ti - ful for spa - cious skies, For am - ber waves of grain, ___
2. O beau - ti - ful for Pil - grim feet, Whose stern im - pas - sioned stress ___
3. O beau - ti - ful for pa - triot dream That sees be - yond the years ___

5

For pur - ple moun-tain maj - es - ties A - bove the fruit - ed plain! ___
A thor - ough-fare for free - dom beat A - cross the wil - der - ness! ___
Thine al - a - bas - ter cit - ies gleam, Un - dimmed by hu - man tears! ___

9

A - mer - i - ca! A - mer - i - ca! God shed His grace on thee ___
A - mer - i - ca! A - mer - i - ca! God mend thine ev - 'ry flaw, ___
A - mer - i - ca! A - mer - i - ca! God shed His grace on thee ___

13

And crown thy good with broth - er - hood From sea to shin - ing sea!
Con - firm thy soul in self con - trol, Thy lib - er - ty in law!
And crown thy good with broth - er - hood From sea to shin - ing sea!

Conduct a 4-Beat Pattern

Conductors show performers the beat, meter, tempo, and dynamics of music by moving their hands in specific patterns. Look at the time signature of "America, the Beautiful."
Conduct a 4-beat pattern. What tempo will you choose for your performance? How and when will you change your movements to show the performers how loudly or softly to sing? Practice conducting this pattern. Then take turns leading your group.

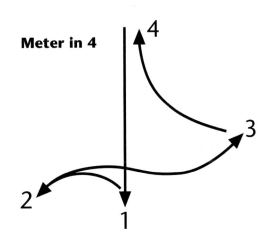

Meter in 4

4

3

2

1

I've Got the Blues

Have you ever felt sad or lonely? Some people might say that you have "the blues." The blues, an American song form, is also a song style that expresses a melancholy state of being. The blues style has had a major influence on popular music styles in the United States.

Follow the song notation as you **listen** to "Blues with a Feeling."
Analyze the chords to discover the blues progression.

CD 13-5

Blues with a Feeling

Words and Music by Walter Jacobs

Swing style

1. Blues with a feel-ing, that's what I have to-day. ___
2. What a lone-some feel-ing, when you're by your-self. ___

Blues with a feel-ing, that's what I have to-day. ___ I'm gon-na
What a lone-some feel-ing, when you're by your-self. ___ When the

find my ba-by, if it takes all night and day. 3. Well, you
one that you're lov-in' has gone a-way and left.

know I love you, ba-by, I won-der the rea-son why? You told me you loved me, ba-by, and you

left me here to cry. ___ Blues with a feel-ing, that's what I have to-day, __ I'm gon-na

find my ba-by, if it takes all night and day.

Voices

Analyze these vocal harmony parts. **Identify** the part that uses the fewest pitches. Choose the part that fits your voice the best. Then **sing** the harmony parts for "Blues with a Feeling."

Keyboards

Look at page E-32 in Keys and Chords. Review the chords and their positions for "Blues with a Feeling." Then **play** the song using those chords.

Guitars

Review the information on page F-26 in Power Strumming. Practice the chords. Decide whether you will play standard or power chords. Then **play** "Blues with a Feeling" with your chosen chord style.

Bass

Identify the repeated patterns in this bass part. Practice the patterns you find. Then **play** this bass part to accompany "Blues with a Feeling."

PRO TIPS

How do blues musicians stay and play together when performing? They watch and listen to each other. As you perform "Blues with a Feeling," watch and listen to your fellow ensemble members to keep your group together.

Winds

This soprano recorder part uses only a few pitches. Check the fingering for each note. Then **play** while a partner **sings** the song. When you are familiar with how the part fits the melody, **improvise** your own part using the same pitches.

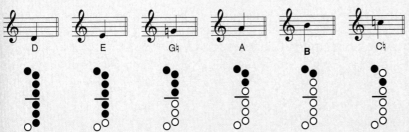

D   E   G♯   A   B   C♯

Recorder

Swing style

On Your Own

Many people have blues music in their personal music collections. Look for other blues selections at home and compare them to "Blues with a Feeling."

Ride the Rhythms

A typical music ensemble in Venezuela and Colombia is the *llanera* [yah-NE-ra] ensemble. The *arpa llanera*, or traditional harp, serves as leader and is supported by several types of small, guitar-like instruments. Rattles called *capachos* are the only percussion instruments. These groups commonly play the *joropo*, a music and dance style of the high plains of Colombia and Venezuela.

"*Canto del agua*" is a song from Venezuela in *joropo* style. Follow the chord changes as you **listen** to "*Canto del agua*." Then **sing** the song in harmony.

Note This

The lyrics of the song probably refer to the Orinoco River, which divides the areas of lower elevation from the higher grasslands of Venezuela.

CD 13-7

Canto del agua
(Song of the Water)

English Words by Alice Firgau

Joropo from Venezuela

1. Es un can-to ma-ña-ne-ro _____ a la o-ri-lli-ta _____ del rí-o. _____ Es un can-to ma-ña-ne-ro _____ a la o-ri-lli-ta _____ del rí-o Que te va di-cien-do, ne-gra, tá-pa-me que ten-go frí-o. Que te va di-cien-do, ne-gra, va-ma-nos a e-na-mo-rar. _____

1. You can hear me sing _ a love song _____ as I stand be-side _ the riv-er. _____ You can hear me sing _ a love song _____ as I stand be-side _ the riv-er. In the ear-ly morn-ing hours, _ feel-ing cold, I sing _ and shiv-er. In the ear-ly morn-ing hours, _ feel-ing cold, I sing _ and shiv-er. _____

2. Ay yai yai es - ta no - che yo ____ me voy,
2. Ay yai yai for to - night I'll roam ____ the dunes,
3. Ay yai yai yo no sé lo que ____ me pa - sa,
3. Ay yai yai when I'm there out by ____ the sea,

Ay yai yai a pa - sear - me en - tre ____ las du - nas,
Ay yai yai by the light of the ____ full moon. ____
Ay yai yai cuan - do es - toy cer - ca ____ del mar. ____
Ay yai yai there's a spell comes o - ver me. ____

Ay yai yai prés - ta - me, ne - gra, ____ tus o - jos, prés - ta -
Ay yai yai stay by me, dear one, ____ I need you close to
Ay yai yai stay by me, dear one, ____ I need you close to

me, ne - gra, ____ tus o - jos, por - que se es - con - de ____ la lu - na.
me, dear one, ____ Your eyes will lead the way for me, ____ my dear one.
me, dear one, ____ Your eyes are bright - er

second time Fine   **7**   D.S. al Fine

se es - con - de ____ la lu - na.
than the wan - ing moon - light.

Guitars

Review the Em and Am chords on page F-14 and the B₇ chord on page F-16 in Power Strumming. Then practice this strumming pattern.

Play "Canto del agua" by playing the chord progression shown in the notation, using this strumming pattern.

▲ Orinoco River, Venezuela

Winds

Recorder and flute add a lyrical line to the accompaniment. **Play** this part during the introduction, the interludes, and the *Coda*.

Bass

Play this bass part on any bass instrument. If you are using a multi-timbral keyboard, choose a bass guitar, cello, or other bass sound.

Percussion

Play this maracas part with small, even shakes. Begin playing during the introduction and continue throughout the song.

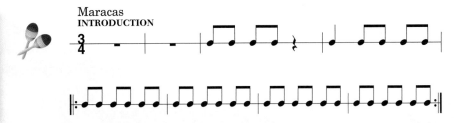

Mallets

This xylophone pattern adds harmony to the song. Practice the part carefully. Then **play** it while you listen to the recording. You may also separate the harmony into two parts to play with a partner.

Moon and Water

Listen to this folk tune from Venezuela. **Compare** it to "*Canto del agua.*" In what ways are they similar?

🎧 ***Luna hermosa (Beautiful Moon)***

13-12 Folk tune from Venezuela
as performed by Los Guayaki
This song features syncopated melodic patterns.

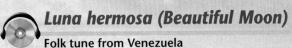

◀ Couple dancing the *joropo*

Capachos ▶

Color in Culture

"De colores" is a famous song from the sixteenth century. It is now a familiar song in Spanish-speaking cultures all over the world. Sing *"De colores"* in harmony.

CD 13-13
MIDI 19

De colores

English Words by Alice Firgau

Folk Song from Mexico
Arranged by Rick Bassett and Buddy Skipper

De _____ co - lo - res, _____ de co - lo - res se vis - ten los
When _____ the mead - ows, _____ when the mead - ows burst forth in the

cam - pos en la pri - ma - ve - ra, _____
cool, dew - y col - ors of spring - time; _____

De _____ co - lo - res, _____ De co - lo - res son los pa - ja -
When _____ the swal - lows, _____ When the swal - lows come wing - ing in

ri - tos que vie - nen de a - fue - ra, _____
clouds of bright col - ors from far off; _____

De _____ co - lo - res, _____ De co - lo - res es el ar - co i - ris que ve - mos lu - cir, _____
When _____ the rain - bow, _____ when the rain - bow spreads rib - bons of col - or all o - ver the sky _____

y por e - so los gran - des a - mo - res de mu - chos co - lo - res me
Then I know why the splen - dors of true love are great, and their col - ors, the

1.
gus - tan a mí. _____
best ones of all. _____

2.
gus - tan a mí. _____
best ones of all. _____

Keyboards

Review how to play a keyboard accompaniment for "*De colores*" on page E-14 of Keys and Chords. Then **play** your part while the rest of the class sings the song.

page E-14

Guitars

Guitars are often used to accompany "*De colores.*" Practice this strumming pattern. Then use that pattern to **play** "*De colores*" following the chord symbols in the song notation.

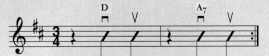

> ### Note This
>
> "*De colores*" is the anthem of the United Farm Workers of America. The UFW is a union that was founded in California by Cesar E. Chavez.

Bass

The bass part for "*De colores*" can be played on a *guitarrón*, a string bass, a bass guitar, a piano, or a multitimbral keyboard. **Analyze** the music and look for patterns. Then **play** with the song.

Mariachi Style

For a *mariachi* style performance of *"De colores,"* add trumpets and violins to the musical ensemble.

Take It to Heart

"Deep in the Heart of Texas" is one of the most beloved songs of Texas, the Lone Star State. Follow the notation as you listen to the recording. Notice that the song contains two chords—F and C₇.

CD 13-18

Deep in the Heart of Texas

Words by June Hershey

Music by Don Swander

Guitar capo 1:

The stars at night are big and bright, Deep in the heart of Tex - as; _____

The prai - rie sky is wide and high, Deep in the heart of Tex - as. _____

The sage in bloom is like per - fume, Deep in the heart of Tex - as; _____

Re - minds me of the one I love, Deep in the heart of Tex - as. _____

◀ McDonald Observatory, Davis Mountains, Texas

Keyboards

Review how to play "Deep in the Heart of Texas" on page E-22 of Chords and Keys. Review the F and C₇ chords before accompanying the song.

Voices

Practice this descant for "Deep in the Heart of Texas."
Then **sing** it while others sing the song. You can also
play this part on a C wind instrument.

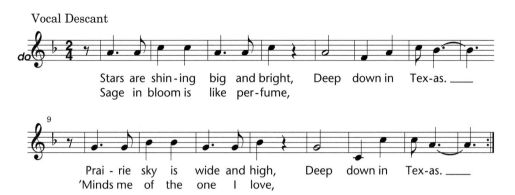

Vocal Descant

Stars are shin-ing   big and bright,   Deep   down in   Tex-as. ____
Sage in bloom is   like per-fume,

Prai - rie sky   is   wide and high,   Deep   down in   Tex-as. ____
'Minds me of the   one   I love,

Guitars

You can play an accompaniment for "Deep in the Heart
of Texas" on guitar. Review these chords.

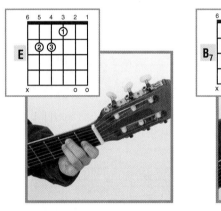

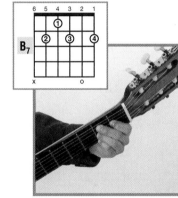

Place a capo at fret 1.
Play a down-down-up
guitar strum as
shown on page F-16
in Power Strumming.
Follow the chord
symbols in the
notation to play
"Deep in the Heart
of Texas" with the
vocal part.

Bass

Play this bass part. Notice that it outlines
the chord roots. The first four measures may
be repeated as an introduction.

Bass

"*Dok djampa*" is a song about the national flower of Laos, the white jasmine frangipani, which represents purity and simplicity. The song has great significance to the people of Laos.

Listen to "*Dok djampa.*" Then **play** the ensemble on the next page with the recording. You may choose to **sing** the melody or to play the violin part.

CD 13-20

Dok djampa
(Jasmine Flower)

English Words by Alice Firgau

Folk Song from Laos

Glockenspiel

Flute/Recorder

Violin

Cello

Woodblock

Triangle

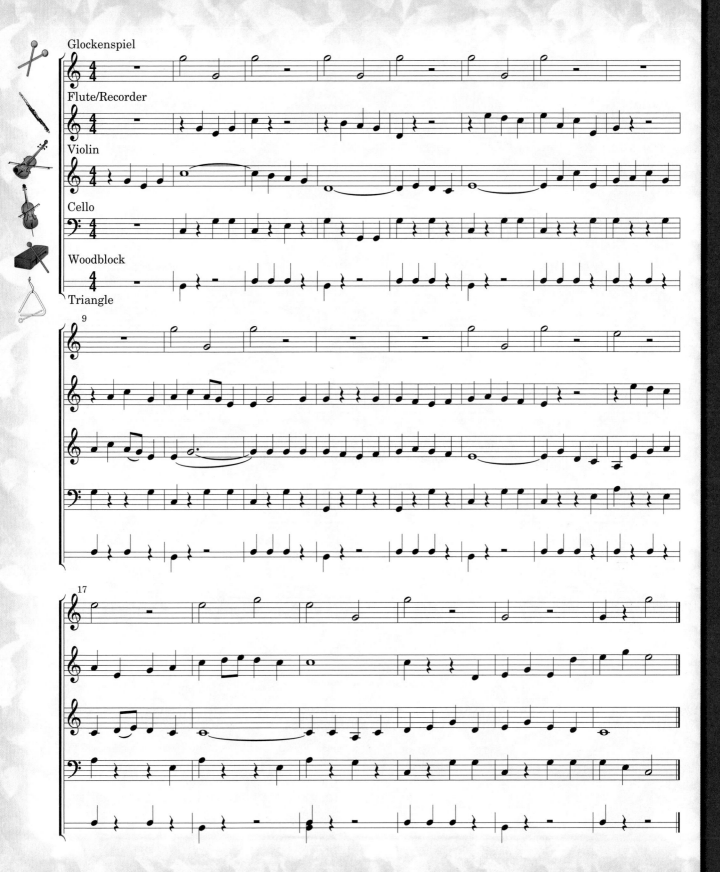

8

DOWN AT THE RANCH

"*El rancho grande*" is a longtime favorite Mexican American song. **Listen** to "*El rancho grande*" and follow the song notation to find the chord changes.

CD 13-24

El rancho grande

(The Big Ranch)

English Words by Alice Firgau

Music by Silvano R. Ramos
Arranged by Buddy Skipper

VERSE

G   C   D₇

A - llá en el ran-cho gran-de, A - llá don-de vi - ví - a, _____
Out yon-der on a prai-rie, The ranch where I was liv - ing, _____

D₇   G

Ha - bía u-na ran-che - ri - ta, Que a-le-gre me de - cí - a, Que a-le-gre me de - cí - a: _____
I heard a pret-ty cow-girl, Who hap-pi - ly was sing-ing, Who hap-pi - ly was sing - ing: _____

REFRAIN

G   D₇   G

Te voy ha - cer   tus cal - zo - nes, Co - mo los u - sa el ran - che - ro;
A pair of chaps   I will make you, Just like the ones for a ranch-er;

G   D₇   G

Te los co - mien - zo de la - na, Te los a - ca - bo de cue - ro.
With wool and leath - er I'll make them. Oh, do please give me your an-swer.

Listen to *Los machetes*. Although the tempo is very fast, you can hear the guitar accompaniment playing on the off beats.

Los machetes

by Mariachi Vargas de Tecalitlan

13-28 *Los machetes* is from a collection of dances considered by many Mexican Americans to be one of the best *mariachi* recordings of all time.

Guitars

Play this guitar part for the song. Practice the pattern of the basic thumb-strum pattern, but omit the thumb. Count *one-and-two-and* as you play on *and*, or the second half of each beat. Playing on the off beats is very common for the guitar parts of a *mariachi* ensemble.

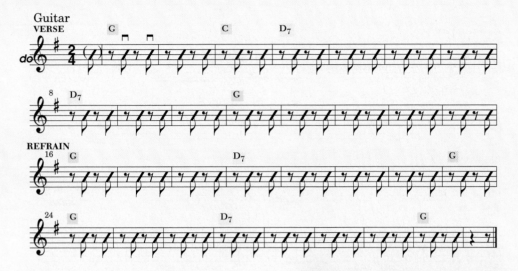

Bass

Add a bass part to "*El rancho grande.*" The bass plays on the beat so that the guitar and bass alternate. Practice the bass and guitar parts together until both players are secure. Do not wait for the other player to play first. Rely on your own sense of timing so that the tempo remains steady.

PRO TIPS

If you play this bass part on bass guitar, dampen the string to make a short sound in one of two ways. Stop the string with your plucking hand, or relax your fretting finger off the fingerboard while still touching the string.

Mariachi

Add a trumpet part to "El rancho grande." If no trumpet players are available, the part may be played on an electronic keyboard in the key of G. Before playing, **read** through the notation and locate the markings that indicate the two types of **articulation** you will use.

Read the notation in the violin part. **Compare** it to the trumpet part. Violins and trumpets often play parallel thirds in *mariachi* music. Again, review how to play the articulation shown in the music. Practice your part with the trumpet, and then add the bass and guitar parts to complete the ensemble.

Compare the rests in the trumpet and violin parts to the melody of the song. Notice that the trumpet and violin often play in the rests of the melody. This alternation of song and instrumental accompaniment is typical of *mariachi* music. When you play, adjust your dynamics to other instruments and voices.

---

articulation The manner in which notes are joined in succession. For example, *staccato* and *legato* are types of articulation.

Keyboards

"*El rancho grande*" uses I, IV, and V$_7$ chords in G major.
Practice playing these chords.

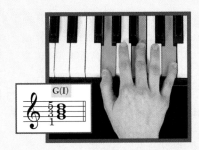

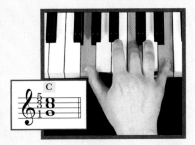

Now **play** "*El rancho grande*," following the lead sheet below.
Notice that you play the same rhythm as the guitars.

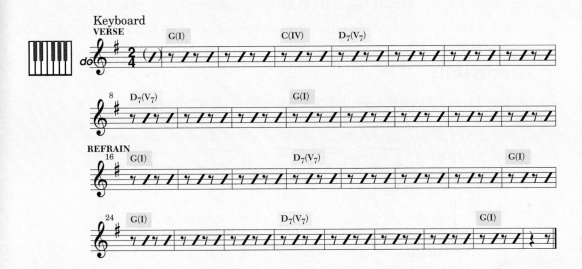

Arrange It

Create your own arrangement of "*El rancho grande*."
Make the following decisions.

- How many verses will we play?
- Will we sing the song in English or Spanish or both?
- Shall we play the melody on an instrument for a verse?
  Which instrument will we use?
- Will we include the violin and trumpet parts during all verses
  or just some verses?
- What dynamics and tempo will we use?

Work with your classmates to make these choices. Then **play**
"*El rancho grande*" for a class performance.

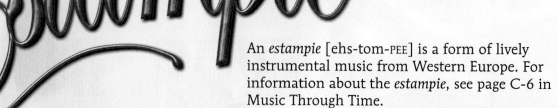

9

Estampie

An *estampie* [ehs-tom-PEE] is a form of lively instrumental music from Western Europe. For information about the *estampie*, see page C-6 in Music Through Time.

An *estampie* consists of short repeating solo phrases with 1st and 2nd endings that are like refrains. A percussion ostinato plays throughout. Here is a possible order.

- Percussion ostinato introduction.
- Eight-measure solo.
- 1st ending - Refrain 1.
- Eight-measure solo.
- 2nd ending-refrain 2.
- Repeat the routine with new eight-measure solos

The music you will play is taken from *La tierche estampie real*, found on page C-6.

How will you know which percussion ostinato to play with the solos and first and second endings?

Percussion

Practice these percussion ostinatos. **Play** with a classmate.

PRO TIPS

During the solos, members of your class can play the tambourine or drum parts, or they may improvise an accompaniment. Experiment with a different small percussion instrument.

Solo Time!

Choose one of these solos to **perform** between the Refrains.

Mallets, Strings, and Winds

Read the refrains below. Choose the part you wish to play. Then select an instrument from the choices given. Practice your part alone. Then **play** your part with two other classmates playing the other parts. Experiment with various instruments. Consider timbre, range, and how long the pitch rings. Which instrument groupings do you prefer?

Practice this refrain next. When you are comfortable with Refrain 2, practice Refrain 1 and Refrain 2 in succession. Then **play** the *estampie* with your classmates, following the typical order.

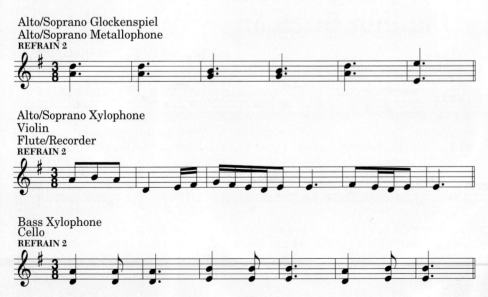

10

Sing of the Sunset

"It is a well-known fact that the folk singer attaches far more importance to the words of his song than to its tune..."

—Cecil J. Sharp (English Folk Songs, Some Conclusions, 1907)

"Every Night When the Sun Goes In" is a folk song from the southern Appalachian Mountains. People in the region are descendants of Scottish, Irish, English, Welsh, German, and French immigrants who crossed the Atlantic Ocean 200 years ago. People of African and Cherokee heritage also lived in the southern Appalachians. Many songs from this region are passed on through **aural tradition.**

Listen to "Every Night When the Sun Goes In." What pitch do you hear that is unusual?

CD 14-1

Every Night When the Sun Goes In

Folk Song from the Southern Appalachians

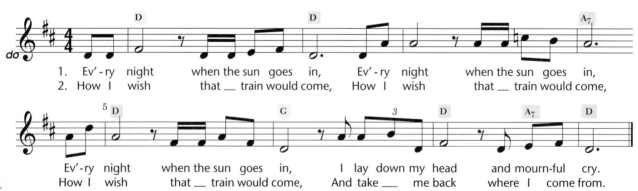

1. Ev'-ry night when the sun goes in, Ev'-ry night when the sun goes in,
2. How I wish that __ train would come, How I wish that __ train would come,

Ev'-ry night when the sun goes in, I lay down my head and mourn-ful cry.
How I wish that __ train would come, And take __ me back where I come from.

Voices

Sing the melody of "Every Night When the Sun Goes In" as an echo.
Look at the score below to see how the echo begins.

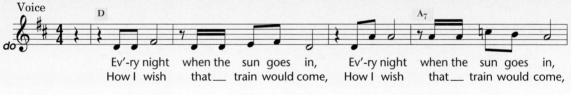

Ev'-ry night   when the   sun goes   in,   Ev'-ry night   when the   sun goes   in,
How I wish   that__ train would come,   How I wish   that__ train would come,

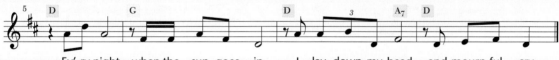

Ev'-ry night   when the   sun goes   in,   I lay down my head   and mourn-ful   cry.
How I wish   that__ train would come, And take __ me back   where I   come from.

Another Version

Listen for the variations in pitch and rhythm in
Every Night When the Sun Goes Down.

Every Night When the Sun Goes Down

arranged and adapted by Sylvia Fricker
14-3   as performed by Ian & Sylvia
Note the blues style of this rendition.

ON YOUR OWN

"Every Night When the Sun Goes In" is just one example of a song handed down through aural tradition. Research other favorite songs to discover their origins.

▲ **Sunset over the Great Smoky Mountains**

Winds

Play these pitches on a soprano recorder.

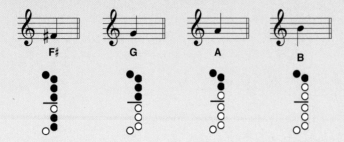

Clap the rhythm of the recorder part below to discover the syncopated rhythm. Now **play** the part, articulating the syncopations clearly.

Analyze the rhythm of this flute part. **Identify** and practice the phrases with dotted rhythms and a triplet. Then **play** this part to accompany the song.

Keyboards

"Every Night When the Sun Goes In" uses a I-IV-V$_7$ chord progression in D major. Review this chord progression on page E-14 of Keys and Chords. Then **play** the song, following the chord symbols in the song notation.

Guitars

"Every Night When the Sun Goes In" uses just D, G, and A$_7$ chords. Review the chords used in this progression on page F-4 of Power Strumming. Then **play** the song with the strumming pattern of your choice. Follow the chord symbols in the song notation.

Mallets

Perform an instrumental version of "Every Night When the Sun Goes In." If you are playing melody set up your instrument with F♯ and C♮.
Perform the melody on various instruments before deciding which you prefer. Extend your performance by playing the ensemble as written, followed by soloists improvising for eight measures, and then playing the ensemble again.

Voices • Percussion • Keyboards • Guitars • Bass • Mallets • Mariachi • Bells or Chimes • Winds • Strings

11

Island Music

"*Guantanamera*" is a well known song that is heard in many countries. The title refers to Guantanamo Bay near Havana, the capital city of Cuba. The words are from a poem by José Martí, Cuba's national poet. What message is Martí sending?

CD 14-4

Guantanamera

Words by José Martí, adapted by Julián Orbón
English Words by Aura Kontra

Music by José Fernández Díaz
Music adapted by Pete Seeger and Julián Orbón

REFRAIN

Guan - ta - na - me - ra, gua - ji - ra, Guan - ta - na - me - ra.

(Melody)

Guan - ta - na - me - ra, gua - ji - ra, Guan - ta - na - me - ra.

VERSE

1. Yo soy un hom - bre sin - cer - o   De don - de cre - ce la pal - ma;
1. I'm just a man from the is - lands   Born in the shade of the palm tree.
2. Mi ver - sos es de un ver - de cla - ro,   Y de un car - mín en - cen - di - do.
2. My words are spo - ken sin - cere - ly   And ring with hope for to - mor - row.

Yo soy un hom - bre sin - cer - o   De don - de cre - ce la pal - ma;
I'm just a man from the is - lands,   Born in the shade of the palm tree.
Mi ver - sos es de un ver - de cla - ro,   Y de un car - mín en - cen - di - do.
My words are spo - ken sin - cere - ly   And ring with hope for to - mor - row.

Y an - tes de mor - ir - me quie - ro   E - char mis ver - sos del al - ma.
In - spired to tell of my long - ing,   I'll leave my sto - ries be - hind me.
Mi ver - sos es un cier - vo heri - do   Que bus - ca en al mon - te am - par - o.
I speak of life and its pro - mise.   I know its joy and its sor - row.

REFRAIN

Guan - ta - na - me - ra, gua - ji - ra, Guan - ta - na - me - ra.

Guan - ta - na - me - ra, gua - ji - ra, Guan - ta - na - me - ra.

3. Con los pobres de la tierra
Quiero yo mi suerte echar.
Con los pobres de la tierra
Quiero yo mi suerte echar.
El arroyo de la sierra
Me complace más que el mar.   Refrain

3. I choose the poor as my people
And share their dreams and their troubles.
I choose the poor as my people
And share their dreams and their troubles.
I'd rather lose ev'ry comfort
Than turn away from their struggles.   Refrain

A Different Version

Listen to another version of *Guantanamera*. What is different about this recording?

Guantanamera

by José Fernandez Díaz
14-8   **as performed by Celia Cruz**
The vocal rhythms in this version are very syncopated.

Keyboards

Play this I-IV-V$_7$ chord progression on keyboard.

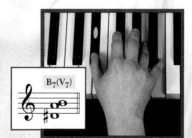

Then follow the chord symbols in the song notation to **play** "*Guantanamera*."

Celia Cruz ▶

Bass

This bass part consists of the roots of the chords in "Guantanamera."
Choose a bass instrument and then **play** your part with the recording.

Guitars

In order to accompany "Guantanamera," you will need to know how to
play three chords—E, A, and B₇ chords. Review how to play these
chords below.

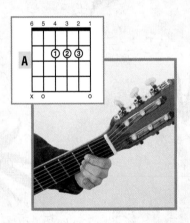
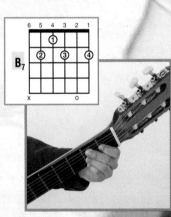

Now practice this strumming pattern. Refer to page F-16 in Power
Strumming to learn how to play it.

Practice the strumming pattern with the
chord changes until you are able to strum
the chord changes smoothly. Then **play** a
guitar accompaniment, following the chord
symbols in the song notation on page I-32.

Percussion

This percussion part can be played throughout "*Guantanamera*." Choose an instrument and practice the rhythms for that instrument. **Identify** markings that indicate stroke direction (D=down, U=up) or which drum head to hit (H=high, L=low). Work with three classmates to **play** the ensemble parts together. Listen to each other to maintain a steady tempo and to balance the parts. Stop just before the *Coda*.

Winds

Play these parts on a soprano recorder or any C instrument. Play the second line whenever the refrain begins. Note that this part is not played during the verse.

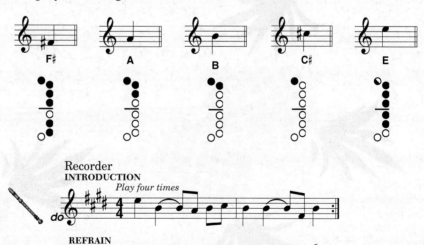

12

Eight Days of Chanukah

"*Hanuka, Hanuka*" is a song for the Jewish holiday of Chanukah. This song is written in Ladino, the traditional language of Sephardic Jews living in Spain.

Listen to the song and follow the notation. Where do the rhythm patterns repeat?

Hanuka, Hanuka

Words and Music by Flory Jagoda

VERSE

1. Ha - nu - ka, Ha - nu - ka, O - cho __ di - yas de fe - li - si - ta.
1. Ha - nu - ka, Ha - nu - ka, eight days of joy __ for __ Ha - nu - ka.

Ha - nu - ka, Ha - nu - ka, O - cho __ di - yas de fe - li - si - ta.
Ha - nu - ka, Ha - nu - ka, eight days of joy __ for __ Ha - nu - ka.

REFRAIN

lai lai lai lai lai lai lai lai lai lai lai lai lai lai lai lai lai lai lai lai lai

lai lai lai lai lai lai lai lai lai lai lai lai lai lai lai lai lai

2. Hanuka, Hanuka,
   Ocho diyas de kantar.
   Hanuka, Hanuka,
   Ocho diyas de kantar.
   Refrain

3. Hanuka, Hanuka,
   Ocho diyas de bailar.
   Hanuka, Hanuka,
   Ocho diyas de bailar.
   Refrain

4. Hanuka, Hanuka,
   Ocho diyas di guzar.
   Hanuka, Hanuka,
   Ocho diyas di guzar.
   Refrain

2. Hanuka, Hanuka,
   Eight days of singing for Hanuka.
   Everyone sing, let voices ring.
   Eight days of singing for Hanuka.
   Refrain

3. Hanuka, Hanuka,
   Eight days of dancing for Hanuka.
   Raise arms high, let feet fly.
   Eight days of dancing for Hanuka.
   Refrain

4. Hanuka, Hanuka,
   Eight happy days of Hanuka.
   Play, dance and sing, let voices ring.
   Eight happy days of Hanuka.
   Refrain

Percussion

Read these percussion parts. Then select an instrument and **play** one of the parts as your classmates play the other parts. **Listen** to how the rhythm patterns interweave as you play.

Mallets

Analyze these mallet instrument parts. Notice that the alto metallophone plays the introduction and the bass xylophone plays the song accompaniment. Choose an instrument and practice your part. Then **play** to accompany *"Hanuka, Hanuka."*

Move On

Create a movement to perform with *"Hanuka, Hanuka."* **Move** in a circle, using movements similar to a grapevine step or hora. Then **perform** your dance while others sing and play the song.

13

Singing – for the Fun of It

People of many countries and cultures sing when they make music. **Listen** to "I Shall Sing." Then **sing** it with the recording.

CD 14-13

I Shall Sing

Words and Music by Van Morrison

VERSE
Guitar capo 3:

1. I shall sing, ___ sing my song, _ be it right, ___ be it wrong. _
heart, ___ with my soul, _ for the young, _ for the old. ___

In the night, ___ in the day, _ an-y-how, ___ an-y-way. _ I shall sing:
When I'm hap-py, when I'm low, _ when I'm fast, ___ when I'm slow. _ I shall sing:

REFRAIN

La la la la la la la la, La la la la la la la la, La la la la la la la ___ la la la ___ la.

La la la la la la la la, La la la la la la la la, La la la la la la la ___ la la la ___ la.

3   1.   2.   *Repeat and fade*

2. With my   La la la la la la la la,

La la la la la la la la, La la la la la la la ___ la la la ___ la.

Voices

Analyze this harmony part for "I Shall Sing." Is it higher or lower than the melody? Practice the harmony part. Then **sing** it while others sing the melody.

1. I'll sing my song, _   or be it wrong. _
2. or with my soul, _   or for the old. _

or in the day, _   sing an - y - way. _   I shall sing:
or when I'm low, _   or when I'm slow. _   I shall sing:

Keyboards

This song uses only two chords—F(I) and $C_7(V_7)$. Review I and V_7 chords on page E-3 of Keys and Chords. Then **play** the song, following the chord changes in the notation on page I-38.

Guitars

Review how to play "I Shall Sing" on page F-17 in Power Strumming. Place a capo at fret 3. Then follow the capo chords in the notation on page I-38.

Percussion

Choose one of these percussion parts. Practice speaking your part using rhythm syllables. Then **play** your part for "I Shall Sing" while your classmates **sing** the song and **play** the other accompaniment parts.

Maracas

Cabasa

Bongo

"Singing is an instinctive activity of the human species, a natural means of self-expression common to all races."

—The Oxford Companion to Music

Bass

Before playing this part on a bass instrument, learn the harmony by
singing the chord tones using letter names. Then **play** this part on a
bass instrument of your choice.

Winds

Practice these pitches on a soprano recorder.

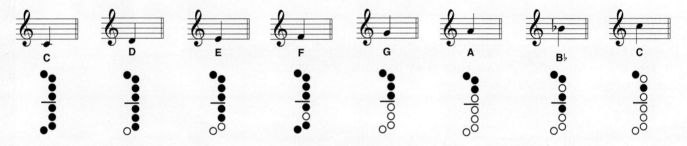

Play this recorder duet during the refrain. Which part has the melody?
Notice that both parts have the same rhythm. These parts may also be
played on other C instruments such as flutes or xylophones.

PRO TIPS

Practice the recorder
harmony parts at a slow
tempo to begin. Increase
the tempo as your playing
becomes more fluent.

Mallets

Select a mallet instrument part. **Analyze** the rhythms and **identify** the pitches. Then **play** your part while others sing with the recording.

Another Rendition

Listen to this famous South African vocalist perform *I Shall Sing*. How is Makeba's version different from the song recording on page I-38?

I Shall Sing

14-15

by Van Morrison as performed by Miriam Makeba

This rendition demonstrates variety in the rhythms and melody.

◀ Miriam Makeba

On the Wings of Song

"I'll Fly Away" is the most famous song written by Albert E. Brumley, a gospel musician and song writer from Oklahoma and Missouri. Brumley thought of the song in 1929 while he was picking cotton and wishing he could "fly away" from the field. He wrote down his song in 1931 and sent it to a publisher the following year. **Listen** to "I'll Fly Away." Then **sing** it in harmony. How many different styles do you hear in this recording?

 CD 14-16

I'll Fly Away

Words and Music by Albert E. Brumley
Arranged by Buryl Red

1. Some glad morn-ing when this life is o'er, I'll fly a - way;
2. When the shad-ows of this life have grown,
3. Just a few more wea - ry days and then,

Oh, I'll fly a - way, fly a - way, fly a - way;

To a home on God's ce - les - tial shore, I'll fly a - way,
Like a bird from pris - on bars has flown,
To a land where joys shall nev - er end,

Oh, __ I'll fly a - way, fly a - way, fly a - way,

Hear It Again

"I'll Fly Away" has become one of the most recorded gospel songs of all time. It has been performed by gospel groups and bluegrass bands. It has been printed in hymnals and used in the musical score for the film *O Brother, Where Art Thou?* **Listen** to another version of this famous song. Which style do you prefer? Why?

I'll Fly Away

by Albert E. Brumley
14-18 as performed by the Trumpeteers
This *a cappella* version is written for all male voices.

Voices

Singers often improvise vocal harmonies to gospel songs they know. Sometimes, repeated words or phrases, such as *I'll fly away*, are the best places for vocal harmony. **Improvise** harmony on the *I'll fly away* phrases.

▲ Albert E. Brumley

I'll fly a-way, O glo-ry, I'll fly a-way;

I'll fly a-way fly a-way, O glo-ry, I'll fly a-way, fly a-way in the morn-ing;

When I die, Hal-le-lu-jah, by and by, I'll fly a-way.

When I die, Hal-le-lu-jah, by and by, Oh, _ I'll fly a-way, fly a-way, fly a-way.

Keyboards

"I'll Fly Away" uses only I, IV, and V_7 chords in the key of G. Review these chords. Then **play** the song, following the chord changes in the notation.

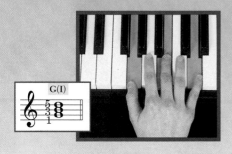
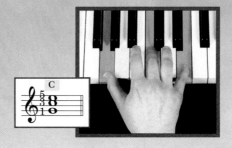

Guitars

You can play an accompaniment for "I'll Fly Away" with three chords—G, C, and D_7. Review how to play these chords on pages F-3, F-4, and F-8 of Power Strumming. Use these for strumming patterns and **play** the song, following the chords in the notation.

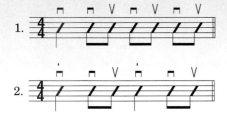

Scene from *O, Brother, Where art Thou?*, 2000 ▶

Bass

Analyze the bass part for "I'll Fly Away." Look for repeated measures and repeated patterns. **Play** the bass part to accompany the song.

Winds and Strings

Create an instrumental version of "I'll Fly Away" by playing the melody and vocal harmony parts on instruments. For example, play the melody below using recorder, flute, or violin.

You may also **improvise** ornaments to the melody using these pitches below. The fingerings shown are for soprano recorder.

15

A Bayou Rhythm Gumbo

"Jambalaya" is a song full of references to Cajun cooking and life in Louisiana. Listen to "Jambalaya." What words are new to you?

CD 14-19

Jambalaya
(On the Bayou)

Words and Music by Hank Williams

VERSE

1. Good-bye, Joe, me gotta go, me oh my oh.
2. *Thi-bo-daux, Fon-tain-eaux,* the place is buzz-in'.

Me gotta go pole the *pi-rogue* down the bay-ou.
Kin-folk come to see Y-vonne by the doz-en.

My Y-vonne, the sweet-est one, me oh my oh.
Dress in style and go hog wild, me oh my oh.

Son of a gun, we'll have big fun on the bay-ou.

REFRAIN

Jam-ba-la-ya and a craw-fish pie and fi-let gum-bo,

'Cause to-night I'm gon-na see my *ma cher a-mi-o.*

Pick gui-tar, fill fruit jar, and be gay-o,

Son of a gun, we'll have big fun on the bay-ou.

. . . I walked through my childhood believing everyone enjoyed the pleasure of preparing and consuming jambalaya, crawfish bisque, and stewed okra."

— Marcelle Bienvenu

Percussion

Create a percussion ostinato. Here is an example. Practice speaking the words in rhythm before playing with instruments.

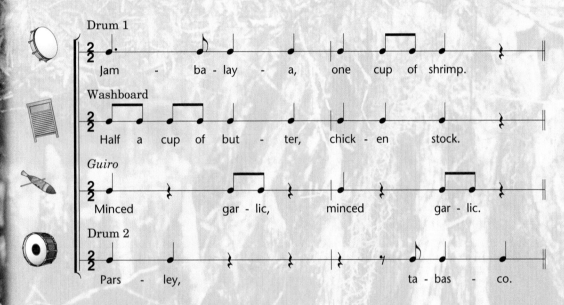

You can also combine portions of two lines to create a percussion gumbo, like this.

Note This

Here are some definitions of words in the song text that might be unfamiliar to you.

A **pirogue** is a dugout canoe that is propelled by the driver standing at the end and pushing a pole to the river bottom.

A **bayou** is a sluggish stream that meanders through marshes.

Jambalaya is a creole dish made of seafood, meat, and spices.

Crawfish pie is a casserole made of crayfish.

Ma cher ami(o) is French for "my dear friend."

Voices

Add this alto part during the second and fourth phrases of the verse of "Jambalaya." Practice the part to see if it fits your voice range. Then **sing** this part or the melody with the rest of the class.

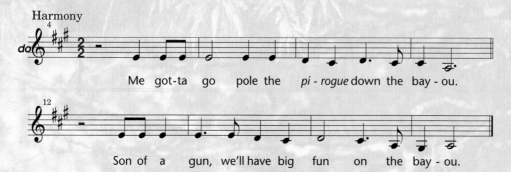

Harmony

Me got-ta go pole the *pi-rogue* down the bay-ou.

Son of a gun, we'll have big fun on the bay-ou.

Winds

Challenge yourself with this countermelody to play during the refrain. **Play** it on flute or recorder while the rest of the class sings the refrain.

Countermelody
REFRAIN

Mallets

"Jambalaya" can also be accompanied by a mallet ensemble. Choose a part to learn. Practice your part separately until you can play it comfortably. Then **play** your part with the other mallet parts.

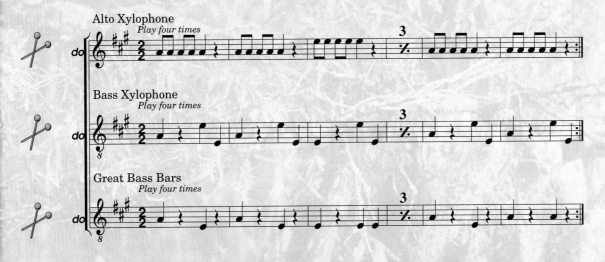

▲ Jambalaya

16

"*La golondrina*" is a well known Mexican song that is often performed in *mariachi* style. Read the lyrics. What is the meaning of "*La golondrina*"?

Listen to "*La golondrina*." **Analyze** the chord changes. What instrumentation do you hear in the recording?

 CD 15-1

La golondrina

(The Swallow)

Spanish Words by Martinéz de la Rosa
Based on a French poem by Niceto de Zamaçois
English Words by Aura Kontra

Music by Narciso Serradell

¿A - dón - de i - rá _____ ve - loz y fa - ti - ga _____ da,
Oh, where, oh, where _____ has sum - mer's swal - low flown, _____

la go - lon - dri _____ na que de a - quí se va? _____
So swift in flight, _____ yet wear - y and a - lone? _____

O si en el vien _____ to se ha - lla - rá ex - tra - via _____ da
Oh, should the wind _____ y skies lead her a - stray, _____

bus - can - do a - bri _____ go y no lo en - con - tra - rá. _____
she'll nev - er find _____ a place where she can stay. _____

Jun - to a mi le _____ cho le pon - dré _____ su ni _____ do,
As I lie sleep _____ ing she'll re - turn to me safe - _____ ly;

en	don	- de	pue	- da	la	es - ta	- ción___	pa -	sar.___
Here,	she	can	lin	- ger	till	morn-ing	calls	her a	- way.___

Tam	- bién	yo es	- toy___		en	la	re - gión___	per - di - do,
I,	too,	have	wan	-	dered,	leav - ing	home far	be - hind___ me;

¡Oh!	cie	- lo	san	- to y	sin	po -	der	vo - lar.___
Since	I'm	not	free, ___		I	know	I'm here	to stay.___

Guitars

Practice these chords.

To play a guitar part for "*La golondrina*," place your capo at fret 3. The A, D, and E$_7$ chords will sound like C, F, and G$_7$. Using the capo will also make your guitar sound like a *vihuela*, a traditional *mariachi* instrument. **Play** a bass-strum-strum pattern, following the chord symbols in the song notation.

Note This

The *guitarrón* replaced the harp in *mariachi* ensembles. The harp was harder to hear and not very portable for the strolling style of *mariachi*.

▲ *Mariachi band*

Bass

Play this bass part on an acoustic or electric bass. The bass part is usually played by the *guitarrón*, a large guitar-like instrument that keeps the beat and highlights the chord changes.

Note This

Olvera Street in Los Angeles, houses the famous *La Golondrina* restaurant, one of the first to serve Mexican food in the city. Strolling musicians sing this song every night.

Mariachi

Add a trumpet part to the accompaniment for an authentic *mariachi* sound. Note the staccato articulations.

Continue the trumpet part on Page I-53 ▶

Play a *mariachi* violin part. Use short, firm bow strokes for repeated notes, and one long bow for slurs. **Listen** for the contrast between long and short bow strokes.

Notice how the violin and trumpet parts trade off musical lines, which is another characteristic of *mariachi* music.

17

Sing Together

"Lift Ev'ry Voice and Sing" was composed by two brothers, composer John Rosamond Johnson and poet James Weldon Johnson. Nearly a century later, it is considered by some to be the African American "national anthem." **Sing** "Lift Ev'ry Voice and Sing" in the octave that is best for your voice.

◄ J. Rosamond Johnson   James Weldon Johnson ►

CD 15-6
MIDI 20

Lift Ev'ry Voice and Sing

Words by James Weldon Johnson   *Music by J. Rosamond Johnson*

1. Lift ev - 'ry voice and sing, till earth and heav - en ring,
2. Ston - y the road we trod, bit - ter the chas - t'ning rod

Ring with the har - mo - nies of lib - er - ty.
Felt in the days when hope un - born had died.

Let our re - joic - ing rise high as the lis - t'ning skies,
Yet with a stead - y beat have not our wea - ry feet

Let it re - sound loud as the roll - ing sea.
Come to the place for which our fa - thers died.

Sing a song full of the faith that the dark past has taught us;
We have come o - ver a way that with tears has been wa - tered;

Sing a song full of the hope that the pres-ent has brought us;
We have come tread-ing our path through the blood of the slaugh - tered;

Fac - ing the ris - ing sun of our new day be - gun,
Out from the gloom - y past, till now we stand at _____ last

Let us march on till vic - to - ry _____ is won.
Where the white gleam of our bright star _____ is cast.

Move with the Rhythm

Create a body percussion ostinato for "Lift Ev'ry Voice and Sing." Begin by stepping to the beat. Here is how the beat would look in notation.

Clap this rhythm while you step to the beat. **Perform** the rhythm as you sing the song.

The next two rhythms are challenging! Choose one of these patterns to clap as you step the beat.

Percussion

Enhance your performance of "Lift Ev'ry Voice and Sing" by adding percussion instruments. Transfer the patterns you practiced above to a percussion instrument of your choice, or **create** your own percussion ostinato. What instruments will you choose? Why? What rhythms will you play?

18

The Lion Sleeps Tonight

"The Lion Sleeps Tonight" was originally recorded in 1939 by South African singer-songwriter Solomon Linda. He recalled a boyhood episode of chasing lions away from cattle. Pete Seeger and the Weavers began performing the song in the 1950s. A pop group called the Tokens made it a number one hit in 1961. **Listen** for the South African influences in the recording of "The Lion Sleeps Tonight."

CD 15-8

The Lion Sleeps Tonight

(Wimoweh) (Mbube)

Words and Revised Music by George David Weiss,
Hugo Peretti, and Luigi Creatore

REFRAIN
Guitar: capo 3

Wim - o - weh, o - wim - o - weh, o - wim - o - weh, o - wim - o - weh, o -

wim - o - weh, o - wim - o - weh, o - wim - o - weh, o - wim - o - weh,

Fine

VERSE

1. In the jun - gle, the might - y jun - gle, the li - on sleeps to - night. _
2. Near the vil - lage, the peace - ful vil - lage, the li - on sleeps to - night. _
3. Hush, my dar - ling, don't fear, my dar - ling, the li - on sleeps to - night. _

D.C al Fine

In the jun - gle, the qui - et jun - gle, the li - on sleeps to - night. _
Near the vil - lage, the qui - et vil - lage, the li - on sleeps to - night. _
Hush, my dar - ling, don't fear, my dar - ling, the li - on sleeps to - night. _

Keyboards

Learn how to play a keyboard part for "The Lion Sleeps Tonight" on page E-8 in Keys and Chords. Then **play** the accompaniment while others sing the song.

Note This

Mbube (pronounced MM-boo-beh) is the Zulu word for lion. The Zulu *uyimbube* on the original recording was interpreted as *ah-wimoweh* by English-speaking musicians.

Guitars

"The Lion Sleeps Tonight" uses just three chords. Refer to page F-5 in Power Strumming to review these chords. Then **play** the song, following the chord changes in the song notation on page I-56.

Voices

Sing a harmony part for "The Lion Sleeps Tonight." **Listen** to the voices on the recording. Then choose the part that best suits your voice.

INTRODUCTION

Wim-o-weh   Wim-o-weh   Wim-o-weh   Wim-o-weh, Wim-o-weh

REFRAIN

Wim - o - weh, a - wim - o - weh, a - wim - o - weh a - wim - o - weh, a

wim - o - weh, a wim - o - weh, a wim - o - weh a wim - o - weh, a

Move to the Beat

Listen to the recording of "The Lion Sleeps Tonight" and **create** a movement for the song. **Move** and **sing** at the same time.

19

Three Kings' Day

"*Los reyes de Oriente*" is an *aguinaldo* (carol) sung to commemorate the festival of the Three Kings. Listen to the melody and harmony voices in "*Los reyes de Oriente*," and then sing the song.

CD 15-10
MIDI 21

Los reyes de Oriente
(The Kings from the East)

English Words by Aura Kontra

Aguinaldo from Puerto Rico

De tie - rra le - ja - na ve - ni - mos a ver - te,
From a dis - tant land, we come in ad - o - ra - tion,

Nos sir - ve de guí - a la es - tre - lla de O - rien - te.
Fol - low - ing a star, a star of fas - ci - na - tion,

¡Oh, bri - llan - te es - tre - lla que a - nun - cias la au - ro - ra,
Shin - ing star so bright, till dawn you rule the night, _____

No me fal - te nun - ca tu luz bien - he - cho - ra!
Nev - er cease to guide us with your kind - ly light. _____

Keyboards

You will need to play the Dm and A₇ chords to accompany "*Los reyes de Oriente*" on keyboard. Review minor chords on page E-19 of Keys and Chords. Read the chord progression in the song notation, and then **play** an accompaniment to the song.

Percussion

Listen to the recording of "*Los reyes de Oriente*" and **identify** the sound of the *guiro*. **Play** one of the percussion ostinatos below. Decide whether you will play during the song, the interludes, or both.

Bass

Analyze this bass part. What patterns can you find in the music? Practice the bass part using a keyboard, *guitarrón,* or another bass instrument. Then **play** the bass part to accompany "*Los reyes de Oriente.*"

Winds

Identify the interludes and *Coda* as you listen to "*Los reyes de Oriente.*" Practice this recorder duet slowly with a partner. Then **play** the duet during the interludes and *coda* of "*Los reyes de Oriente.*"

20

'Round & 'Round

Rundadinella is a lively tune from the seventeenth century. The melody is an eight-measure theme that repeats. **Listen** for the repeating theme in *Rundadinella*.

Rundadinella

15-15 Seventeenth century melody as arranged by Carl Orff

The round is sung by a chorus of boys' and men's voices.

Read the notation of *Rundadinella* below. **Identify** the *staccato* markings. Then **sing** with the recording.

▲ Carl Orff

Run - da, run - da, run - da, run - da - di - nel - la, Run -

da, run - da, run - da, run - da - di - nel - la.

Bass

Analyze the bass part below. Practice the part on any bass instrument. Then **play** it with the recording.

Bass

Mallets

Play *Rundadinella* on mallet instruments. Use soprano and alto xylophones to play the unison melody. Replace all the B bars with B♭ bars on both xylophones.

Soprano/Alto Xylophone

Now work with a classmate to **play** an accompaniment. Notice that you will need two mallets.

Soprano Xylophone 1 & 2

Alto Xylophone 1 & 2

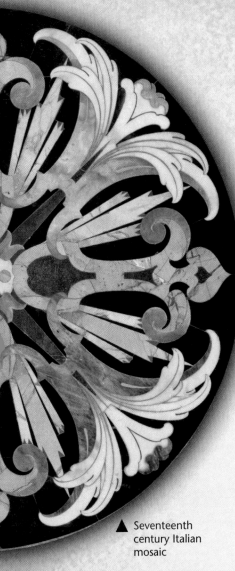

▲ Seventeenth century Italian mosaic

Play and **sing** *Rundadinella*. Choose one of the instrument parts to play with your classmates. Then **play** *Rundadinella* together as an ensemble.

Dance for Fun

These steps were used in dances from the seventeenth century. Perform this movement while others **play** the piece.

- Step on the right foot, and with the weight still on the right, hop on the same foot.
- Repeat with left foot.

Move slowly at first for practice, and then speed up to match the tempo of the recording. Keep your knees flexible as you hop.

21

Our National Anthem

Most nations have songs or anthems that represent their country at special events and ceremonies. The Congress of the United States declared "The Star-Spangled Banner" the national anthem of the United States on March 3, 1931. **Sing** "The Star-Spangled Banner."

CD 15-16

The Star-Spangled Banner

Words by Francis Scott Key

Music by John Stafford Smith

Oh, say! can you see, by the dawn's ear-ly light,
stripes and bright stars, through the per-il-ous fight,

What so proud-ly we hailed at the twi-light's last gleam-ing, Whose broad
O'er the ram-parts we watched were so gal-lant-ly

stream-ing? And the rock-ets' red glare, the bombs burst-ing in air,

Gave proof through the night that our flag was still there.

Oh, say, does that __ Star-Span-gled Ban-ner __ yet __ wave __

O'er the land ___ of the free and the home of the brave?

Voices

Analyze this vocal harmony part for "The Star-Spangled Banner." It has a limited range. What is the highest note? What is the lowest note? Look for phrases that are the same. **Identify** the slurs and the fermata. **Sing** the harmony part as others sing the melody.

Note This

Francis Scott Key wrote the words to "The Star-Spangled Banner" while he watched the British attack on Fort McHenry near Baltimore in 1814.

◀ Engraving of Francis Scott Key, circa 1840s

PRO TIPS

Challenge yourself to conduct a three-beat pattern as you sing "The Star-Spangled Banner."

22

An Important Spiritual

African American spirituals are an important part of the musical heritage of the United States. "Wade in the Water" is a very old and powerful spiritual. It is said that Harriet Tubman sang it as she led slaves to freedom through the Underground Railroad. **Listen** to "Wade in the Water." Then **sing** the song in call-and-response style.

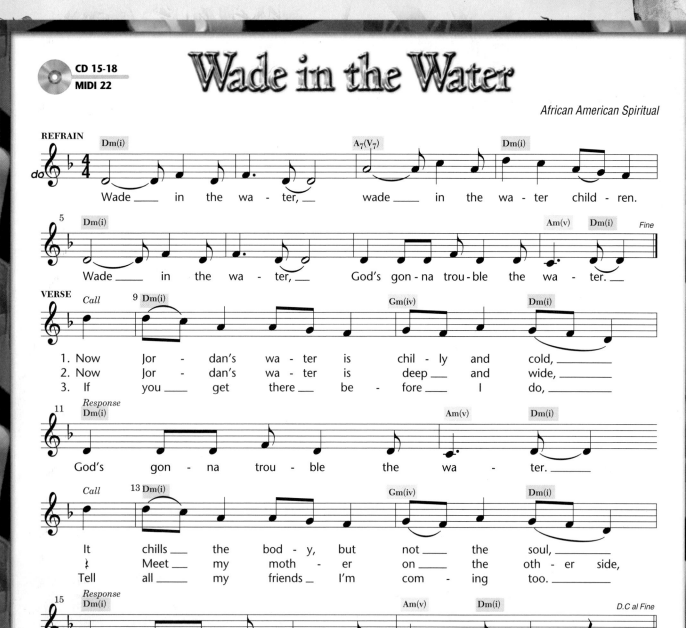

CD 15-18
MIDI 22

Wade in the Water

African American Spiritual

REFRAIN

Wade ___ in the wa-ter, ___ wade ___ in the wa-ter child-ren.

Wade ___ in the wa-ter, ___ God's gon-na trou-ble the wa-ter. ___

VERSE   *Call*

1. Now   Jor-dan's   wa-ter   is   chil-ly   and   cold, ___
2. Now   Jor-dan's   wa-ter   is   deep ___ and   wide, ___
3. If   you ___ get   there ___ be-fore ___ I   do, ___

Response

God's   gon-na   trou-ble   the   wa-ter.

Call

It   chills ___ the   bod-y,   but   not ___ the   soul, ___
Meet ___ my   moth-er   on ___ the   oth-er   side,
Tell   all ___ my   friends ___ I'm   com-ing   too. ___

Response

God's   gon-na   trou-ble   the   wa-ter. ___

▲ **Jordan River below Lake Tiberius**

"Spirituals sing of woe triumphantly, knowing well that all rivers will be crossed, and the Promised Land is just beyond the stream. The Spirituals ask no pity for our words, and on the strongest of melodies give melody of faith. That is why there is joy in their singing, peace in their music and strength in their soul."

—Langston Hughes

▲ Langston Hughes

How Is It Built?

Analyze the melody of "Wade in the Water." The notes of the melody come from the minor pentatonic scale.

Improvise a melody using the notes in the scale shown above. **Play** your melody on recorder, xylophone, or keyboard. You can also sing your melody on a neutral syllable.

Winds

Practice these soprano recorder fingerings in the D minor pentatonic scale.

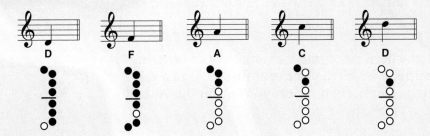

Analyze the soprano recorder melody. **Identify** the measures that are the same. Practice the melody, then **play** it during the refrain of "Wade in the Water."

▲ *The Harriet Tubman Series Number One*, 1939–40, by Jacob Lawrence (1917–2000)

Keyboards

"Wade in the Water" is in a minor key. Review minor keys on page E-19 of Keys and Chords and on page H-22 of Sounds and Symbols. Practice this chord progression on your keyboard.

Notice that the fourth chord is a minor v chord. Use the fingering shown above to determine where to place your fingers. When you are comfortable making the chord changes, **play** "Wade in the Water" following the chord symbols in the notation.

Guitars

"Wade in the Water" can be played on guitar using power chords. See page F-25 in Power Strumming to practice chords that you can use with this song. Then follow the chord symbols in the notation to **play** this song while others sing it.

Mallets

Accompany "Wade in the Water" using the mallet instrument parts on page I-67. **Identify** the refrain and verse in the score. How do the parts change between sections? Choose a part and practice it. Then **play** it with the song.

PRO TIPS

A right-handed player using three mallets can hold two in the right hand and one in the left. A left-handed player can hold two in the left hand and one in the right.

Sea Island Spiritual

"Yonder Come Day" is a spiritual from the Georgia Sea Islands. The Georgia Sea Island Singers perform music like this to help preserve the culture and the Gullah language still spoken on these islands. **Sing** "Yonder Come Day" as you perform this step-clap movement pattern.

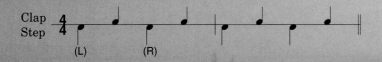

Clap
Step
(L) (R)

Yonder Come Day

CD 15-20

Additional Words and Arrangement by Judith Cook Tucker

Spiritual from the Georgia Sea Islands

Voices • Percussion • Keyboards • Guitars • Bass • Mallets • Mariachi • Bells or Chimes • Winds • Strings

Add a Beat

Perform the body percussion ostinatos below with "Yonder Come Day." Listen to the recording to decide when you will start your ostinato. Then **perform** the ostinatos with two of your classmates while others sing the song.

PRO TIPS

Before learning to play a new melody, it is always a good idea to speak or clap the rhythm first.

Listening Selections by

Listening selections appear in *italics*.

Composer

Index of Songs